A Focus on the Family Resource Published
by Tyndale House Publishers, Inc.
FocusOnTheFamily.com

Tyndale House Publishers, Inc.
Carol Stream, Illinois

HANDBOOK on

THRIVING as an ADOPTIVE FAMILY

Real-Life Solutions to Common Challenges

David and **Renée**
Sanford
General Editors

A Focus on the Family book published by
Tyndale House Publishers, Inc., Carol Stream, Illinois 60188

Focus on the Family and the accompanying logo and design are trademarks of Focus on the Family,
Colorado Springs, CO 80995.

TYNDALE and Tyndale's quill logo are registered trademarks of Tyndale House Publishers, Inc.

All Scripture quotations, unless otherwise indicated, are taken from the *Holy Bible, New International Version*®. NIV®. Copyright © 1973, 1978, 1984 by International Bible Society. Used by permission of Zondervan Publishing House. All rights reserved. Scripture quotations marked (KJV) are taken from the *King James Version*. Scripture quotations marked (NKJV) are taken from the *New King James Version*. Copyright © 1982 by Thomas Nelson, Inc. Used by permission. All rights reserved. Scripture quotations marked (NASB) are taken from the *New American Standard Bible*®. Copyright The Lockman Foundation 1960, 1962, 1963, 1968, 1971, 1972, 1973, 1975, 1977, 1995. Used by permission. (www.Lockman.org)

Certain people's names and details of their stories have been changed to protect the privacy of the individuals involved.

The use or recommendation of material from various Web sites does not imply endorsement of those sites in their entirety.

Editor: Brandy Bruce
Cover designed by Joseph Sapulich
Cover photograph of hands copyright © by Michael Kemter/iStockphoto. All rights reserved.
Cover artwork copyright © by iStockphoto. All rights reserved.
Photo of David and Renée Sanford taken by Damon Evans, Mind's Eye Productions, Glendale, Arizona,
http://www.mindseyeproduction.com. Used by permission.

Library of Congress Cataloging-in-Publication Data
Handbook on thriving as an adoptive family / by David and Renée Sanford, general editors.
   p. cm.
 ISBN-13: 978-1-58997-338-1
 ISBN-10: 1-58997-338-0
 1. Adoption. 2. Adopted children. 3. Adoptive parents. 4. Family. I. Sanford, David. II. Sanford, Renée.
 HV875.H277 2008
 362.734—dc22
                    2008026054
Printed in the United States of America
1 2 3 4 5 6 7 8 9 / 14 13 12 11 10 09 08

Contents

Part IV: Special Challenges

Religion that God our Father accepts as pure and faultless is this:
to look after orphans and widows in their distress
and to keep oneself from being polluted by the world.
—JAMES 1:27

Acknowledgments

Praise be to the God and Father of our Lord Jesus Christ,
who has blessed us in the heavenly realms with every
spiritual blessing in Christ. For he chose us in him before the
creation of the world to be holy and blameless in his sight.
In love he predestined us to be adopted as his sons through
Jesus Christ, in accordance with his pleasure and will.
—EPHESIANS 1:3–5

Lord, we thank You for our own adoption into Your heavenly family. It is out of gratitude and love that we partner with those who parent the parentless.

Our heartfelt thanks to each of the adoption experts who lent their time and energy writing chapters and contributing in other ways to this comprehensive new adoption handbook.

Our thanks to the many families who graciously shared their stories of joy and sorrow, and allowed us to celebrate and grieve with you. We so admire your unending love for the Lord and for your children. Thank you for offering your stories in hope that other families might learn and grow from your sometimes comical, often tearful, and always inspiring stories.

Our special thanks to Debi Grebenik, Mardie Caldwell, Jayne Schooler, and the many others who wrote the bonus chapters and stories posted online (see page 267 for more details).

Our sincere thanks to the editorial reviewers for this volume—especially Barbara Testa Butz, Mardie Caldwell, Jill Otis, Susan TeBos, Laura Wassink-Erkeneff, and Carissa Woodwyk. Your compassionate hearts for this project have encouraged us and reminded us how necessary this work is. Thank you for your careful attention to detail and commitment to making this book the most useful resource it could be.

Thanks to the others who have coached our editorial team at various critical steps—particularly Cynthia Bigelow, Sherrie Eldridge, and Kelly Martindale.

Our enthusiastic thanks and applause to our Sanford Communications, Inc. team—Alyssa Hoekman, Amanda Bird, Elizabeth Honeycutt, Elizabeth Jones, Rebekah Clark, Robin Banks. Above all, our deep thanks to Beyth Hogue—your work as managing editor was phenomenal. We couldn't have done this project without you!

And, finally, sincere thanks to our champions at Focus on the Family: Brandy Bruce, Larry Weeden, Katie Porter, and Kelly Rosati. May your vision and commitment to strengthening and supporting adoptive families bless many generations to come.

Introduction

When did you first start thinking about growing your family through adoption? What was the first gift God gave you in your parenting journey of faith?

As a couple, David and I [Renée] knew adoption was our heart's desire for our family long before we were married.

How did David know? First, he loved children! Second, he strongly resonated with God's call to care for orphans and widows in their distress (James 1:27). Third, adoption played an important role in his extended family.

I felt the same. Among other things, I loved being the oldest sister in a larger family—with two siblings by birth and three by adoption. Little did I know my heart's desire would one day open up the door for David and me to serve as general editors for this post-adoption handbook!

Each person's story is different, but every contributor to this handbook has demonstrated a personal commitment to adoption in God's plan for families. For us, adoption isn't theoretical. It's reality.

My family first grew by adoption when I was nine. My parents heard about a little boy who was going to be placed in foster care because his mother's degenerative disease had left her unable to properly care for her children. Through no moral fault of his mother, this little boy had experienced profound neglect. My parents welcomed that little boy into our home and later adopted him.

Several years later, other families from our church were adopting children from the Philippines where missionary friends lived and served. Again, my parents felt God's leading to meet the needs of an orphan child. A little girl this time, they decided. When they wrote to the orphanage, they happened to say, "If you have sisters, we'll take two." Two it was—two darling girls, aged one and a half and three years old. For me, as an almost 13-year-old girl, it was like having two pretty dolls (except when the littlest one threw tantrums!). For my parents, however, it meant embarking on an uncharted journey into parenting children who were adorable on the outside and hurting deeply on the inside. Little did my parents know what they were getting into.

At that time, I remember my mother started listening to a new radio broadcast hosted by Dr. James Dobson. Because my parents had grown up in broken and neglectful homes, they took in whatever they could learn from God's Word and ministries like Focus on the Family. God's grace proved to be abundant as they poured into us children the love and nurturing they themselves had not received as children.

Still, the tools that my parents needed for the particular challenges of raising adopted children were just not available. They did the best they could, but they wish they had known more. Looking back, they would have done some things differently and, perhaps, everyone would have experienced a bit less pain.

Thankfully, much research and attention has been given to the unique needs and concerns of children who are adopted and their families. Careful study and insightful listening has led to a better understanding of how to more effectively parent children who have experienced the loss of their birth family and/or the horrors of abuse. Resources and support that were nonexistent or hard to find in years past are now available to adoptive families.

For those parents thinking of adopting, the material in this book will help you make an informed decision. For those families who have already adopted, we want this book to lay a solid foundation upon which you can build your family, strengthen your parenting skills, and feel supported and encouraged. And for those adoptive parents who are struggling at the moment, we want you to know that there's hope and help available and that you are not alone. Whether you read the book from start to finish (which we recommend!) or read a particularly appropriate chapter here and there, we trust you will find this book helpful at every turn.

To say the least, we're delighted that adoption is coming to the forefront of the Christian community as a way to minister to the orphans God so highly values. Now we want to make sure that children are not just placed, but that families prosper in every way possible.

All parenting is a brave journey of faith. After all, God alone can work the miracles of healing, health, and faith that we desire to see in our children and in our own hearts and lives. So, when God gives us the opportunity to truly meet our children's needs and better love them in ways they understand, let's receive those gifts with thanksgiving and praise.

May this book and the ongoing ministry of Focus on the Family supply many such gifts to you and your family today and for generations to come.

Part I
Becoming an Adoptive Family

Welcome Home

by Paul Batura

To God be the glory
great things He hath done.
—FANNY J. CROSBY

The light of the long day was fading just as the clouds began to clear. Turning into our neighborhood, we saw that a typical late summer thunderstorm had soaked and saturated the blacktop streets. To the west, the sky was ablaze in an orange glow as the sun settled just beyond the summit of Pikes Peak. We were at the end of a 10-hour drive and two-week trip. Pulling within sight of our home, we spotted a giant blue banner draped across the front of the house. Large white lettering proclaimed the warmest greeting of our lives:

WELCOME TO YOUR NEW HOME, RILEY HAMILTON!
7 Lbs 10 Ounces

Our 10-day-old adopted son stirred in the backseat of a borrowed green Subaru station wagon. In the blink of an eye, the hopes and dreams of all our years were beginning to be fulfilled.

Like many couples, we had desired children for a long time, only to be met with a series of disappointments. "Just be patient," physician after physician counseled. Of course, this is always easier said than done. We lost our first baby at 12 weeks in utero. Then after two invasive surgeries over the course of a year, our doctor informed us that "success" was very likely. Yet, one month later, my wife inexplicably suffered a grand-mal seizure and we were thrown once again into a cycle of tests, procedures, and consultations. More months passed. More disappointment. We would lose two more preborn babies at only two weeks gestation.

Meanwhile, our young couples Sunday school class continued to celebrate the announcements of expectant mothers almost on a bimonthly basis. At one point, nine of the women in class were pregnant at the same time, eliciting a crack from a father that "there must be something in the water!"

We laughed, but unfortunately, Julie and I weren't drinking from the same tap.

And so, for four long years, our house remained quiet.

"Have you ever considered adoption?" asked my friend Marlen, just two weeks after the latest disappointment.

The fact is that we had—but the costs associated with adoption, both emotional and financial, intimidated us.

"My wife and I know a family whose daughter is thinking about placing her baby up for adoption," said Marlen.

That evening, I arrived home and shared the news with Julie.

"Are you kidding?" she said, wide-eyed. "This is just what we have long fantasized about . . . remember? We've said, 'If only we knew someone who knew someone who wanted to give us their child!'"

I remembered.

"For this to happen," she said, "we're going to need a miracle."

For us, the miracle—our son, Riley—safely secured in his car seat for the long drive home, now seemed so obvious.

THE ADOPTION JOURNEY

Congratulations! You've made it. Can you believe it? It's happened. You're now an adoptive parent. Really! Truly. After years or months of waiting and the seemingly countless hours of painstaking preparations—the forms and files, the background checks and baby classes, the scrimping and saving, the travel, and yes, even the tears borne of joy and sadness, you've finally arrived home with junior in tow!

If you feel as though you've just emerged from weeks in the wilderness, your feelings and emotions are well placed. Are you worn out? The fatigue of parenting will often manifest itself on various levels: physical, emotional, and spiritual, to name just a few. Now would be a good time to catch your breath and assess your condition. Enjoying the luxury of hours of uninterrupted rest might not be an option, but the book you now hold in your hands is a good place to start!

The paradox of parenting by adoption is now your story. At once, it's been both exhausting and exhilarating. It's been joyous and heartbreaking. You've given everything you've had to give, yet your cup is now overflowing with much more than you ever knew you had to offer. And it's only just begun.

It's critically important to consider the adoption journey much like the many miles of a circuitous mountainous marathon. The journey is long. It'll take your breath away. It can be unpredictable or maybe even frustrating and fascinating all at the same time. Eager as you are to finish, you can run only one mile at a time. You've already covered a lot of ground and exerted a significant amount of energy. Don't lose sight of your commendable progress thus far, but don't rest comfortably on your laurels either. It's time to keep moving, and you should be applauded for considering how best to approach and run the miles that lie ahead. Let's get started.

Transitioning an Infant from the Birthmother to Your Family

The 33-year-old couple stood alone at the front of Henderson Hills Baptist Church in Edmond, Oklahoma, on a hot midsummer evening. Their eyes gazed out at the hundreds of empty seats in the cavernous auditorium. Never had they felt so alone and small and unprepared for what was about to take place. The back center door of the church swung open. In a silent, somber, and slow procession, the birth family of the boy they planned to adopt made their way down the aisle to the front of the sanctuary.

Three-day-old Konipher James was swaddled in a yellow and white blanket in his bassinet. His birthmother placed him beside the hesitant couple and knelt down to adjust his jumper. He was sound asleep, seemingly oblivious to the significance of the moment. The tears of the young woman who had given birth to him just two nights earlier fell softly on his tiny pink cheek. The only sounds in the air were the quiet sobs of those gathered in a small circle just beyond the first row.

The transfer and transition of an infant from his birthparent(s) to the adoptive family is likely to be a trail watered with tears and swollen with emotion almost beyond human comprehension. What is a gain for one family is a loss for someone else.

An entrustment or relinquishment ceremony as described above might sound like an awkward and emotionally laden step. Many adoptive couples would prefer to receive their child in a far more private setting. And each situation is unique, of course. But if given the opportunity, you might want to consider planning and holding such an event. Over time, the process appears to increase the likelihood of long-term adoptive success for several key reasons:

1. Though it's a potentially awkward and heart-wrenching occasion, it actually helps to ease the transition for both the birthmother and the adoptive couple. The birthmother is less likely to feel as if she is abandoning her baby.

2. It personalizes adoption and removes the impersonal and sometimes offensive influence of the law on the process. It's no longer simply a legal transaction but a heartfelt, personal decision.

3. It provides a significant event for both parties and an opportunity to state publicly their respective intentions, hopes, and plans for the years that lie ahead.

As it would turn out, the specific ceremony noted above played a key role two days later in reminding the heartbroken birthmother that her original selfless decision was a good choice made in the best interest of her child. "I reread the letter I read to my son on that dark night," the birthmother reflected, "and realized that if I meant what I said—that adoption was the best thing for him—then I couldn't change my mind and call the whole thing off."

OTHER OPTIONS

Circumstances might not allow for such a ceremony, but it will be important to plan ahead and consider how best to ease the transition between caregivers. In some states, it's illegal for a birthmother to relinquish a baby to the parents in a hospital. As such, transfers have been known to occur in hospital parking lots, adding insult to injury. Consult with your agency or attorney, but remember that the method utilized may be more important to the birthmother and child than to you.

In the event of a closed adoption, ask the social worker (or placement agency) as many questions about the birthparents as possible. Even if you get few answers, you may receive something your child will cling to later as information you otherwise would not have to share.

In a semi-closed adoption, you might want to consider exchanging letters to be read in private and later shared with your child at an age-appropriate time. Again, the ultimate goal is to help mitigate the pain the birthmother will experience. If she is able to communicate her thoughts and feelings at the time of relinquishment, the chances of her changing her mind will be significantly reduced.

TIPS FOR HELPING YOUR ADOPTED CHILD
ADJUST TO A NEW HOME

Whether you're adopting an infant shortly after birth or receiving a child who has spent some time in either foster care or a traditional orphanage, the transition to your home can be a difficult time in a young person's life.

Here are a few suggestions to help ease this transition *if you're adopting an infant* (you'll find more help on this subject in chapter 6):

Clear your calendar: Be careful not to consider the arrival of your newly adopted child as clearance to return to your normally hectic schedule. Take time and allow the child to familiarize himself with your eyes, touch, scent, and sound.

Establish yourself as the primary caregiver: At the outset, at least for the first month if at all possible, it's best to limit the circle of care to only parents when it comes to bathing, diapering, feeding, and comforting. There will be plenty of time to introduce your newest family member to other adults.

Don't underestimate the value of soothing music: Classical music has been shown not only to reduce anxiety but also to contribute to intellectual and cultural development.

If possible, consult with the previous caregiver: Ask for documentation/notes the foster family may have kept (e.g., feeding records, sleeping habits, and baby's "firsts"). This should be available even if the foster family needs to be contacted to obtain it. It's worth asking and waiting for. Typically, the foster family returns all notes along with the child so this should not be difficult. While you shouldn't feel bound by the old traditions and habits of a previous foster family, changing everything all at once can be incredibly tough for a young child to handle. Incremental adjustments tend to work best.

Establish your home as a place of grace: Regardless of how well you plan and how many experts you consult with, transitioning a child into a new home can still be a volatile and unpredictable season of great challenge. Do the best you can and prepare yourself for the inevitability of falling short from time to time.

And here are some general guidelines ***if you're adopting an older child***:

1. Unlike the adoption of an infant or toddler, an older child is likely to be far more observant to the physical and practical order of the home. For example, if you already have children in the family and they each have their own room, it's a good idea to try and provide a similar level of accommodation for your new arrival. Be very deliberate about making the new child feel welcome and avoid signs of favoritism.

2. It's also a good idea to consult with the new child on room décor; older boys may be less inclined to participate in paint and furniture selection but if you're looking to maximize the new child's comfort and "buy-in" to the family, involving him or her in personal decisions is well advised.

3. Adoption experts warn, however, that when establishing the routines and rhythms of the household, don't necessarily expect a 13-year-old adopted child to act like a typical child of his or her age. It's not uncommon for an older adopted child to be developmentally challenged. In other words, be prepared to expect the unexpected.

4. Tracey Gee, a home study coordinator with Chicago's Finally Family adoption agency, stresses the need to tackle the safety issues. "You have to put yourself in the mind-set of an exploring five-year-old or eight-year-old," she said. "Put dangerous cleaning supplies out of reach. You should keep prescription medications up and out of the way. You have to look at safety issues as you would with any child, but you have to keep in mind the child's mental age as well as his or her physical age."[1]

5. The seemingly simple matter of food choices can be an incredibly frustrating issue when adopting an older child. Going well beyond the matter of picky eating, some older children might come from orphanages where food was so scarce that they grew accustomed to hoarding whatever they were able to get hold of. Still others may have developed hard-to-break bad habits. It's wise to keep healthy snacks handy and above all, exercise patience in the kitchen and at the table. Even the most vexing dietary "demand" can be adjusted over time.

In such a short space, it's impossible to address the obstacles you might encounter during the initial period of transition of life with an older child. We'll look at more possibilities in chapters 7–9. You can, however, take comfort in knowing that an important decision on your part has forever changed your destiny and the destiny of your newly adopted son or daughter.

We cannot change a child's past, but we can cooperate with the Holy Spirit and help to affect the years to come with God's grace and guidance.

RESPONDING TO QUESTIONS THAT DON'T WARRANT ANSWERS

If you've already arrived home with your child, the chances are good you've encountered some of the most common awkward questions along with some very sincere and legitimate inquiries. Some of them might have touched on your initial motivations surrounding this entire adventure and maybe caused you to cringe when they were first posed: *Why don't you just have your own? What kind are you getting?* Maybe many were purely factual: *How much does it cost? How long will it take?* Those are fairly easy ones to answer, yet can still be insensitive or inappropriate.

Once your child is home, you've now crossed a bridge and such questions are no longer theoretical or hypothetical. Some of them may be asked in the presence of your son or daughter. It's good to be prepared with appropriate and pithy answers when faced with some of the uncomfortable queries well-meaning people will inevitably ask.

Before we tackle a few of the most common questions, consider again the words of King Solomon: "Reckless words pierce like a sword, but the tongue of the wise brings healing."[2] It should be your goal to extend grace to the person asking a given question.

Where applicable, consider the following commonly asked questions and suggested answers:

Q: *Do you know his real mother or father?*

A: Jimmy's birthparents have offered us an opportunity to be his mom and dad. We are grateful for the privilege.

Q: *Do you have any children of your own?*

A: Including our newest one, we have _____.

Q: *I didn't even know you were pregnant.*

A: The Lord had something else in mind. We were given an opportunity to adopt!

Q: *It must have been nice not to endure nine months of pregnancy and give birth.*

A: Adoption is a labor of the heart.

It's important to maintain a sense of humor along the way. One newly adoptive mother said she used to fantasize about strolling through a store with her newborn child and having people ask her how she was able to get back into shape so quickly after the birth. The moment arrived in aisle four of the local supermarket, but she couldn't pull it off. She was just so proud of her newly adopted son.

An adoptive father is often asked if his son gets his eyes from him or his mother. He might reply, "God gave him his beautiful eyes."

Sometimes the easiest way to respond to questions or comments that have complicated answers is to simply respond with two words: *Thank you* or *Good question.*

It's Time to Celebrate

Remember that if you're going to treat the newest member of your family just as you would a child born to you, don't forget to allow other people to do likewise. Some couples, nervous about the instability and uncertainty of a pending adoption, will decline invitations to participate in baby showers or other celebratory events. But once home and settled in, hope and expect your family and friends will treat you as they would any other new parents and welcome your newest family member with as much fanfare and joy as they deem appropriate.

Depending upon your schedules and the proximity of loved ones, some couples enjoy holding a dedicatory service at their church or they might host a more intimate gathering in their home. Whatever your approach, keep this in mind: There is no right or wrong way to celebrate!

Coming Home Day

Each family will have to decide for themselves how and when to celebrate the anniversary of their child's entry into the family. Some will simply mark the child's actual birthday as the date to set aside to give thanks and remember. Others will often remember the actual day they received their child from his or her birthmother or from the orphanage. If it was an international adoption, some will mark the day their child first stepped foot on American soil. Whenever you decide to remember this historic milestone, it's wise to make it special. Here are a few suggestions:

Tell them their story. In an age-appropriate fashion, tell them about the day your family grew and your life changed forever. Children love detail and will latch on to things that might surprise you, such as the name of their first teddy bear or the flavor of their first ice cream cake. If you have video footage of the day you received your child, you might watch this together.

Dr. James Dobson, founder and chairman of Focus on the Family, tells the story of how he and his wife, Shirley, used to tell their son, Ryan, in great detail about the day they brought him home from the orphanage. For years, little Ryan would say, "Daddy, tell me again about the big white building . . ."

Many families create a "life storybook," chronicling their adopted child's journey in becoming a part of their family. This might be a scrapbook or an album where you write an age-appropriate account or story version of your child's adoption journey and keep pictures and unique facts about your child, special details about the adoption, information regarding his or her birthparents, and letters or mementos from the birth family.

You can continue to add to the life storybook over the years and enjoy going through it together from time to time. Pull the book out on the day you celebrate and remember all the special milestones that you and your child have reached together. (You might consider making two copies—one for Mom and Dad to keep safe and protected, and another version for your child to keep.)

Treat it like a birthday. Make a big deal out of it; buy some balloons and make his or her favorite meal.

Make it a family day. Incorporate the whole clan into the mix by setting aside time to go to an amusement or a local park.

"Gotcha Day" by Kelly Bard

Our daughter Lydia's "Gotcha Day" is November 16, 1999. On that day, our seven-month-old baby was carried off a plane from Korea and into our arms for the first time. Every year we celebrate that day by watching video clips of the first "Gotcha Day," enjoying Korean or Thai food with the family, and eating a "Happy Gotcha Day" cake, complete with candles representing each year.

"Gotcha Day" gives us the opportunity to continue celebrating the wonder of adoption—the day our daughter became a part of our family. We might not have video of my pregnant tummy or of her birth, but we do have photos, videos, and wonderful memories that we renew each year—the day we gained a daughter and new member of our family to love.

AND SO, WE BEGIN

At the Lord Mayor's Luncheon on November 10, 1942, the dishes from the main entrée were being cleared from the tables when Great Britain's prime minister, Winston Churchill, strolled to the podium. World War II had been raging in Europe for over two years and victories had been few and far between. But on this day, there was good news to celebrate. The Allies had achieved a significant victory over the Germans at El Alamein in North Africa. The prime minister's remarks were cautious but precise: "Now this is not the end, it is not even the beginning of the end. But it is, perhaps, the end of the beginning."[3]

The arrival home and subsequent first year as parents is a season to celebrate. But as noted earlier, it's not the end of a long race, but rather the start of a lifelong love affair with your precious child. As Sir Winston urged the faithful, the first year is merely the end of the beginning, not the beginning of the end.

■■■

Paul Batura and his wife, Julie, are delighted to be adoptive parents and live in Colorado Springs, Colorado, with their three-year-old son, Riley Hamilton, along with his adopted dog, R. H. Macy. Paul serves as the senior assistant for research to Dr. James Dobson at Focus on the Family. He is the author of *Gadzooks! The Highly Practical Life and Leadership Principles of Dr. James Dobson*, in addition to numerous award-winning essays and short stories.

Phoebe's Story
by Greg Hartman

Guo Qiao Hong was born somewhere in China's Hunan Province. Two weeks later, she was abandoned in Zhuzhou City square—no note or anything—she was simply left on a bench in a basket.

I do not know if her birthparents ever named her, much less why they abandoned her. Maybe they desperately wanted a boy; maybe Guo was an accidental pregnancy, and they chose abandonment over abortion.

Guo Qiao Hong spent most of her first year in Zhuzhou Social Work Institute, an orphanage that named her and added her name to a very long waiting list. The orphanage is a modest four-story building with tiled floors and walls. Wooden high chairs surround big buckets of toys; the babies sit in chairs most of the day and play with the toys as over-worked nannies run around wiping runny noses and changing diapers.

I have a photo of Guo's crib—it is about as big as a case of soda, with spotless sheets and a teddy bear comforter. Just like baby beds you have seen before, except this one shares a room with 50 more just like it. Zhuzhou Social Work Institute is nothing fancy—the babies are clean and well fed, but Guo Qiao Hong was only one out of hundreds of thousands of babies China can't afford to feed.

On April 8, 2002, one of Guo's nannies bundled her up and took her on a 90-minute bus ride to Changsha, Hunan Province's capitol city. The nanny carried Guo through the lobby of the Grand Sun Hotel, took an elevator to the 21st floor, and handed her to me and my wife, Sarah. Nothing fancy, just a simple, unceremonious moment that changed all of our lives forever.

From Changsha, we took Guo to the American consulate in Ghuangzho, changed her name to Phoebe Ruth Qiao Hartman, finalized the adoption, then took Phoebe home to her new family.

Ever notice that God's most exciting work is, on the surface, nothing fancy? A shepherd boy, anointed Israel's greatest king with no one but his brothers in attendance (1 Samuel 16:13); the blind, healed with mud and spit (John 9:11). Our Savior, entering the world in a manger and paying the whole world's debt upon a cross. Sinners, saved by grace with nothing more than a humble prayer.

Adoption is nothing fancy, either. We complicate it with paperwork, but it boils down to this: A child has no family; a family opens its arms. The Bible says that God adopts us into His family when we are born again (Ephesians 1:5).

When we adopted Phoebe, I caught a glimpse of what it must be like for God when someone asks Jesus into his or her heart. Think about it: Someone spends everything he has to save a person the world was ready to throw away. A life everyone thinks worthless is suddenly worth everything. No wonder there is joy in the presence of the angels when sinners repent!

Now that God has given Phoebe a family, I am looking forward to seeing what He will do with her. I suspect it will be nothing fancy—but glorious.

Attachment and Bonding

by Debi Grebenik

*Love is patient, love is kind. It does not envy, it does
not boast, it is not proud. It is not rude, it is not self-seeking,
it is not easily angered, it keeps no record of wrongs. . . .
It always protects, always trusts, always hopes, always perseveres.*
—1 CORINTHIANS 13:4–5, 7

One family with whom I worked wanted to expand their family by adopting a child from another country. Their family consisted of the parents and two sweet-natured little girls. The parents wanted to adopt a younger male child. The little boy they adopted came into their lives through much perseverance in the adoptive process. They were thrilled to have him join their family.

Then, a few months after the adoption, he began to act out. His behaviors were targeted on the primary caregiver, his mother. He would yell at and hit her; defecate and urinate on the floor; cry and scream instead of sleep at night; and he wouldn't allow anyone to touch or attempt to calm him. As a result of his escalating behaviors, the mother began to react to him and became angry with herself for her negative thoughts toward him.

When I met them, she felt as though her son was in the process of ruining her family. She expressed how much she despised how he changed their family. She found herself yelling at him in response. The father became the only one who could soothe the child. Without his presence, the boy's behaviors continued to escalate.

The emotionally drained family needed answers. Why was this happening? What could they do?

First, I explained the issue of attachment and bonding. As parents interact with and relate to their children, children reflect what they see. They model facial expressions, voice intonations, and physical gestures, and these elements contribute to the child's developing attachment capabilities. For some of us, this process is second nature; for others, it is unknown territory.

Attachment can be a complex concept. To understand, let's look for it in everyday life. The face of attachment is evident in children who, while playing with other children, go to their parent(s) and touch them or stand near them to "touch base" and then return to playing with their friends. Attachment is also seen when children run to their parent(s) when hurt, sad, afraid, or overwhelmed. When attachment is present, the parent(s) can soothe this child. A child who is not attached may be hypervigilant; always on guard out of fear; or they may not respond to the parent's words, sounds, or gestures.

All different degrees of attachment exist. A child may have experienced an intermittent attachment process such as when parents are deployed, divorced, or depressed. If there is even one significant adult in a child's life who will provide consistency and unconditional love and support, that child can attach. Attachment is based on the needs of the child.

Bruce Perry, M.D., a specialist in child development and trauma, defines attachment as "a special enduring form of 'emotional' relationship with a specific person which involves soothing, comfort and pleasure."[1] An attached child finds security and safety in context of this special relationship. It is within this secure and safe relationship that a child is able to develop emotionally, physically, socially, culturally, intellectually, and spiritually. This connectedness provides the context for a child to learn, love, survive, work, create, and grow.

Attachment is also demonstrated when the loss or threat of loss of the specific person evokes distress. Distress is manifested through behaviors: bouts of crying, throwing tantrums, periods of hoarding, moments of withdrawing, actions of self-mutilating, and other significant behaviors.

A New Definition of Attachment/Regulation

Psychoanalyst John Bowlby, drawing on concepts from ethology, cybernetics, information processing, developmental psychology, and psychoanalysis, formulated the basic tenets of attachment theory. He defined attachment as the affectional tie between two people. It begins with the bond between the infant and mother. This bond then represents how the child's life relationships will be formed. Bowlby stated, "The initial relationship between self and others serves as a blueprint for all future relationships."[2] In other words, it is at this beginning stage that a baby learns how to relate to others. Initially, his or her world is very small and focused only on the parents or primary caretakers. Their response to the baby will determine the baby's ability to attach.

In attachment interactions between baby and mother, the secure mother regulates (calms) the baby's shifting arousal levels, which affects the baby's emotional states.[3] If, during stressful events, a sustained calm stage can be reached due to parental soothing, the child develops self-regulation skills. The child begins to learn how to self-soothe, and these skills form the building blocks of healthy and significant future relationships. The ability to self-regulate and be regulated is a prerequisite to the ability to form healthy attachments.[4] This process is easy to observe when a mother rocks, holds, or bounces her child; perhaps coupled with a shushing sound while the baby calms. Some babies settle down just at the touch, smell, or sound of their mothers.

Babies, children, and youth who did not experience this soothing process find it difficult to calm down in moments of stress. These are the individuals who may react with only a minor provocation. An adolescent who begins yelling, cursing, or crying when asked to complete a task or chore provides an example of someone who is not able to self-soothe. Attachment can thus be defined as the dyadic regulation of emotion.[5]

Bonding involves a set of behaviors that leads to an emotional connection, (which is also known as attachment).[6] Understanding this process is key to helping a child with attachment disorder.

The Positive Interaction (Needs-Arousal) Cycle

As we've mentioned, attachment occurs when the caregivers, primarily parents, provide stable and consistent responses to the child's distress. Distress occurs when a baby or child experiences hunger, fatigue, illness, or any other type of discomfort.

An emotionally healthy adult delights in taking care of his or her baby or child. The mother and father respond to their child with eye contact, cooing sounds, physical snuggling, and rocking movements. In turn, the child responds with smiling, gurgling, clinging, sucking, and playing. This reciprocal interaction creates the basis for attachment. See the diagram below.

Healthy Attachment Cycle[7]

The safety and security that a strong attachment builds creates healthy cognitive, social, emotional, and spiritual development for the child as he matures.

Children (biological or adopted) who do not get their needs met as babies and small children typically do not form a strong attachment with their parents. Even when adopting a baby, it is important to consider that the removal of a child from his or her biological mother creates a traumatic event in the life of the child.

One experienced mother, Amber Bartell, discovered this when she took little Amy into her home. As an infant, Amy had been passed from friend to friend by her mother. So when Amy was placed with Amber's family, bonding was anything but natural. In fact, Amy constantly pulled away from Amber. Whenever Amber tried to lay Amy on her shoulder, for instance, Amy held her body rigidly away from Amber. This continued until Amy was 11 months old.

So keep in mind that attachment with the new parents may not be automatic. Knowing this, parents need to understand not only the truth that establishing an attached, loving, and committed relationship with their child is key, but also the fact that this may take some considerable time and effort. The adoptive parents' investment in fostering attachment can mitigate the trauma experienced by the child in the removal from her biological mother.

It is also important to note that adopted children (who suffer from attachment problems) may experience difficulties during certain developmental phases such as adolescence. These difficulties occur because of the youth's inability to meet her own needs. Out of her frustration, she might express her anger by yelling, hitting, vandalizing, threatening, or withdrawing.

As well, the parent of an adopted child may have missed out on some significant aspects of attachment in his or her own upbringing. The adoption process thus may trigger unresolved emotions for the parents. It is important for parents to be self-aware, understanding the challenges and blessings of their own childhoods. When beginning the process to adopt a child, parents often prepare financially, physically, and spiritually, without considering what effect the adoption will have emotionally.

Remember the family mentioned at the beginning of the chapter? By the time I saw them in family therapy, the situation had escalated and they were almost ready to dissolve the adoption. As we plowed through what was going on in their lives, we were able to discover the real issues. Throughout the mother's life, people at every stage had given up on her and cast her aside. That's all she knew in relationships—rejection.

Instead of responding as the parent when things became difficult with her son, she became that little girl and felt rejected once again. As the mother understood and expressed her pain and hurts, her heart began to mend, and her ability to feel and express love to her son began to swell. She experienced her son for who he was—a little child who needed her calm presence, realistic expectations, unconditional love, and unlimited patience. She could now respond to his broken and wounded soul as his mother instead of as another broken child.

Through the power of prayer, processing pain with another person, and the presence of the Holy Spirit, healing can occur—both for the parent and the child. That is the quiet beauty of parenting hand in hand with God. This is also what gives hope; you can make a difference in the life of a child and, at the same time, you can become more of the parent God intends for you to be.

DEALING WITH TRUST
AND CONTROL ISSUES

One family had a 12-year-old son they adopted at age six. He was adopted previously at age three when the rights of his birthparents were terminated; but unfortunately, the adoption dissolved and he lived in a residential treatment center until he was adopted by his new family. Obviously, this young boy had experienced multiple traumas in his brief life. As a result, he exhibited significant behavioral issues. Most notably, he acted as though he were a two- or three-year-old. He was not able to interact socially with children his own age. In addition, he could not identify or express feelings and his cognitive delays were evident. Even his motor skills were compromised.

To their credit, the parents did not focus on some of his challenging behaviors. Instead, they provided him with unconditional love and acceptance, much like God does for us every day. Part of what these parents did was rock and cuddle with this boy to provide him with some of the connections he missed as a baby. They also told him how sad they were that they did not get to take care of him as a baby, protect him, and nurture him. They created new bonds with him as they talked constantly about how special he was to them—and they saw enormous progress in his behaviors.

The sensitive parent is attuned to his or her child's natural rhythms and responds to those appropriately and timely.[8] This attunement, which is primarily nonverbal communication, is paramount to secure attachment. A parent's ability to be attuned is contingent on his or her own experiences of trust, attachment, and bonding. When children have parents who respond sensitively to their signals and provide comforting bodily contact, the children can then respond readily and appropriately to the distress of others, thus demonstrating the ability to empathize.[9] As a result, positive patterns of interaction are deposited in the brain's limbic system, providing a repertoire of experiences for the child to build upon. The child begins to trust and relate to his parents emotionally. This is where the healing begins.

Each child needs to make a connection with a significant adult with whom he or she can feel safe and process his or her hurts, fears, and hopes.

The Three A's of Attachment

Let's take a look at the three A's of Attachment as offered by Dr. B. Bryan Post:
- Attention: spending time, talking, singing, interacting
- Affection: holding, rocking, kissing, carrying
- Attunement: feeding, making eye contact, soothing, attentiveness[10]

Take a moment, read those, take a deep breath, and read them again. Certainly, you are providing most, if not all, of these key components. But if there is a lack in any of these areas, become proactive in emphasizing this in your relationship with your child. For most of us, this process comes naturally; for some, however, this process is difficult.

While it would be easy to be judgmental toward parents unable to provide this secure base, we must remember that some parents enter into the parenting chapter of their lives without the experience of having been adequately parented themselves. They bring their crippling pasts to the parenting role. Some come with histories of physical abuse, sexual exploitation, extreme neglect, domestic violence, drug exposure, economic deprivation, medical trauma, or parental absence. Due to the significance of these backgrounds, some will be crippled in their ability to respond sensitively to their child's needs. They may not understand the potential harm that their actions or inactions may have on a child in their care.

Attachment disorder can be transmitted intergenerationally. Children lacking secure attachments with caregivers commonly grow up to be parents who are incapable of establishing this crucial foundation with their own children. Instead of acknowledging, understanding, and following the instinct to protect, nurture, and love their children, they abuse, neglect, and abandon. But with self-awareness and help, parents can and do break these cycles. It is vital that we work together to break such cycles.

Reactive Attachment Disorder—Understanding, Recognizing, and Treating

When attachment is interrupted or incomplete, resulting in behavioral responses that meet specified criteria, the diagnosis of Reactive Attachment Disorder may be given. According to the Diagnostic and Statistical Manual of Mental Disorders (DSM-IV-TR, Fourth Edition, Text Revision), Reactive Attachment Disorder is a disorder caused by a lack of attachment to any specific caregiver at an early age, and it results in the inability of the child to form normal, loving relationships with others. Because Reactive Attachment Disorder results from an interruption in the bonding cycle, the interruptions may be caused by various factors such as in-utero substance abuse, parental neglect, and physical abuse. Additional factors include maternal ambivalence, depression, or illness, which all alter the baby's growth and development.

Adopted children are more likely to exhibit emotional, behavioral, and educational problems than children who are raised by their biological parents.[11] This is due to the fact that, on average, they have experienced an interruption in attachment. For example, having a greater number of caregivers may have prevented them from having that crucial experience of forming a strong, secure attachment in infancy.

But whether adopted or not, any child may experience stressors such as abuse, neglect, or trauma, prenatally or during the first years of their lives. The most damage or benefit is realized during the first 36 months of a child's life, during which time the human brain develops to 90 percent of its adult size. This is also the time when the brain builds the systems and structures that will lay down future tracts for social, emotional, behavioral, and intellectual responses.[12]

It is during this crucial period of brain development that a child can be scarred significantly. When the primary needs for survival are not met consistently and appropriately, the effects are significant, even if those effects may take some time to become apparent. As the behaviors surface, a therapist should assess if the child meets the threshold for a diagnosis of Reactive Attachment Disorder. The child must meet the criteria as identified by the Diagnostic and Statistical Manual of Mental Disorders. Children may experience attachment challenges, but it is only when the attachment challenges begin to affect the child's life negatively that it is considered a disorder.

It is important to note that when a child experiences significant neglect, holes are created in the brain, interfering with a child's ability to think consequentially.[13] The beauty is that these holes can be healed (over time) through restorative and regulated relationships with parents who are calm, peaceful, and committed. This peace comes from more than just an emotionally healthy life. Ultimately, it comes through Jesus Christ our Lord. As He promises in John 14:27, "Peace I leave with you; my peace I give you. I do not give to you as the world gives. Do not let your hearts be troubled, and do not be afraid." Typically (but not always), healing takes about 15 to 18 months to occur.

While most families want their attachment-challenged child to be in therapy—and it's true that therapy is beneficial—keep in mind that the child's most effective therapists are the parents, guided by God, the loving Father. This healing can be a slow, evolving process; however, be encouraged that some progress can be seen early on. Parents need to remember that parenting an attachment-challenged child is a marathon, not a sprint. Parents, with the support of a specially trained Christian therapist, can give the child the loving, calm, and consistent environment needed to bring about the child's emotional and spiritual healing.

It is also important to remember that parenting will bring up our own fears: Am I doing the right thing? How can I keep my child safe? What if my child acts out in church? In public? What will others think? How will this affect my other children? My marriage? Do I have what it takes? Once again Scripture points us down the right path in 1 John 4:18, "There is no fear in love. But perfect love drives out fear, because fear has to do with punishment. The one who fears is not made perfect in love." Those fears can be mitigated within the context of relationship. These relationships include friends, family, and church. Within these relationships fears can be expressed, processed, and understood.

Armed with understanding, parents will not be crippled by their own fears. Most of us know the value of "venting" our emotions to a good friend, spouse, pastor, or therapist. This venting provides a therapeutic opportunity to express our emotions that prevents us from becoming emotionally frozen or handicapped.

The key here is to bask in the perfect love of the Father, while realizing that His love will fill the spaces where fear formerly resided. When we live this way, we can parent our children from a place of love, not of fear; responding to their needs before they even know they have a need, rather than reacting from a place of fear.

PROMOTING HEALTHY ATTACHMENT
IN ADOPTED CHILDREN

Knowing the prenatal and early history of any child that you adopt is important; this information helps guide the parents' responses to the hurting child. Many interventions mitigate the effects of early trauma. When a baby is placed in your arms for adoption, it is important that the parents give their baby the time needed to bond with them. If the child is older, some modification of these suggestions can be implemented. For babies, suggestions for an effective bonding experience include:

- Skin-to-skin time (make sure that the baby is against both parents' chests without clothes on to allow for maximum closeness). Remember that skin is our largest organ and both parents need to have skin-to-skin contact with their new baby.
- Minimize stress or chaos in the home.
- Provide a calm and nurturing environment for the baby.
- Be vigilant to follow through with promises or stated intentions as you build a relationship of trust and hope.
- Incorporate soft music, soft lights, and muted sounds in the home.
- Minimize the number of visitors coming to the home; while everyone is excited about your new baby, you need time to bond and too many adults in the child's life makes that process confusing.
- Keep the child at home as much as possible, to make the schedule predictable and calm.
- Quantity of time does matter—it is important to spend a lot of time with your new baby or child. He or she needs you to be established as the primary caretaker in his or her life.
- Begin to take on the role of protector and keep your child safe. Compare this to a child who has a disease with a suppressed immune system and you are trying to guard him from infection. You can do this by keeping him safe and protected, similar to protecting the emotional health of your new child. Be diligent in your efforts and you will reap the benefits of the attachment process.

- Pray and trust God to equip you with the wisdom you need to do what is best for your particular child.
- Realize that you are building the template for future relationships that the child will have.

Parenting children of all ages is dependent on the developmental age of the child. If you adopt an older child, the preceding principles are still relevant. Remember that your child may be at a much younger age emotionally.

For toddlers, it is imperative to remember that toddlers' verbal skills can be limited, inhibiting their ability to express their feelings. With this limitation, parents need to allow toddlers to vent their emotions while continually being present in the moment. For example, if a toddler begins to cry, scream, or act out, the parent can sit down next to the child and calmly say that she is right there and she's not leaving. This statement needs to be repeated in a quiet voice until the child calms down.

For older children, it is important to work toward building a strong relationship with them. In addition, when working with youth, it is imperative to focus on their stressors, not their behaviors, and to respond in love, not react out of our own fears and emotions. Older children also need a contained, stress-free environment with calm, loving parents. One family that I worked with adopted an adolescent girl. I encouraged both parents to spend one-on-one time with her daily, particularly during times of transition such as waking up in the morning, coming home after school, and at bedtime. These times were to calm her fears and build her trust in their presence and care for her.

Other soothing options include quiet music, soft lights, and calming scents. Touch also provides a venue for soothing. Touch, rocking, and massage are tools that parents use to provide relaxing and comforting opportunities for children. It is within the loving relationship between parents and their child that a child is healed.

You may want to seek therapy if you are overwhelmed and stressed and feel as though your child is struggling. If possible, seek out a Christian therapist with experience in working with adoptions or attachment. Ask other parents which therapist they used. Call the adoption agency and seek referrals. You might consider joining a support group—online or near your home. Don't walk this road alone. Remember to seek a therapist who will work with the family, not just the child; one who will not shame or blame your child and who will see God's plan for you and your family.

Hope for Parents

As Christian parents, we have a significant, life-changing resource in the presence of the Holy Spirit. As promised by the Lord Jesus Christ, the Holy Spirit brings peace—He is the one who provides a defense against the current stressors of life and the power of past trauma events. As parents, you can learn and invest all that you can for your child to be healthy and whole. But the Lord alone can reach into the depths of your child's heart and psyche where no one else can reach and bring healing.

Remember the wise words of James 1:4, "Perseverance must finish its work so that you may be mature and complete, not lacking anything." That verse encapsulates the parenting process: Endure. Trust. Relate. Grow. Enjoy.

Sow the seeds of attachment and you will reap the harvest of a meaningful and peaceful relationship with your child.

▄ ▄ ▄

Debi Grebenik is the Executive Director of a foster care and adoption agency. She is a licensed clinical social worker, trained as a specialized attachment therapist. With this knowledge and experience base, she's built a private practice of adoptive parents experiencing challenges with their children. She obtained her Ph.D. in Educational Leadership and provides training and consultation throughout the United States.

Bonding with Lily
by Dawn Gasser

We were prepared to win a small child over with our love when we set off to China to bring our one-year-old daughter home. Though I knew it would be difficult for Lily to trust anyone, I naively felt ready for the challenge. Unfortunately, like many parents, I was anything but pre-pared for the long journey ahead.

It became clear to us during the first weeks of getting to know Lily that she did not receive much, if any, physical or social contact while in the orphanage. The nannies that we met there cared deeply for the chil-dren, but there just were not enough of them to go around. Our daugh-ter, like the other adopted girls in our travel group, did not like being held or being close to anyone. Throughout the day, Lily would tolerate us trying to engage her, but you could tell it was with a conscious aware-ness and a protective stance.

Going to or awakening from sleep are often when we are at our most vulnerable as humans, and this was the time when Lily was her most fragile. We would watch her cry every morning for what seemed like forever as she awoke. Not wanting us to be near her, any effort to comfort her always made it worse. Nighttime was equally daunting. She wanted and needed us to be out of the room, enabling her to fall asleep on her own.

Amid our attempts to make an effort with Lily each day, small steps seemed to make no difference. With time, I learned not to expect much and to give everything I had. In an effort to promote rest for Lily, we changed her nighttime routine. We began just standing in the hallway and talking quietly to her as our bedtime routine. After many nights we were able to stand in her room, and then gradually stand closer and closer to her crib. Finally, we were able to sit in the rocker beside her crib while she lay quietly.

We tried to rock Lily by holding her close in a tight blanket, but she would forcefully turn her body away from us with her legs sticking straight out like a board. It was impossible to hold her comfortably like that for very long and she would point to her crib—our cue to put her down and leave her alone. One thing I learned over the following months was that the end of the day was not the time to deal with rejection on a routine basis. It has a way of making the soul weary. Night after night, I practiced leaving my heart at the door when I entered her room for the seemingly loveless bedtime ritual.

Many nights when it was my turn to put Lily to bed, I felt like I was putting in time. In deafening silence I would plan the following day, reflect on what needed to be done, and pray when I felt strong enough. Mostly, I sat in silence until I heard Lily say, "Momma." To which I would whisper with hope in my breath, "Yes, baby. I am right here." Then I would be casually dismissed with the words, "Go now, I tired."

One night as I was sitting alone in the rocker just inches from Lily's crib, I asked her in a whisper if she would hold my hand. There was a long silence. I told her I was afraid and asked her again. Still nothing. Then I told her if she held my hand just for a minute I would then leave so she could sleep. Suddenly, I saw a couple of fingers peeking through the crib rails. I gently grabbed hold of her hand with my two fingers. Slowly, I worked my hand into a position that would allow me to hold hers in a full handshake. Within minutes she pulled her hand back; I stifled my tears and took my cue to leave.

Each night I would ask for the same handshake through the crib rails, trying to hold and caress her hand a little longer each night. I was not simply putting in time anymore . . . I was trying hard.

Lily had been with us for over a year, and one day we had had an overscheduled day together. We were both tired and just going through the motions of our nighttime routine. I sat in the rocker, folded my arms across my chest, and tilted my head back to relax. Before long I heard, "Momma." I knew what was coming, so I sat forward to stand up and leave. Then I heard a louder, "Momma." As I looked back at the crib, I saw a hand stretched through the rails as if reaching for something.

I quickly reached back, grasped Lily's hand, and sat back down. She squeezed my hand tightly, let out a deep breath, and smacked her lips a little. I stayed frozen in position for a long time not wanting to move away. I could hear her breathing slowly, deeply, and then she fell asleep, tightly holding her momma's hand.

In that moment, I thought my heart would burst as tears streamed down my face in a silent celebration. It was like watching the first brave crocus leaf push through the frozen ground toward the warmth of the sun at the first sign of spring. My heart was filled with hope for our future. Exhausted from the day, Lily left her heart open to be loved by me for the first time, and I knew that I would guard it with my life.

Sibling and Extended Family Relationships

by Rob Flanegin

Home is where you can go
without being a guest.
—R. B. MITCHELL, *CASTAWAY KID*

Preparing older children to receive a family member through adoption represents a milestone moment in your family's history. Investing wisely in this process will maximize the positive long-term effect on your family life and on the next generation.

Upon reflection, my wife and I began to lay a foundation years before we ultimately decided to pursue adoption. It first started with our decision to host exchange students in our home.

These young people came to live in our homes, not as renters, but as members of our family. We were their parents for a short time period and we poured love and support into their lives. Over the years, we have visited them in their home countries to mark key milestones in their lives.

Our birth children and extended family quickly learned that the world contains many different types of people. People who look different from us, people who speak a different language from ours. Each one of them is a gift from God. They learned that family meant much more than just those who were born to Mom and Dad. This experience paved the way for people to accept our decision to grow our family through adoption.

Many families will not have the time to pursue this kind of preparatory experience. Indeed, for most, the arrival of a new child into your family has already occurred or may be just a few short months away. How you talk to your children about your decision to pursue adoption will depend on a number of factors—the ages of your children, ages of the prospective children coming into your family, your children's personality types, and so on. Here are a few pointers to consider before you launch into a discussion with your children:

Approach the subject gradually. Don't dump a huge amount of information on them all at once. Lead into the discussion over time. Start with the basics. Answer the primary questions and move on when they are ready.

Prepare for the inevitable questions. Get educated on what children are most likely to ask, be concerned about, want reassurance on, and so on. Here are a few examples:

- Will Mom and Dad have enough time to spend with us when these new children come to live in our home?
- What will happen if (when) we do not get along?
- What if they don't like me?
- Do we have room for another person?
- Will we have enough money?

Seize the day. Try to maximize the learning potential of the moment. You may not be able to see it right now, but your decision to pursue adoption will have huge implications for the way your children view the world they live in.

- Use the opportunity as a way to teach your children about orphans in our world. Who are they? Where do they live (thousands of miles away or maybe right down our street)? What does God say about the orphan?
- Do some research and identify people who have been adopted. You will be surprised to read about all the people of the Bible who have been adopted (Moses, Esther, Jesus). Who are some of the famous people in today's culture who have been adopted? Has anyone been adopted in your extended family or close friendships? Discover their story and share it with your children.
- Discuss how God builds families. Some children are born into a family while others come into a family through a process known as adoption.

Adoption is not a last option for having a family. Adoption may represent God's best option for some couples to have children.

If you made it this far, you've successfully set the stage for the discussion of your decision to grow your family through adoption. It's time to openly discuss your decision with your children.

Discuss your plans as well as their concerns in a normal, neutral setting. In our family, we have found that the dinner hour represents a great time to ask questions and get feedback. If you have a large family, watch out for the child who has nothing to say. He just might be the one who is struggling with this decision. Make sure you have interacted personally with each child to hear his hopes, fears, and concerns. Be open to hearing their good and bad thoughts. The way you respond will tell your kids if you really want to know what they are thinking. Ensure that your body language matches your words.

As you move down the adoption path, periodically ask your children questions about how this would affect your family. As they start to comprehend what this means to the family, they will no doubt have more questions for you.

Be careful not to imply that your children have a yes or no vote in the decision. It's ultimately Mom and Dad's choice. Emphasize that you care about what your children think, but it's a decision you're making for your family.

What do you do when one or more of your children openly objects to the idea of adoption? First of all, don't dismiss their concerns as selfish or uninformed. Take care not to say something such as "grow up!" or "you'll get over it." Most of the time, a heartfelt one-on-one discussion is all that is needed to address their very real concerns. More than likely they are not too excited about the thought of sharing Mom and Dad with anyone else. Maybe they experienced a child at school or church who was adopted and struggled to fit into the classroom setting. Ask them to talk about their objection and how they came to the conclusion that adoption is not a good thing. Dig a little under the surface to uncover your child's true objection, not just the concerns that she is able to articulate. Then, as the adoption happens and the weeks and months go by, keep talking with your child so that she knows you still care deeply about her struggles.

Our children were quite different in their responses and questions. Let's look at a few real-life examples.

Kyle is our "the entire world is either black or white" child. If he sees any gray, it's just a small sliver. Kyle is also a math genius. He was straight with me one night when we were discussing the good and bad of moving forward with the adoption of two more children. "Dad, do the math. It means less time for you and me!"

Kevin, on the other hand, is our "the whole world is gray" child. If there is a way for Kevin to find a path to negotiate from, he will! He could only see great things with having more kids in the family. He would say, "Hey Dad, we will finally have enough kids to have a really good family baseball game."

When we were pursuing our third adoption, Lada, one of two in a sibling group we adopted earlier, immediately saw a child who needed a loving home. "Dad, she needs a home; why not ours?"

Anticipate and prepare for the fact that the children already in the home will experience just as much adjustment as the parents, and they will do so with very little education or training. The fantasy of having a new brother or sister may be fostered by the honeymoon phase during the first few weeks once the child comes home. This will then be replaced with reality when the new family member decides he also wants to play with that new toy or be cuddled by Mom or Dad.

Another issue to consider is how much to tell your children about their new sibling. Discuss with your spouse what information you will agree to share with your children. The reality is that too much information is not always a good thing. Don't share intimate details about the adoptive child that you don't want spread outside of the home or that could potentially hurt or embarrass your adopted child. You want your children to tell the adoption story to family and friends without having to keep track of what is safe and what is not safe to tell others.

FOR ONLY CHILD SITUATIONS

If you have an only child aged two to eight years old, you will almost undoubtedly experience additional issues with this new brother or sister. Sharing space and things, let alone Mom and Dad, with someone else at this age is very hard for someone who has never had to do that before. If possible, before the adoption, try to get your child used to having to share things and your time with others. This might include: joining a playgroup, enrolling your son or daughter on a sports team, or having your son or daughter attend Sunday school or a Bible study group like AWANA. Another neat idea we learned from another family was instituting the "new toy" rule. It goes something like this. Every time a child in the family gets a new toy (birthday, Christmas, etc.) he is required to give one of his other toys away to someone in need (Goodwill, Salvation Army, church clothing drive, etc.).

You may also want to explore getting your only child involved in the process of adoption. Think of creative ways she can participate in the process. This might include selecting toys or clothes for the new brother or sister or creating a family picture collage to be given as a present. A little work during this pre-adoption phase will go a long way once the new child has entered your family.

WHAT YOUR CHILDREN NEED FROM YOU

It is really quite simple. What your other children need from you as you prepare for and after the new child enters your family through the process of adoption is no different from what they needed from you before the word *adoption* ever came into their vocabulary. They need *love*, and it is always spelled T-I-M-E. Your children need to be constantly reassured with your words and actions that growing your family through adoption will not affect how you love them.

During the adoption process, you will no doubt spend a lot of time getting paperwork completed, attending training classes, and talking to agency personnel on the phone. It is easy, as you get into the process, to start to slight your kids each evening as you get closer to milestone dates of the adoption process.

Don't let the process and paperwork of adoption send the wrong message to your children. Find a way to purposefully schedule time with your kids. Prepare a schedule to ensure that you are not squeezing out your children. They need to know that this adoption is not going to change the love you have for the children already in your family.

PHASES OF ADJUSTMENT

Your family may experience some or all of four major adjustment phases when a new family member enters your home through adoption. Again, the ages and personalities of the children involved will have a definite effect on the length of each stage. It's obvious that infants adopted close to birth will exhibit very few of these distinct stages while an older teen may exhibit most of these stages.

The four distinct stages are:

1. *The Honeymoon Period.* The new family member has arrived. Your new child will explore this new environment, but in a very timid fashion. One of your other children might say, "Wow, he seems different from the picture you shared with us, Mom." Each of your children will be sensitive to interactions and more attuned to this new child's behavior during the first few weeks after he comes home. You will not see many issues during this time frame. Everything is new and interesting to everyone in the family. Depending on the ages of the children involved, this period can last anywhere from two to eight weeks.

2. *The Settling-in Period.* From the beginning, it's vital that schedule and routine be established. Basic rules around the house need to be communicated verbally. It's important that you watch everyone's body language and facial expressions during this time. Your new child may give you key nonverbal cues that something is amiss. Past memories, missing friends, homesickness, and reality of this new world slowly sinks in, and grief begins to rise to the surface. Your other children will no doubt spend less time, again depending on their age, with the new child as the newness of the family change starts to dissipate. This stage usually lasts for another two to eight weeks, depending on your child's age.

3. *The Testing Period.* This can be the critical stage of integration of your new family member. One to three months have gone by, and specific issues cannot help but rise to the surface. During this period, it's critical that you watch where you are spending your time. Am I favoring one child over another? Am I disciplining fairly? All of your children will be looking for obvious, unexplained differences. You might even hear an occasional "You let them get away with everything, how come they don't get grounded?"

It's important to find a private spot to talk to the child who objects during this period. Let your child express herself and discuss openly why she is feeling this way. Once she has finished, let her know that you understand what she is saying and that you appreciate her unique perspective. Don't force your child to feel the same empathy you have for his new brother or sister. He might not have the emotional maturity yet. Besides, he's the brother, not the mother or father.

4. *"I'm more a part of the family than not" stage.* This stage develops over time as your child gains more of his identity as "a member of your family" and less as "a person living in your home." This stage doesn't follow the testing stage because . . . guess what . . . the testing stage never ends! While age is always a factor, some keys to identifying this stage include:

- The ease at which the new child gives Mom or Dad a hug when she sees them
- Lack (or drastic reduction) of overt manipulation by the child to get her way
- Sharing with other children in the home
- Ability to celebrate other children's birthdays or successes—to see them as separate and good and not as a deprivation or slight against the adopted child. (This goes both ways—for the birth child to feel this toward the adopted child, too.)
- You find that you do not have to engage in every little argument or conflict that arises during the day and that the children start to work it out themselves

It's important to note that several situations may cause your child to jump right past the honeymoon and settling-in period. I've seen this, more often than not, in situations where the age of the child entering the home is very close to the age(s) of the oldest child or other children in the home. In these cases, the honeymoon may be brief or nonexistent. Past a certain age, children work quickly to establish a pecking order between them.

You may want to consider birth order resources to understand certain dynamics. Questions to consider: Could the age combination of the children involved create a challenge for the oldest in the family? Which children tend to be more aggressive around other children? Which children tend to sit back and watch from afar when confronted with a conflict situation?

Of course, most children who have suffered extensive trauma prior to adoption can benefit from appropriate counseling. But it's also a wise decision to invest in a few hours—or even a few months—of counseling for you and your spouse. Incorporating a child with adoptive or trauma issues can bring your own unresolved issues to the surface. The same is true for supporting your other children, or the family as a whole, with qualified, professional help.

Handling Conflict between Your Other Children and Their Newly Adopted Sibling

Okay, the honeymoon period is over and just when you think, "Hey, we've got this thing licked," it happens. Get this one fact into your head right now. It is not a matter of *if*; it's a matter of *when*. Conflict will happen and you, as the parent, need to be prepared to handle it when it does.

If you prepare for and expect issues to surface, you will be more able to handle conflict when it arises. Certainly, there will be fewer issues when the child first enters your home. This will change with time depending on the level of trauma experienced by the child. Expect more issues with more intensity as the child settles into your home. Again, your child's age, temperament, personality, and trauma experienced will all influence the type of issues your family will experience.

Let's take a look at a few common responses by your other children to the new child:

What if my biological child is showing jealousy or hostility to the new child?

Jealousy or hostility to a new family member is almost always a function of not wanting to share Mom or Dad with someone else. As we have discussed, find some time to get alone with your child and discuss his feelings. What is driving the jealous feelings? Why is the new child making him mad? Be sensitive to his feelings as they are very real to your child. Again, don't dismiss or judge. Usually some one-on-one time is all that is needed to address these issues.

What if my kids have to share a room and do not get along?

The first thing to remember is that every child who has had to share a room with another sibling has experienced times where they do not get along. If your other children had their own room to themselves, they may be missing the privacy or not liking the fact that they now have to share with the new family member. Have another one-on-one with your child (you see this should happen on a regular basis!). Acknowledge his or her feelings. Help identify any needed rules of the room. Involve both children in setting up room rules to which they both can agree.

What if my biological children start saying that our adopted children are not really a part of the family?

This situation calls for immediate action. You have got to arrest your child's behavior before it causes permanent damage to your new child. Many adopted children have their radar constantly scanning for messages that tell them that they are worth less than everyone else. These kinds of comments will validate those feelings and cause harm that may take months or even years to redress.

Adjusting to the New Child by Amber Bartell

When our three teens began rejecting our newly adopted seven-year-old son, Jake, we laid down the law on referring to him as an outsider. But no matter what we tried, nothing seemed to help.

Finally, we decided that we needed to act like a family whether we felt like a family or not. We mandated dinnertime. We made a rule that no one could leave the table until everyone was finished. In addition, we assigned seats during meal times and car rides, drastically reducing arguing and resentment.

Whenever our older children started talking about how they wished they could go back to the way things had been before, we reminded them that we are a family and nothing is going to change that. We also told them that our family would grow again someday as each of them married and had children of their own, adding that they would not get to choose those relatives, either, and their dad and I never chose our siblings and their spouses.

Changes and adjustments are never easy, but a few modifications to our family traditions allowed each of us the opportunity to appreciate our role within the family while valuing one another individually.

Quickly pull aside the child that is verbalizing these feelings. Address the "under the cover" issue of why she is feeling hurt enough to act out in this manner. Then talk about how her words can seriously hurt your new child. You may want to explain how she (or you, for that matter) may feel frustrated or hurt by your adopted child's words or actions, but that she is not truly damaged. But the unkind, hurtful words *will* do actual damage to your adopted child.

You may or may not want to give your child a consequence for her words, but for sure, you need to assist her in asking forgiveness for what she has said. You may want to have your child express to other family members, not just the adopted child, that what she said is not really true. Either way, make sure you walk with your child and participate in each of these discussions so that the outcome brings more help rather than further harm.

Remember, regardless of age, children who are brought into the family through the process of adoption are screaming out from inside, "Can I trust you to be in charge of me, to take care of my needs, to love me when I'm not so loveable?" They have high expectations of you. You need to rise to the challenge. Gaining trust doesn't happen by simply giving the adopted child emotional space to get used to everyone else.

Preparing Your Extended Family—Explaining Your Decision, Gaining Support

As you head down the adoption path, it's best to be prepared for the responses you will most likely hear from others. Openness to adoption with your extended family and friends is usually a function of several factors. These factors include:

- Do they know anyone who has ever been adopted? Any family members or friends?
- Has their view of adoption been colored by a bad incident or news story?
- Do they have prejudices about people of a different color or from a different country?
- What are the specific generational differences? Younger generations appear to be much more open to bringing in children of a different nationality, race, or ethnic origin.

- What is the closeness to your family—both physical distance and relational intimacy? Grandparents or extended families that can drop by for a visit will have many more opportunities to connect with and influence your children than those who live far away.

Before you make the call, e-mail, or write a card, understand that the recipients of your message will be dealing with your decision to adopt on two distinct levels. First, they really do want to know what you're doing. Did you really think this through? Is this really just some kind of emotional reaction? Is your decision to head down this path final? Where are you in the process? How long will it take? How is it going so far?

Second, they will be interpreting what you say through a lens of what adoption means for your family, for them as an individual, and for the extended family relationships as a whole. Prepare yourself for a few negative or even hurtful comments. This is the time to extend grace. Give them time to let your family's decision sink in. If necessary, help them explore adoption. Point them to resources that will help answer those same questions you had when you began the education process.

OUR STORY

Once my wife and I decided to move forward with growing our family through adoption, we knew we would have to make that call to our parents to explain to them what we were doing. In my case, it would be with my mom. After my father passed away, my mom remarried. She lives several states away—too far to drop in unannounced, not so far that she cannot manage to come up for a few days each year to keep up with her grandchildren.

My mom has already put up with a lot from our family: our moves to foreign countries, several career changes, the news of unexpected pregnancies, and so on. I'm sure she's a little on edge when we phone her up instead of sending her an e-mail. But believe me, for her, the phone is the way to go with this news. And we know that Mom tends to be more of an analyzer than an on-the-spot processor. She needs time to let the news sink in before she is able to get on board. She often expresses doubts about a decision until she has enough information to develop an informed opinion.

When I talked with her about our family's decision to adopt a child from a foreign land, she was, to say the least, a bit stunned. Why not another birth child? Why a foreign country? How does it all work? How fast will this happen?

After sharing our decision, I told her about a good book we found to be extremely helpful in understanding how the process worked. I could hear her quickly writing down the title, "Now what was that book called again?" The analysis had already started. (Today, of course, I'd recommend *this* book!)

After my mother digested the book I recommended, she was now much more aware of the adoption process and, therefore, more ready to take in our decision on a heart level. After a few conversations, it was apparent that she was supportive of our decision. It was now something real for her and she could ask questions from a position of knowledge rather than being a total outsider to what adoption was all about.

Lesson learned: Don't assume that everyone out there is knowledgeable about the process of adoption. It's true that most people will understand the word *adoption*, but don't think that they know any more than that unless you know they have experienced it within their family.

DEALING WITH AN UNSUPPORTIVE EXTENDED FAMILY

Over the years, I've met and talked with dozens of adoptive families. A large majority of them have supportive families and they express the tremendous difference this makes both during and after the adoptive child came to live in their family.

On occasion, however, I've met a couple of families who were not supported by their extended families. My heart instantly goes out to these families. No doubt this lack of support became a significant obstacle to ensuring that this adopted child experiences the full benefit of a new loving family. Extended family members express these common objections:

- I'd never do something like that.
- Don't you have enough kids to worry about already?
- How could you ever love a child that's not your own?
- What if the child's problems can't be fixed—will they ruin your family and maybe ours?
- You're making me feel bad for not doing something like this.

Dealing with an unsupportive extended family is crucial—ignoring or mishandling the issue will make life much more difficult for you and your family. You can't control their attitudes. Here are a few suggestions for what you *can* do:

- Pray . . . always and often.
- Educate your family on your view of adoption.
- Remind them that a number of key biblical characters were adopted, including Moses (by Pharaoh's daughter) and Jesus (by Joseph, His earthly father).
- Model love toward others while protecting your children and holding to your family values.

While you might not be able to change your family's minds about adoption, make sure they know that you and your spouse have not made this decision on a whim, but have prayed about this for countless hours. Become an excellent listener if a family member expresses resistance to your plan to adopt. People don't always need—or get—to have their way, but they do want to be heard. Fight the urge to cut them off and correct each misconception they express.

After they are done talking about their concerns with your plan, you will be ready to respond. First, repeat back the issues they have raised to ensure you heard them accurately. When that is complete, you will be ready to discuss your response.

You will no doubt be able to address most of the issues extended family members might raise based on the information you've gathered, but there may be one or two items to which you don't have answers. Don't be afraid to say that you really don't have a good answer at the moment, but that you will get back to them after you've studied the issue. The key is to stay calm, speak clearly, and don't let your feelings overstep your discussion. Of course, it's your family, so it's your decision, but try to approach extended family members in a way you would want to be treated if you had concerns about decisions they were making.

It takes time for people to process the information provided. So be patient. Be available to answer additional questions. Follow up with extended family members to see if their perspective has changed.

What happens when you make every effort to help extended family members understand and process your family adoption, but they still refuse to support you, your family, or your new child?

Ouch! It hurts just to say it, doesn't it? At this point, there are only a few things you can and must do. The section below tells us where to begin.

Things to Consider When Dealing with Unsupportive Family Members

1. First, you will have to put the needs of your immediate family, including your new child, first. Let unsupportive family members know that you will not sit by if an inappropriate comment is made about your family. If they disagree with your family's decision to adopt, then it's their responsibility to keep their comments to themselves.

2. If you think extended family members will not be able to keep these feelings to themselves, then you have little choice but to avoid family gatherings where they are present. The truth is that negative or hurtful comments have the effect of undoing months, or even years, of hard work on your part to make your new child feel welcome and wanted.

3. If you find yourself at a family gathering and you hear an inappropriate comment being made about your family or your children, deal with it quickly and firmly. Your children need to know that you can be trusted to correct inappropriate comments and that you will stand up for them in all circumstances.

If you plan your response ahead of time, you will be ready when it happens. Role-play with your spouse to ensure you are both able to handle general adoption questions or awkward situations from your family.

4. Don't let your extended family play favorites. Never let them treat your children differently based on their birth status. You may not be able to fix someone else's prejudices, but you don't have to let those prejudices hurt your child.

If this is happening, find a private setting to talk with the individual about your concerns. He or she may be unaware of how his or her actions are affecting your family. Be prepared to give suggestions on how he or she can "even it out," so to speak. If it continues to be a problem, clearly define the behavior that is not acceptable around your family. Remember, you have to put your family first, above extended family.

Preparing extended family for your decision to provide a home to a child in need should be thought through before you make the first call. Time and effort invested in preparing your children and extended family will yield countless blessings to the new family member who comes into your home through adoption.

■■■

Rob Flanegin is the global strategy and business services director for Compassion International. Rob is married to his wife of 20 years, Tresa, and together they have five children—Anastasia, Lada, Kyle, Kevin, and Katerina. They have had the distinct privilege of welcoming three older-aged children into their family via an international adoption process.

Life in the Middle
by Tracy Waal

Our oldest daughter, Bethany, and our adopted daughter Meke are still the oldest and youngest sisters, respectively. They've faced the adjustment of adding two new sisters to the bunch, but our adopted daughter Neti and biological daughter Kailey have faced the most radical change in birth order. They're fighting for territory unfamiliar to them, this role of middle sister.

Just the other night there was another territorial battle. Kailey was upstairs reading a bedtime story to Neti and Meke—something I asked her to do so I could spend a little bit of time with Bethany. But, instead of reading, I heard the battle lines being drawn again.

"Noooo! You said, 'Nyah nyah nyah nyah NYAH!'"

"No I didn't, Kailey! Nyah nyah nyah NYAH nyah nyah!"

Bethany and I stopped talking so we could hear what was going on. As the yells bounced back and forth several more times, I caught myself thinking, *Wow, Neti's English is getting really good.*

And then I thought, *Wow, they're really sisters!*

Realizing that intervention was needed, I walked upstairs and calmly ordered both girls to bed immediately. Kailey complied without question, realizing that it was only five minutes before bedtime anyway. Neti hasn't figured out how to tell time yet, so she began sobbing uncontrollably.

The dispute was over a silly little ball. Mommy had allegedly asked Kailey to put it away twice. But she didn't, so Neti, feeling like two warnings were enough, decided that Kailey had forfeited ownership of said ball. Now being public property, Neti snatched the ball up in her purse and took it to her room, claiming it as her own, thus firing the first shot of the battle.

I spent 10 minutes talking to each girl separately as she lay in her own bed, working our way through what had happened. Neti and I talked about ownership rights and eminent domain (in six-year-old vocabulary, of course). With Kailey, I talked about responsibility, understanding, and respect.

I ended my conversation with Neti by saying, "It's a little bit hard to be a little sister, isn't it?" Whatever control she had found was lost again as her daddy verbalized her new reality. Her little body began involuntarily trembling as her lungs gasped for air in a series of short bursts. She buried her head in her pillow and let out a long howl.

It's gotta be tough.

We spent the last five minutes listing the good things AND the hard things about being a little sister. (She filed getting cool, hand-me-down clothes in the positive column.)

Before going to sleep, Neti regained control, and maybe a touch of her own identity.

Developing a Support Network

by Laura Christianson

Carry each other's burdens, and in this way
you will fulfill the law of Christ.
—GALATIANS 6:2

Katie, a single mom of a toddler adopted from China, longed to connect with other adoptive parents. When a friend from work told her about a group for new adoptive parents meeting at a local church, Katie's eyes lit up, then clouded.

"A group for adoptive parents sounds good, but it meets at a church? I haven't darkened the doors of a church since I attended my grandma's funeral when I was eight years old."

"Just give it a try," urged her friend. "They offer free childcare."

Katie grudgingly agreed to check it out. "But if they try to convert me, I'm out of there," she vowed.

On the evening the group met, Katie slipped into the church classroom and found a seat near the back. She folded her arms and stared, stone-faced, at the speaker, who glanced her way with a welcoming smile.

For the next hour and a half, Katie sat, arms crossed, mentally daring the speaker to preach at her. It didn't happen. Near the end of the evening, the speaker asked whether anyone had prayer requests. One parent spoke up: "Please pray for our two-year-old daughter, whom we adopted from foster care. She's really struggling with anger and won't let us hug her."

Another parent chimed in: "Pray for me, too. I'm single and just took three months off work. I dread the thought of returning to my job and sending my daughter to day care."

Katie's eyes widened and a tear slipped, unbidden, down her cheek. While these people were more "churchy" than she was accustomed to, they were real, with struggles just like hers.

At the close of the meeting, as parents began trickling out of the room, Katie made her way to the front and waited for the speaker to finish chatting with several parents. Katie introduced herself to the speaker and said, "Thank you for not calling on me. Thank you for not asking me to talk." She paused, and then breathed, "It's so good to know I'm not alone."

Parents who have adopted often feel isolated and misunderstood. Convinced others don't empathize with the unique challenges adoptive families face, they attempt to gut it out on their own. But then something happens that helps them realize how crucial a community of support really is.

Debbie, who adopted a five-year-old boy and an 11-year-old girl from Russia, recalls the first weeks after her children arrived home:

It was like moving them into Disney World. They came from an orphanage—where they'd barely scrounged enough to eat—to our home, with a fridge full of food, a pantry full of more food, a microwave, and an oven. Every moment was thrilling for them, but it exhausted me, a mom in my late 40s.

The first time I took my five-year-old son to the grocery store he was so excited. He'd shout, "Look, Mama, look!" Then he'd start yelling, in Russian, "Oranges! Oranges! Look at the oranges!"

A fellow shopper who observed the uproar approached us and asked, "Who's this?"

Somewhat frazzled by my son's shouting, I replied, "My son; my husband and I just adopted him from Russia."

The woman paused, and with a thoughtful look on her face, asked, "Aren't you concerned he's going to grow up to be an alcoholic?"

"That instant, I knew I needed support," says Debbie. She not only needed a crash course in how to respond to insensitive questions, but she also needed support for her children, who were suffering from information overload and struggling to adjust to a foreign lifestyle.

"We searched for somebody in our kids' age group who spoke Russian," says Debbie. "We even visited a Russian-speaking church to see whether they had a playgroup." Unfortunately, most people who had adopted from Russia had young children who no longer spoke the language. The adoptive family functions in Debbie's area catered to families with infants and toddlers. Undaunted, Debbie started her own adoption support group.

Connecting with others who get it—whether they're friends, teachers, therapists, or fellow parents who have adopted—nourishes your family's emotional and spiritual health. Let's explore several key ways you can develop community during your journey through adoptive parenthood.

FAMILY, FRIENDS, AND NEIGHBORS

When a woman gives birth, it's common practice for her mom—or someone who plays a motherly role—to show up for a week or two and help prepare meals, clean house, and care for the baby. Friends and neighbors arrive in a steady stream, bearing casseroles and baby gifts.

Parents who adopt experience a different scenario. Because their children often arrive unexpectedly, grandparents may not have made travel plans. When parents adopt older children, others imagine the kids must be capable of caring for themselves, and they assume help isn't needed or they believe the parents have everything under control and don't want help.

While parents who adopt don't experience the physical strain of pregnancy, labor, and delivery, their emotional stress is every bit as intense as that of a parent who gives birth. In addition, these new parents might be:
- Caring for a child who is malnourished or who has medical complications
- Learning to communicate with a child who speaks a different language
- Adjusting to becoming a transracial family
- Establishing firm boundaries with a child who's been bounced among foster homes
- Grieving the loss their child's birth family is feeling
- Helping siblings adjust to the arrival of the adopted child

- Worrying when bonding doesn't occur instantly—even after several months
- Feeling off-balance, sleep-deprived, and overwhelmed
- Wondering, "What have I gotten myself into?"

Post-adoptive families crave the healing balm that friends, extended family, and members of their faith community offer. If you're feeling isolated and overwhelmed, don't be afraid to ask for assistance; people are willing to lend a hand when they understand your needs. Ask trusted friends, members of your small group, or your pastor to take turns phoning you—just to check in—on a weekly basis.

Though you may feel awkward and selfish for doing so, contact your church and request that meals be delivered to your home during your first week or two of parenting, just as they are for other new parents.

If you're a single parent, having a strong support system in place is even more critical. Ellen, a single mom who adopted an 18-month-old from Cambodia, says, "Before I adopted my daughter, people told me, 'I will raise your child with you.' And they really meant it. But once my child arrived home, most of those friends were too busy with their own lives to help."

Ellen and several other single adoptive moms from her church formed a support group; the moms scheduled play dates and swapped childcare. But most importantly, they found sustenance as they walked through the unique challenges faced by single parents who adopt—together.

Whether you're single or married, it's important to set up respite care providers. These people should be trusted individuals who know your child's needs and can be a regular part of your child's life. Whether it's a babysitter for the evening or a couple who will take your child overnight, in the beginning, it's better for your child's security needs to be cared for by a limited number of people.

Most importantly, let your friends and family members know how they can be praying for you during your first months of adoptive parenthood. Consider starting an e-mail prayer letter, a blog, or a newsletter that regularly updates your child's progress and lists specific ways people can pray on behalf of your family.

If you're home all day with your child, plan some outings. Take your child to a park and play in the sandbox, toss a ball together, or simply load your child into a stroller and walk. The fresh air and exercise will do you both good.

Your public library stocks free regional parenting magazines that list play-groups for children. The listings often include groups for adopted children. The YMCA, Boys & Girls Club, churches, and adoption agencies can also alert you to playgroups in your area.

Whether you have a laid-back child or an extremely active one, consider joining a water fitness class—many pools offer parent and child swim programs for children ages 12 weeks and older. The classes focus on acclimating your baby to water, helping you and your child develop bonds of trust, and having fun together. Since classes are age-based, they are great places to meet parents whose children are your child's age.

HEALTH CARE PROFESSIONALS

Either before or immediately after adopting, contact your employee benefits department and learn when you must add your child to your health benefits policy. It may need to happen within 30 days to be effective.

You'll also need to visit a pediatrician. You're going to get to know your child's pediatrician quite well over the next few years, so interview several pediatricians before choosing one you think will be the best fit for your child.

The American Academy of Pediatrics section on Adoption and Foster Care (www.aap.org/sections/adoption) has a state-by-state directory that lists more than two hundred professionals who specialize in adoption medicine. The directory specifies the types of services each member provides, which include:

- Post-adoption health services
- Infectious disease consultation
- Primary care for adopted children
- Follow-up care for children with special needs
- Cognitive, developmental, and behavioral testing and monitoring
- Early Intervention (EI) programming and consulting
- Testing and Individualized Education Program (IEP) consulting for school-aged children

If you're having trouble locating a pediatrician experienced in working with adopted children, ask for recommendations from your adoption service provider, other parents, or your regional children's hospital.

During your first pediatrician appointment, acquaint your child's doctor with the pertinent details about the adoption and share any medical information you have about your child. If your child was adopted internationally, ask the pediatrician to run a full battery of diagnostic tests, which will identify infectious diseases or other health problems common among children adopted from a particular country.

If you are worried that your child may not be attaching normally or you've noticed that your child acts extremely hyperactive (two common challenges adopted children face), voice your concerns. The doctor will help you set up a system for documenting your child's behaviors so you'll have a baseline from which to measure. Your child's pediatrician may also refer you to a specialist who will conduct behavior-specific tests to determine whether your child needs short- or long-term therapy for issues such as:

• Transition/cultural adjustment
• Identity development
• Attachment difficulties
• Learning differences
• Attention Deficit Hyperactivity Disorder (ADHD)
• Sensory Processing Disorder
• Emotional wounds resulting from grief, loss, abandonment, abuse, or neglect

Your child's pediatrician can recommend Early Intervention programs, which provide a wide range of therapy, counseling, and support services for children from birth through age three. Your adoption social worker can refer you to clinical psychologists, Christian counselors, attachment therapists, and other mental health professionals who specialize in adoption.

Your adoption service provider and other parents who have adopted can also offer you tips for how and when to apply for financial assistance—in the form of grants, discounted fees, or state and federal subsidies—for medical care, therapy, or counseling.

While you can't control what happened in your child's past, you can help shape your child's current and future mental and physical health. God has given you a privilege and a responsibility to advocate for your child. If you suspect anything unusual about your child's development or behavior, don't hesitate to consult with a health care professional.

CHILDCARE PROVIDERS AND EDUCATORS

Cheryl and Ken had been waiting for two years to adopt an infant. Knowing she wanted to take six weeks off work as soon as their baby arrived, Cheryl warned her boss, "I may give you only one day's notice before I bring home my child."

"Yeah, right." Her boss rolled his eyes.

Then Cheryl and Ken received the call. Their baby was due in two days and they needed to travel across the country to meet their soon-to-be daughter. "I gave my boss twice as much notice as I had promised," Cheryl recalls, laughing.

Because adopted children often arrive unexpectedly, parents must sometimes scramble to make decisions regarding schools and educational programs. And for those families who choose to use childcare providers, many day care centers have waiting lists that stretch two years or longer. Parents who have recently adopted and seek immediate openings may be turned away. Cheryl spent much of her six-week adoption leave scouring the phone book and visiting day cares until she found a warm, loving facility that had an opening.

Parents who adopt children with physical or behavior problems have even more trouble locating a provider who will take on their child. In my book *The Adoption Decision,* I share the story of Kym and Mike, parents who couldn't find a day care equipped to handle their 22-month-old son's Attention Deficit Hyperactivity Disorder (ADHD) and sensory integration disorder. Their son lasted less than a week in most of his day care placements, two weeks in a Christian school, and less than an hour in Sunday school. He was most successful when they enrolled him in a state-funded therapeutic preschool program and later, in a self-contained public school classroom for children with behavioral challenges.[1]

If you need to find a childcare provider, Early Intervention program, or school for your child, prepare to spend a significant chunk of time exploring your options, particularly if you adopted a child who has special needs. First, learn what services your child is legally entitled to (such as English as a Second

Language, speech therapy, or an Individualized Education Program), and then visit facilities that offer those services.

During your visit, observe the behavior of the children the provider cares for, and find out how the provider determines placement in the program. Ask the following questions:

- What is your discipline policy? (Obtain a written copy of the policy and study it carefully to determine whether the provider's discipline strategy meshes with yours.)
- What is your child-to-staff ratio? (The American Academy of Pediatrics recommends one staff person for every three-to-five small children and one staff person for every seven to ten older children.[2])
- Are children separated by age? (Separating older children from younger children can reduce the amount of infectious illnesses and the severity of discipline issues.)
- What staff training is required? Are staff members trained in child development? (All staff members should be certified in basic first aid, at the very least.)
- What is your staff turnover rate? (While childcare providers typically have a fairly high turnover, a consistently high turnover rate is a red flag. Ask other parents who use this provider to share their opinions about the staff and any other concerns they have.)
- What experience does your staff have working with adopted children? Working with children who have special needs? (Some providers are not well-versed in adoption issues, and many are not equipped to care for children who have special physical, emotional, or cognitive needs.)

An increasing number of parents who adopt homeschool their child—at least temporarily—to compensate for the child's developmental delays and to strengthen attachments during the child's transition into the family.

SUPPORT GROUPS

It's daunting—not to mention emotionally draining—to choose among pediatricians, therapists, caregivers, and educational options. An adoption support group is one of the best places to get advice and encouragement from others who have been there, done that.

Whether they're church-based, community-based, or Web-based, every group has a unique flavor. Some host regular social events, outings, playgroups, and cultural activities. Others provide one-to-one mentoring. Still others focus on small group sharing, educational workshops, prayer teams, orphan care, or community outreach.

The church-based ministry described at the beginning of this chapter provides practical parenting advice for new parents and reaches out to unchurched community members. "We do fun things, like scrapbook parties, and we ease into our devotional and prayer request time, so those coming from outside the church aren't offended," reports the Tennessee-based group's founder. "We gently weave in aspects of our faith and we don't judge people. We let them know that if they feel called to adopt, they are welcome to attend our meetings."

Parents who have adopted lead the Tennessee-based group. "Most of our leaders and guest speakers are parents who have adopted and who have a heart to reach out to others who are adopting in order to share what they've learned."

A church of two hundred members in Possum Trot, Texas, collectively adopted 72 older children from foster care. In his book, *Small Town, Big Miracle,* Bishop W. C. Martin explains how his congregation parents these children as a community. He writes:

> We're really one big family here—through the thick and thin of life, right up till death itself. If a family is having trouble with a child and needs some help, they don't call Child Protective Services. They call on a neighbor or a nearby relative. Sometimes, that child may stay with someone else for a while till things get straightened out. It's how we relate as family. We're in this together.[3]

Together, the community of Possum Trot relies on God to give them the tools, the knowledge, the perseverance, and a deep-rooted commitment to positively shape the lives and futures of their kids. Bishop Martin urges the church to "come out of its addiction to comfort," take up the cause of children who are languishing without a home, and "make a difference in the world."

A growing number of churches are responding to the call. Some clergy create awareness about foster care and adoption through preaching about the topic. Many churches provide training for caregivers and teachers, so they are better equipped to interact with children who have special needs. Some churches have special prayer services for families who are waiting to adopt, or blessing services for new adoptive families. My book *The Adoption Network: Your Guide to Starting a Support System* details many ways individuals and churches can create a vibrant community of support.[4] You can also look to the Resources Guide at the back of this book for a list of organizations involved with adoption.

Worldwide, churches and organizations are utilizing the Internet to offer support targeted to specific types of adoption. Adoption blogs are popular, as well as e-mail discussion groups. Many national adoption groups have local chapters. Member families meet regularly to socialize, to celebrate their children's cultural heritage, to attend seminars about adoption issues, and to offer small group support. You can ask your adoption service provider for a list of support groups, organizations, and Web links.

If you live in a small, isolated community, finding adoption support can be challenging. In fact, the knowledge and experience you gained while navigating the adoption process may just qualify *you* as the community expert in adoption issues. If support isn't readily available, take charge and create your own support base. Start by scheduling a visit with your clergyperson. Explain to your pastor that one-third of all Americans are touched by adoption within their immediate families.[5] Help your pastor do the math; the average attendance at a Protestant church is 124, which means that 41 people in a typical congregation have direct ties to adoption.[6]

Apply these statistics to your own faith community and determine how many people within your congregation are affected by adoption. Once your clergyperson realizes that adoptive families represent a fast-growing segment of your church's population, he or she will be more likely to back an adoption support ministry. Your clergyperson—who has influence within your community and beyond—can help connect you with others who might be willing to serve on an adoption support ministry team.

If you're not ready to start a ministry but need support for your family—now—ask your clergyperson to introduce you to a compassionate listener from within your church or community who will minister to your needs.

Top Ten Things I've Learned About Adoption (and Wish I'd Known Sooner) by Barbara Testa Butz

1. Don't tell people things about your child that you haven't told him. It's his story to tell, not yours.

2. Your child might, for a time, believe that everyone was adopted, and may be surprised and/or confused to learn that's not the case. Your child might think adoption is the best thing in the world—until her peers inform her otherwise.

3. The media are biased against adoption and your child may pick up on that. Be prepared to address it. Silence may convey to your child that you agree with the media.

4. It's okay not to answer people's nosy or too personal questions about adoption or your child, even if it's a question from your mother or mother-in-law!

5. School brings on new issues for the adoptee.

6. So does adolescence.

7. Expect to hear "You're not my real mother" or some variation of this phrase at some point in your parenting experience (usually an angry moment). It's normal.

8. Realize that your child thinks about her birthparents more often than you'd expect. At some point, your child may reflect: "I wish I grew in your tummy." It's okay.

9. Your child's feelings about adoption will be more caught than taught, so remember that it's not just what you say about adoption to your child, it's what you say about adoption to others. Actions speak louder than words, so never forget that your child is watching.

10. Adoption is a journey, not an event. It is a process, not a moment in time. Enjoy the journey and remember that it was your destiny to be a family formed through adoption!

Respite Care for You and Your Spouse

When parents think about creating a community of support, they often neglect to include one of the most important components: caring for themselves. One parent, who assumed adopting a baby would be easier than adopting an older child, wondered why she felt so irritable, fatigued, hopeless, and emotionally unattached to her infant son after six months. She visited her doctor and was diagnosed with Post-Adoption Depression (PAD), an increasingly common anxiety disorder among parents who are emotionally unprepared to cope with the challenges of parenting adopted children.

As you enter adoptive parenthood, assume that frustrations and setbacks will occur. Arm yourself against the onset of parental panic by making an extra effort to care for your emotional, spiritual, and physical needs.

If at all possible, take a leave of absence from your job. If you're feeling overwhelmed, feel free to say no to entertaining, obligations—even visitors. Give yourself quantity time to get to know your child; you'll carry the memories of those first weeks together for the rest of your life.

As you're getting acquainted with your child, let the housework slide. Temporarily hire a cleaning service if you can afford to. If you feel compelled to maintain some semblance of tidiness, create a division of labor with your spouse. Decide who's going to vacuum, scrub toilets, and do dishes. But don't set your jobs in stone—realize that one parent may be more exhausted on certain days, and cut each other some slack. And accept any extra help offered from friends or church members.

Rest whenever you can. When your child naps, instead of rushing to sweep the kitchen floor, take a few minutes to unwind: Read a magazine article or book, walk on your treadmill, soak in the bathtub, or grab a catnap. Consider hiring a sitter once a month—or ask a trusted friend or adult from church to cover for you—and get out of the house for a couple of hours, even if it's just to go on a bike ride or to find a quiet spot to read Scripture and pray. Fresh air, exercise, and "alone" time will rejuvenate your body, mind, and spirit.

Remember that you are not *just* a parent; don't let parenting consume your life or your relationship with your spouse. When our son was an infant, my husband and I bought season tickets to the University of Washington football games. During every home game, we left our son in the care of a grandparent, aunt and uncle, or friend. Not only did my husband and I enjoy a fun outing together, but our loved ones delighted in having one-on-one time with our son.

When our children were preschoolers, we joined a Parents Night Out child care co-op at our church. Every Friday evening, three sets of parents took on babysitting duties for three hours, while the remaining six couples enjoyed a night on the town.

Our sons are now in their teens and tweens, and my husband and I continue to make date night a priority. Once a week, we bring the boys takeout from their favorite teriyaki restaurant, rent them a video, and give them permission to stay up a little later than usual. Then my husband and I dine at a local restaurant, visit the mall together, or catch a movie.

As your family grows up together, don't hesitate to ask for help from the greatest encourager of all: God. While you'll never attain parental perfection, God truly is the perfect parent. Your Heavenly Father waits for you to run into His arms, crying, "Help, Father! Show me how to parent." The Original Adoptive Parent is intimately familiar with every challenge you face, and He celebrates every milestone with you. God's Spirit, who dwells within you, communicates His thoughts to you and breathes life into you when you're exhausted.

Invite God to take charge of your childcare team. His power, at work in you, is able to do immeasurably more than all you ask or imagine (Ephesians 3:20).

●●●

Laura Christianson specializes in writing and speaking about adoption-related issues. She is the author of two books: *The Adoption Decision,* which helps prospective adoptive parents work through insecurities and questions about adoption and adoptive parenting, and *The Adoption Network,* a workbook for those who want to build a support system in their church or community. Laura shares her passion for adoption with a worldwide audience through her award-winning "Exploring Adoption" blog (www.exploringadoptionblog.com). She lives with her husband and their two sons in the Seattle area.

Needing Others
by Amber Bartell

Our adopted daughter, Katie, was a very defiant three-year-old. Unfortunately, she was also a defiant four-year-old, five-year-old, and six-year-old. She didn't outgrow the terrible twos. When she was three, we knew we needed help and that's why we finally went to the doctor and learned that she did, indeed, have ADHD.

Being proactive with our kids meant always anticipating their needs—anticipating meltdowns, establishing routines, protecting a child who seemingly had no fear, dealing with sleep issues, and so on. It was a tough job. By about the time Katie turned four, my self-esteem was really suffering.

So I cried out to God for an older woman to mentor me. God sent two women! One was Katie's Sunday school teacher, Laura, and the other was my first carpool buddy, Meg. Meg's oldest son and my oldest son both entered kindergarten the same year, but Meg had married at about 40 and was over 10 years my senior. She's the only one who really saw all that I was going through at that time. She would tell me to hang in there when she knew I was nearing the end of my rope. She held her kids accountable and she held my kids accountable too. Laura committed to praying for us every day and would call to see how we were doing. We had a standing dinner invitation for her to come over once a week. Her encouragement was invaluable to my husband and me.

Those were the kinds of friends I desperately needed! I didn't need anyone else to critique my kids or my parenting, I needed someone to come alongside me and help.

But by the time our kids were six, seven, and eight, my husband and I were feeling pretty isolated. We had a couple of friends, but didn't really know very many people in our church anymore. We had been in a home group, but standard babysitting protocol was to leave all the kids in a back room with one of the older kids at the hosts' home. That had not gone well with our three! We just dropped out. We tried having the group meet at our house, but that wasn't any better. Our kids needed constant adult supervision.

Still, the isolation was hard. That fall we decided to try a home group again, on our terms this time. We would host it and we would put our kids to bed an hour early. They could read books and listen to music or stories, but they would stay in their rooms. That worked well and got us through those difficult behavior years. The last year that we hosted a group, our kids were old enough to just play in the basement with another family's children while we had our Bible study upstairs. Our kids were warned, of course, that we would go back to the old system if they couldn't handle behaving, but there were rarely any problems with the kids that year.

When we moved, we determined to get to know our new neighbors and, hopefully, establish a positive relationship with them. Katie grew to love the elderly couple across the street; they were like another set of grandparents to her.

It took time and effort to establish relationships and avoid isolation, but it was worth it. Having people in our lives who cared enough to support us and pray for us made all the difference in making it through the tough times.

5

Nurture and Discipline

by Sandra Lundberg

*. . . do not exasperate your children; instead,
bring them up in the training
and instruction of the Lord.*
—EPHESIANS 6:4

Karen is almost finished preparing dinner. "Russell," she calls out to her eight-year-old adopted son, "turn off the TV and put your toys away. It's time to wash up and come to the table. It's almost time to eat." Russell does not move. Karen wonders if he hears her over the television. She calls out to him again, but this time her voice is slightly irritated. Russell squirms but does not move.

Karen's frustration is mounting. She walks over to Russell and stands between him and the TV. "Russell, I've told you to get ready for dinner and you are not even starting to clean up. Look at me when I am talking to you." Russell makes eye contact with his mother, then averts his gaze. Karen interprets Russell's behavior as disrespectful and defiant. Russell has already begun to tune Karen out as she says something about going to his room "by the count of three." When he remains frozen in his seat, Karen grabs him by the arm and pulls him down the hall to his room. She puts him on his bed and pulls the door closed behind her. As she walks down the hall she calls to Russell, "Stay there until I come back for you."

Does this sound like a scene from your own home? You may identify with Karen, or you may believe that she was overreacting to Russell. This chapter will help clarify some of the unique challenges of disciplining children who have been adopted, discipline methods that may or may not be effective, handling differences in discipline among siblings, and the essential component of coming to agreement as parents.

Let me begin by saying that committing to personal prayer and having a support network of people praying for you and supporting you in tangible ways is key throughout parenting. Many people are tempted to isolate themselves when they run into difficulties in childrearing. This can be true in adoptive families due to a perceived lack of understanding, interest, or desire to help. But instead of isolating yourself and your family during difficult times, run to God, through prayer and Bible reading, and run to your friends and family. Pursue professional help if needed. And know that along the way, you and your spouse will continue to learn and grow when it comes to nurture and discipline for your family. A lot of patience and grace will go a long way in maintaining important relationships throughout the journey.

The goal in balancing discipline and nurture is helping your child mature into an emotionally, spiritually, and physically healthy individual. If you only focus on behavior change, you will not raise a healthy individual. You must initiate and develop a deep and abiding connection with your child. Keep in mind that children need to learn to assess situations and take action considering the likely outcome. To do this, a child needs to learn to respond immediately to parental imperatives, choose an option from those given by a parent, and make mistakes that can be corrected in the safety of home and family.

Consider the relationship God wants to have with us. As humans, we respond to His love for us by loving and wanting to please Him in return—not because we have to but because we choose to.

You must reach through your child's hurt and see beyond those behaviors intended to distance you. Remember that the behaviors that frustrate you are very often intended to keep him safe (or to make him *feel* safe). Be patient and stay focused on the long-term goals of connection and relationship. As you do, you will be presenting a model of God's patience and love for us. Sometimes your child will be able to articulate why he disobeyed or misbehaved and other times he may not know or cannot explain it to you. In either case, it is up to you to nurture the connection and help your child to grow in the right direction.

Understanding the reasons for your child's behavior and responses is important, but the truth is that some adoptive parents may never know the full extent
of their child's underlying problems for a number of reasons (e.g., the child being
too young at the time of any abuse to put the experience into words, or the child
having a sparse history due to adoption from overseas or multiple placements).

However, be encouraged that neither parents nor children need to understand or know everything that has happened in the child's past or inside the child
in the present in order for there to be healing and attachment. Now, let's look at
some of the challenges you might run into when dealing with discipline.

THE UNIQUE CHALLENGES OF DISCIPLINING
ADOPTED CHILDREN

Disciplining a child who has been adopted presents a number of unique challenges. You may feel that others are evaluating you as a person and as a parent as
you establish your own family rules and expectations. Many parents find it difficult negotiating this balance between themselves and are even more frustrated
trying to explain their decisions to family and friends.

Another challenge is the fact that children with multiple broken attachments
and abuse often do not respond well to traditional methods of discipline, such
as "time outs," corporal punishment, grounding, or a demand to make eye contact and immediately obey their parents. In fact, these methods may actually
escalate conflict with the child.

And still another challenge to parents in disciplining their adopted child is
that the child may bring pain from his past into the new family. The new family then experiences pain they neither caused nor expected. Many parents become
discouraged and confused when this happens.

Before adoption and early in the adoption process many parents believe the
love they provide their child will heal any early wounds and the adopted child
will respond to them like other securely attached children. However, if and when
this does not happen, the parents may feel hurt and rejected. They may become
angry at this unfair situation and find it difficult to respond to their new son or
daughter with compassion. They may even become angry at God and with each
other. And all the while their new child and any other children in the home need

them to be a team—to be secure, loving, and compassionate toward each other and their family.

Why Some Traditional Methods Do Not Work

Traditional methods of discipline can work well for children adopted at birth or without complicated attachment histories. In these situations, the parents have provided the love and nurture the children need in order to accept discipline as the loving training it is designed to be. On the other hand, children who are adopted when they are older or who have more complicated histories are not likely to respond well to some traditional methods.

Why is this? For one reason, an adopted child with a history of multiple placements and abuse often feels threatened by giving control to parents. This creates an impasse for both the parents and the child. Despite the child's fear and resistance, he needs to allow the parents to be in control. He needs to experience his parents' control as safe and allow them to meet his needs. These experiences help his heart heal. (See chapter 2 for more information on attachment and bonding and the need/arousal cycle.) For this reason, parents need to nurture the child at all times—when she behaves and when she misbehaves. Building trust and attachment must take precedence over "fixing" the child's present behavior.

"Time outs," behavior charts, love withdrawal, deprivation, grounding, and reacting in anger do not work with many adopted children because they often have trouble thinking consequentially, and because isolation feels safe to them (i.e., they fear relationships even though they yearn for relationship).

Remember, this is the bigger picture to keep in mind when you are frustrated by your child's behavior. Rather than fixing the behavior or understanding your child's underlying problems based on his history, you need to create safety and security so that she can experience emotional connectedness and healing. Let's take a closer look at what can go wrong when using traditional discipline methods and some possible alternatives:

Time Outs. "Time outs" are ineffective because adopted children need "time ins." They need ongoing interaction with the people who love them. Sending a child to be alone with instructions to calm down, think about what she has done, and not come back until she's ready to behave makes no sense. A securely attached child responds to a time out from a position of wanting to please his parents and be in their presence. An adopted child with attachment issues may not yet even have this desire. And she often cannot calm herself without help. Before she came to your family, she may never have received the parental comforting she needed that would enable her to internalize that model and calm herself. Time with the parent when she is misbehaving can teach her to calm down and also to engage with people appropriately.

So if your adopted preschooler pokes your dog in the eye, do not send him to another room for a time out. Gently, but firmly, take his hand in yours, possibly look him in the face or have him sit in your lap, and say, "Gentle touches. We don't use hands to hurt." Then help him form an appropriate behavior. For example, if you feel confident he is mad at you for not letting him watch more TV and the dog was safe and easy to hurt, you may tell him, "Say, 'Mom, I'm mad at you,'" with an appropriate scowl on your face. He may react inappropriately again, but he will learn in time that it will not result in you not loving him anymore or sending him away from you. Instead, he'll get increased physical contact with you and emotional connectedness—the very things he needs though he likely does not want.

When might time apart be appropriate? Consider another example. If your teenage son curses at you and slaps you across the face, do not respond in kind. It may feel correct to slap him back, send him to his room, and ground him for life. However, any of these responses will likely provoke further verbal and physical aggression. (Depending on the severity of the situation, recruiting outside help may be necessary.)

In this type of circumstance, it is wise to first remove yourself from the situation until you have both calmed down or you are calm enough to help him calm down. This is most easily done by walking out of the room and not saying any last words. If your child follows you, still trying to provoke you, then you may need to go into a room and lock the door. Although you are not staying with him through the physical and emotional arousal, he will likely calm down with a bit of isolation. Remember, he wants that distance.

When you are ready to re-engage, don't try to immediately talk through what just happened; instead, if possible, do an activity together. He knows what he did was wrong. A lecture won't help at that moment. Later, you can tell him what the consequence of his action will be. (Make sure it is something that requires more time together.)

Behavior Charts. Behavior charts are problematic for adopted children for two reasons. The first is that it seems nonsensical to be rewarded for behaviors that are not exceptional. For example, making the bed, not having a tantrum in a store, taking out the trash—these are behaviors that are reasonable to expect. They are not behaviors that require rewards. The second reason behavior charts do not typically work with these children is that they often have a poor ability to understand time. A goal of earning points all week may seem impossible. The adopted child may perceive this as an expectation of him to be perfect forever. Because this is too much pressure, he will intentionally not earn the reward.

If your elementary-aged child does not throw a tantrum in the store, you can tell his stuffed animals, "Andy did well not yelling in the store." The praise is appropriate to the behavior, not overdone, and given indirectly so the child can overhear the praise without having to "do something" with it. This is the path of least resistance for a child who needs to undermine his achievements or disagree with Mom and Dad. If the child has no problem accepting positive feedback then, of course, address the child directly. Again, keep it low key and appropriate to the behavior. Not yelling may be excellent progress for Andy; however, it is within normal expectations.

Love Withdrawal. Love withdrawal occurs when parents withdraw emotionally and physically to change a child's behavior. This rarely works well as a form of discipline even with well-attached children. It will not work as a form of discipline for adopted children.

The adopted child has already experienced the greatest loss possible when she lost her biological parents. Trying to wait until she demonstrates loving behavior toward you before you show love to her will not work. Because of her previous loss, she can certainly hold out longer than you can. Worse yet, withholding expressions of love only reinforces her belief that she is not lovable, that she cannot be loved, and that love is painful. In the meantime, no healing is taking place and she is not getting any closer to claiming you as her parent.

All children need to know that their parents' love for them is unconditional.

This may not always be easy, but unconditional love modeled by the parents then provides a path to understanding God's unconditional love for us.

Deprivation. Depriving a child of things may be a popular way to change behavior but it does not reach the heart. As you can well imagine, the child may begin to work the system. For example, he may begin to think, *If I feed the dog then I get my computer back.* In this instance, we would want the child to begin to experience some empathy for the hungry dog and possibly desire to please Mom and Dad. However, this is only going to happen over time as the child allows himself to attach to the dog and the parents. In the short term, it's all about the child's wants.

Depriving a child of things seldom works with a previously abused child because the child rarely truly needs whatever is being taken away. He will tell you he didn't want it anyway. In fact, he would rather have control than things any day. Your child needs time interacting with his parents, not with things.

So if your adolescent makes a mess in the family room, don't just tell him, "No more Xbox till you've put everything else away," and expect him to clean up by himself. Instead, say, "I see there is a mess in the family room. Let's clean up together, and then we can have some game time together." The joint effort enhances connection and takes the power struggle out of the interaction.

Grounding. Parents who use grounding as a method of discipline are also working at a disadvantage. The child may be used to doing whatever he wants without getting permission. If he's not grounded he assumes he can still do anything that hasn't been specifically ruled out. Instead, parents need to be the ones who give permission because the child needs limits to be safe. Thus, parents need to be asked on a regular basis for permission to participate in activities. This control may need to last longer for some children than others. For example, a child who has experienced trauma will need to experience the safety of his parents' control in his life, and establishing this sense of safety will take time.

Corporal Punishment. This chapter on nurture and discipline would not be complete without a discussion of spanking. Parents who have ongoing relationships with the adoption agency or social services will need to abide by the agency rules when it comes to spanking. If you have the freedom to make this decision without agency dictates, the following are issues you need to consider when deciding the appropriateness of spanking your adopted child: your primary goal in parenting, your definition of spanking, your guidelines for when to spank and when not to spank, and how your adopted child's age and individual history inform this decision.

Remember, your primary goal is to establish an environment that will encourage attachment and trust. Therefore, consider what your definition of a spanking is and when you believe it is appropriate. For the sake of this discussion, a spank will be defined as a swat with an open palm to the fleshy part of a clothed bottom. A spanking of one to three swats should sting just enough to get the child's attention in order to redirect the child. Spanking should occur infrequently after the age of five and be phased out by 10 years old in favor of other disciplinary skills.[1] A spank is to be used only to shape predetermined behaviors that pose immediate danger to the child or to someone else, or when the child directly, willfully disobeys you.

In light of this, parents should never spank an infant (age range 0–18 months). It is the parents' responsibility to keep the baby safe by maintaining a safe environment. An infant is not being defiant by squirming when having diapers changed or making a mess when being fed. An infant is exploring his environment. Provide distraction while changing diapers so you can get the job done. And plan on cleaning up the kitchen too many times to count.

The decision to spank or not must also be specific to the parents and child. Spanking can escalate or exacerbate the conflict rather than correct a behavior. It must take into account the child's history (abuse, neglect, RAD, etc.). Most experts agree that it is never appropriate to spank a child who has been abused.

You must never spank out of anger. It must only be in response to a predetermined set of behaviors. Traditionally, this has been when the child is putting himself at risk or is being intentionally defiant. Therefore, it is not appropriate to spank if you find yourself reacting to your child pushing your buttons. In this situation, it is not fostering connection and long-term health. You have just lost control and, in so doing, lost your ability to provide safety and security.

Responding to an adopted child in anger or disciplining him while you are angry will not result in the healing and change of behavior that you desire.

Indeed, previously abused children are comfortable with you becoming angry. Anger keeps the emotional distance between you.

If the child was adopted as an infant, then the child may respond to a spanking as another well-attached child would. However, keep in mind that even an adopted infant will grieve his birthmother's voice and heartbeat and can struggle with attachment issues later. The older the child is at the time of adoption and the more complicated his history, however, the more likely he should never be spanked. You may feel that the older child may be the child who could most benefit from spanking; however, that is least likely to be the case and points to anger that is unresolved in you. (If you find yourself struggling in this area, seek professional help from a licensed therapist specializing in adoption issues.)

PROMOTING HEALTHY METHODS OF DISCIPLINE FOR ADOPTED CHILDREN

If possible, understanding any past injuries (emotional or physical) unique to your child will help you as you seek healthy discipline methods. Keep in mind that healthy methods of discipline should account for the child's age and personality and the parents' and the child's needs for control, safety, proximity, and consistency in order to create a new environment where attachment and trust can grow.

Parents often think of their child in terms of her chronological age. When you think of your adopted child, you need to consider her chronological age *and* her emotional age. Her emotional age may be significantly younger than her chronological age. You may have a child who is 10 years old but functions as a four-year-old. You will need to tailor your interactions with her to the level of a four-year-old. This includes not only your expectations for her behavior, but also the words you use to describe those expectations.

In addition, it means setting her boundaries in line with a lower age level. In so doing you will begin to make up for the parental care she needed but did not receive during her early development. As you interact with her according to her emotional age, she will have the chance to "catch up" and thus actually "grow up" in the progressive manner God designed. If you have a six-year-old who functions as a four-year-old, then you will want to set a limit such as, "You may ride your bike to the end of the cul-de-sac while I am watching." As she matures, "You may ride around the block when you have my permission."

You need to help your child out of the aroused state of fear that often comes with discipline and bring him into a calm emotional state with you. If you will decrease your child's stress level, he will have the opportunity to learn from experience, which is necessary for change.

Let's say that Jane's four-year-old daughter picks the deli counter line to lie down on the floor and begin kicking and screaming. What should she do? This is a nightmare for most parents who would rather crawl in a hole than have their child act up in the grocery store. Although it may be very annoying if you are near the end of your shopping trip and the cart is full, your best response is likely to be picking up your child, with special attention to restrain flailing limbs, and carrying her out to the car, leaving the shopping cart for the store attendants to deal with.

Tantrums lose most of their energy without onlookers. When the tantrum is over, you may or may not choose to go back into the store. If you do choose to go back in, remind her what the rules are for grocery stores (for example: stay in the cart at all times, do not take things off the shelves, and no yelling). Usually after a few times of leaving the store the child realizes she can't manipulate you with misbehavior and these outings become easier.

If you're dealing with an older child, obviously you can't keep him buckled in the cart. You can, however, require him to keep a hold of the cart with one hand, not take things off the shelves, and not yell. If the hand comes off the cart, the cart stops moving until the situation is resolved. Again, usually "bad behaviors" decrease without an audience, so rapid departure, child in tow, may still be the best option. Don't start naming off consequences to be expected when you get home, as that will only escalate the arousal level for both of you.

Let's return to the story of Karen and Russell at the beginning of the chapter. We must be aware that Karen is struggling internally because of the pain Russell has brought into her life. She is grieved because she didn't expect the adoption experience to go this way. Karen thought that her love for Russell would knock down all barriers and he would love her in return. She thought about the home where he first lived. She thought of his lengthy abuse history and multiple foster placements. She especially thought about saving him from all that. So why is Russell rejecting and disdaining her?

The key that Karen has not understood yet is that all of Russell's broken attachments and unmet needs have resulted in him feeling terribly threatened and fearful. Russell is not choosing to be defiant in order to "thank" his mom for adopting him. He simply needs different approaches to learning appropriate behavior. He needs approaches that see incremental change as successful.

So, when Karen told Russell to look at her, and he did for a few seconds, but then averted his gaze, that was a positive step for him. She can change the course of the interaction by sitting near him on the couch, taking a moment to calm herself, then saying, "Russell, let's get ready to eat." He may look at her or not and he may or may not say a word. She may then gently put her hand on his and say, "Let's turn off the TV and put the toys away." She can begin to put up the toys, modeling what she wants him to do. She should not put away everything. Russell should help. (This may take some time, so she should turn off the kitchen appliances.) After the room is reasonably clean, they can move to the sink, wash hands, and sit to eat together. This will be different than she expected, but step-by-step they will connect.

It is also very important to consider your child's personality and history when you are going to be transitioning to a new activity (e.g., going somewhere, getting ready for bed, picking up toys, etc.). Some children are able to quickly shift from one activity to another. Other children need a little advance notice of what is coming. This might mean going into the room, making eye contact—or otherwise establishing that what you are saying is being heard—and then saying something like, "Russell, dinner will be ready in about 20 minutes. In about 10 minutes you'll need to start getting ready to come to the table. I'll set the timer to remind you." Timers are helpful because they are objective when we are not. You may still need to come alongside and move through the transition together, but in time it will become easier.

Each approximation is a good thing, not a failure because it did not reach the final goal. As your child's fear lessens, he will not always have an immediate fight, flight, or freeze reaction. He can learn the cause and effect of his actions.

On really hard days, parents who have adopted a child with significant attachment problems need to remember that their child's rejection is not personal. Their child would reject anyone who tried to love her. She does not know what she needs. She fears letting someone else have control. She will protect herself against any further pain by denying that her new parents are important to her. Her thinking may be something like this: *When they get rid of me it will be on my own terms. I made them do it and it doesn't hurt so much because I don't love them.*

Remember, if you use discipline methods that heighten the stress level and physiological arousal, you will reinforce the patterns of brain activity, emotional response, and behavior that you want to extinguish. If you help your child calm down and connect with you even when you are correcting his behavior, you will create an environment where he can flourish.

If your child is acting out more severely than the examples given in this chapter, you will need professional help to devise a workable plan for your family. This chapter is not meant to provide individualized advice. It is impossible to address the numerous unique situations that parents will face. Don't hesitate to seek professional help if the situation is beyond your control.

THE NURTURE AND DISCIPLINE NEEDS OF CHILDREN WHO HAVE BEEN VERBALLY, EMOTIONALLY, PHYSICALLY, OR SEXUALLY ABUSED

For a variety of reasons, the nurture and discipline needs of children who have been verbally, emotionally, physically, or sexually abused are more complicated than those of children who have not been abused. As we delve deeper into this important topic, I want to first establish the keys to nurturing and disciplining the abused child:

- Correct without shaming or breaking your emotional and physical connection
- Be specific with your expectations
- Be flexible
- Be aware of your tone, word choice, and eye contact
- Initiate physical and emotional connection
- Praise your child, indirectly if necessary

By following these keys, you will offer the healing experience of meeting your child's needs. Your child will begin to learn that you, as her parent, can have control and she still can be safe. In time, she can let go of some of her vigilance and attach to you.

In the following paragraphs we'll look deeper at a few of these specific methods:

Correct without shaming or breaking your emotional and physical connection. If a previously sexually abused child begins to stimulate himself while in your lap, then you need to distract the child from that activity; this could be done in several ways and would be determined by you, the parent. You might begin by simply shifting positions. If the child's sexualized behavior continues, you need to correct it verbally. Be sure not to shame your child (verbally or nonverbally) while correcting this behavior. Even if you shame the child nonverbally, the child is likely to internalize this as: *There is something wrong with me.* This is very confusing for the child because this activity may have been encouraged in her previous placement.

You might simply say, "Mommy (or Daddy) loves to snuggle with you. But rubbing like that is not part of snuggling. If you keep doing that you'll have to sit next to me instead of in my lap." Then continue with the story and snuggle time because that continues the nurture and emotional connection.

If the behavior still persists, then stop reading and get up and engage in something more active: walking around the block together, baking cookies, and so on. (Some parents might choose this option first.) Consider the fact that the inappropriate behavior may seem normal to the child and it will take time to reshape the child's understanding of what is appropriate and inappropriate. Or the child may have become bored and so started to stimulate himself. Even children who have never been abused may engage in some type of self-stimulation when bored.

Of course, sometimes parents send a shame message and break the connection physically and emotionally. If this happens for you, then prepare yourself for how you'll handle that situation differently, with compassion, when the opportunity arises again. Practicing your words beforehand can be very helpful. Your child needs to learn about appropriate touch that is not sexualized. Your child also needs to understand that sexualized touching is not appropriate for children. At some point, you can talk about the fact that those people who taught her this behavior were wrong. This lays the groundwork to explain that sexualized touching is only appropriate between husband and wife.

Be specific with your expectations. Your hurt child may not understand that behavior falls on a continuum. You will need to clearly explain what the child needs to do. For example, you might use numbers when talking about expectations: 5 being the best behavior and 1 being unacceptable behavior. For a child of 8 or 10 years old, the expectations for making his bed might be 1) climbing out of bed and leaving it completely unmade; 3) pulling the sheets and blanket up and placing the pillow at the head of the bed; and 5) tucking in the sheets and blanket and smoothing out the comforter, placing the pillow at the head of the bed, and putting the stuffed animals in order. Be very specific in your explanation of desired behaviors. If you want your child to make his bed with the sheets tucked in, say that. If you want the animals nicely displayed, say that. Oftentimes we expect our children to know these things without our saying them. Also, our children may have learned to pretend they know more than they do or have more capabilities than they do. See what they are capable of, and then tailor your requests so they can build self-worth by incremental success.

Be flexible. Remember to be flexible. This is especially important when it comes to things you cannot control. Primary examples of this are eating and bodily functions.

It makes sense to accommodate when it comes to eating. The child may hoard food because she is afraid there won't be any the next time she is hungry. Or she may desire sweets all the time. Do not allow her to have a refrigerator in her room. Instead, keep a good supply of healthy snacks and offer her food throughout the day. Let her know she can ask you anytime she needs something to eat. The significant difference is that *you* are the one providing the food. As she learns that there is food available and that you are safe and not shaming her, this need will pass. Also, meeting these basic needs allows for bonding so that she can move beyond these needs to other, deeper ones.

For the common problem of destroying toys, do not get upset and talk about what the toy was worth or ask your child why he did it. Instead, you could respond with something like, "We can't play with that one anymore. We'll put it in the trash." Then walk to the trash can together and throw the ruined toy away. One less toy is not really a problem. You may be concerned that you'll end up throwing all the toys away. Usually that does not happen. Sometimes saying less and taking immediate action accomplishes more in this situation.

However, you know your child's maturity level best. Talking through situations may work with some children. After seeing the broken toy, you might say, "You must really be hurting; let's talk about it." An emotionally immature child is not likely to respond in a way to clarify why she destroyed the toy. She may be unable to put into words why she is angry or hurting. Again, you know your child best. Keep his maturity level in mind when deciding how to respond.

Be aware of your tone, word choice, and eye contact. Remember that children who have been abused are very vigilant to read their parents' attitudes without a word being spoken. They began doing this to protect themselves, and it is likely to become a skill they sharpen for the rest of their lives. Parents need to be willing to consider what they are communicating to their children through nonverbal as well as verbal cues. This may mean being willing to take feedback from a spouse, social worker, or friend about something that you were not even aware of about yourself. (Chapters 12 and 13 offer more advice on dealing with children who have experienced trauma or abuse.)

Parents of children who have been abused verbally and emotionally need to be cognizant of their tone, word choice, and eye contact. They may learn over time that a certain word or combination of words sets their child off because it always preceded abuse in their biological family, prior placements, or orphanage. Once parents become aware of these triggers, they can creatively work around them.

While these specific methods—and others mentioned—may seem lax in teaching correct behavior, they actually are quite stringent. The focus is not on letting the child do whatever she wants, but on teaching the child in every situation that the parent is ready, willing, and able to be in charge. This loving control prepares the child so she can learn correct behaviors in a meaningful way.

EXPLAINING TO SIBLINGS WHEN YOU USE DIFFERENT METHODS FOR EACH CHILD

Keep in mind that your other children are likely to feel stress and loss when a new child enters the home. This is true even if they have talked about wanting to adopt. The children are the barometers in the home. They will live out for you the increased stress level. Additionally, if you choose to use different methods of discipline, you may have to explain to the children already in the home why you have to discipline this child differently.

Let's take a look at how Karen might handle this with her other son John:

"Mom," John says, "do you still love me?"

Karen says, "Of course I love you, John. I'll always love you."

"But Mom, Russell gets away with all sorts of stuff, and then he still gets dessert."

"I know, John. It's not that he is getting away with stuff; it's that we have to correct him differently."

"But that's just it. You always send me to my room and you're always holding him in your lap. I want to sit in your lap. You don't love me the same."

"Oh, John, I'm sorry, I do love you. And I know it doesn't feel fair. Let's you and I have some snuggle time right now while Russell is sleeping. Would you like to do that?"

"Yes."

"And I'll talk with Dad about us making sure we have special time with you alone while Russell is getting adjusted to our home."

"Okay."

"And during those special times we spend with you, we can talk about ways we are treating you and Russell differently. We are still going to have to treat you differently, but maybe we can help you better understand why we are doing what we are doing."

Some parents may decide to completely revise their methods of discipline for children already in the home. That's okay, too. Other parents may decide to explain to the children that "Johnny gets spankings for disobeying Mommy and Daddy. Russell does not get spankings for disobedience because his birthparent hurt him and so he does not learn well when people correct him physically." Again, these decisions have to be specific to each family and to each child. And remember to use careful discretion when sharing personal information regarding your adopted child with others, including siblings.

Conversations similar to the one we saw between Karen and John foster increased understanding and sensitivity to what a child who has already been living in the home may feel. Parents must not deny that there is a difference in how the children are being treated. Don't dismiss the fact that the difference doesn't feel fair. If you deny it, your children will learn not to believe what you say. Always allow for further discussion later.

In the end, your other children may not need to understand and may not be capable of understanding why the new child gets treated differently. However, all of your children need your love, time, and attention. You may feel like you have nothing more to give. On some days that may be true. Much more often, you must give more than you think you have on reserve so all the children are assured you treasure them. Remember, this will only last for a season. You do not want to regret having one child feel you sacrificed your relationship with him for your relationship with another child.

Why It Is So Important Both Parents Are on the Same Page

It is very likely that your once-stable home and family has been turned upside down during the process of adoption. You long for things to be as they once were. You also long for the desire of your heart to be met in loving, nurturing, and sacrificing for your new child and having her love you in return. I submit for your consideration that you will be able to experience love given and love returned much sooner if you and your spouse take steps *together* to work toward your child's healing.

Just as you pursued adoption together, it is very important that you both commit to nurturing and disciplining your child using the same methods. If you are divided about what techniques to use, your child (or children) will perceive a crack in the unity between Mom and Dad and will find a way to exploit it.

You may have noticed your child giving Mom a harder time than Dad. This is especially true if Mom is the one providing the majority of the child's care. When faced with this situation, parents may disagree about how the child behaves and what needs to be done about it. However, it is vital that Mom and Dad work through these feelings together and find common ground. Having a united front and reinforcing each other's decisions is essential in successfully nurturing and disciplining your children. Those who fail to do this will, along with their children, suffer negative consequences. The worst consequences are: (1) sacrificing the primacy of the marriage and (2) delaying the child's progress to healing.

God has blessed you with this child through adoption. Now you must work together to bless this child by being the parents he so desperately needs.

A FINAL THOUGHT

As you seek to discipline your adopted child in creative ways, keep in mind that the goal is rarely to win this particular battle (though that may be important at certain times). Instead, the ultimate objective is to help your child grow in wisdom and stature, and in favor with God and men (Luke 2:52).

Never forget that when the Bible addresses the responsibility that parents have to discipline their children, "nurture" comes before "the admonition of the Lord" (Ephesians 6:4 KJV). Disciplining with your child's heart needs in mind will bring him or her to a place of wholeness where he or she can truly obey you—and God—from a healthy heart, soul, and mind.

■■■

Sandra Lundberg is a licensed clinical psychologist who works with Focus on the Family. During her training, she became interested in the behavior disturbances of children in residential treatment facilities, foster homes, and adoptive families. She has spent a significant amount of time reviewing research, literature, and more on adoption, abuse, and the origin and treatment of attachment problems.

Trial and Error
by Kelly Rosati

We were blessed to adopt all four of our children through the foster care system. The older two (Daniel, eight years, and Anna, six years) came home as babies and were always very close with each other. When God added three-year-old Joshua and, a year later, two-year-old Hope to our family, dynamics got interesting. At first, the older two welcomed the younger two with a magnificent, spiritual purity that encouraged my husband and me through hard times. Their attitude was: *They need a family. We're a family. They can come with us.* It was beautiful.

So we were somewhat taken by surprise by the intensity of the reaction of our six-year-old daughter to the love expressed by her eight-year-old brother to his now youngest sister. When Daniel would kiss or hug little Hope, Anna would sometimes rage wildly and strike them both, exclaiming that Daniel was the worst brother in the whole world and she would never forgive him. She would further proclaim that Hope was horrible and she didn't want her in our family (poor Hope had just been sitting there, doing nothing except receiving a hug from her brother). Anna is normally a loving and generous girl and these outbursts had us perplexed, to say the least.

After many unsuccessful lectures about hitting and mean words (I'm a slow learner) and some ineffective time-outs in her room (this girl is very attached!), we realized that when Daniel showed Hope affection—but not Anna during the same episode—Anna felt horribly rejected by her brother. Her rejection was expressed through strong, raging anger.

So the next time it happened, we held Anna and asked her if, when Daniel hugged Hope, she felt rejected and as though Daniel loved Hope and not her. Her huge feelings subsiding, she whimpered yes, tears squirting from her eyes. We encouraged her to tell Daniel, "I feel rejected and mad because it seems like you love Hope and not me."

We also explained the whole situation to Daniel, who couldn't understand why Anna whacked him and raged at him when he hugged Hope. He responded that it "didn't make sense" for Anna to get mad when he hugged Hope because hugging Hope didn't mean he didn't love Anna. We told him that while he was right in his logic, Anna couldn't help how she felt, only how she expressed it. We encouraged him to hug Anna, too, each time he showed affection to Hope. He still doesn't think that's logical, but he agreed to do it anyway.

It's not always easy, but learning to respond to our children's individual needs has helped our family experience a tad more peace and love all the way around.

Part II
Life Issues from Birth to Adulthood

6

Infants

by Laura Wassink-Erkeneff

Our society has this love thing all twisted around.
We think the basis of love is our feelings,
but it's not. The New Testament teaches that
love is a decision to act. Love is always about
what you do for others, not what you feel.
—LISA MISRAJE BENTLEY, *SAVING LEVI*

In my counseling practice, I encounter parents who believe that, because they adopted their child as an infant, he is too young to be affected by the loss of birthparents. These parents believe that all their child needs is love and a new opportunity in life. If only this were the case. Instead, parents need to be equipped with information that empowers them to understand all that transpires within their child during the first months of life.

To grasp the full picture of your child, you have to look at adoption from different perspectives. What is involved in your infant's developmental stage? What happens if developmental milestones are not met? What can you do as a parent to help your child? Once you have an understanding of developmental milestones, you can apply this information to a child who was adopted domestically, internationally, or through the state. When a clear picture is formed, parents are better equipped to understand their child and parent him more effectively.

DEVELOPMENTAL MILESTONES

What goes on developmentally, even with an infant, is the foundation for future emotional and physical development.

The first stage of development, infancy (birth to 18 months), is trust versus mistrust. This is a time when the foundational building blocks are laid to determine whether children are going to develop feelings of trust or mistrust toward the world around them. (Refer back to chapter 2 for more on attachment and bonding.)

During this first stage of life, children are in what is referred to as a *sensory stage*. During the sensory stage, an infant's learning is done through senses such as auditory, tactile, and visual. Children are seeking and in need of positive, loving care to develop normally at this stage. This is done through the physical and visual contact with those who are caring for them, forming trust. During this time, many parents choose to keep their child close to their chest so the child can hear the parent's heartbeat.

In addition, many parents who have adopted choose to be the only adults to hold and care for their new infant (or limit the number). This intense focus on bonding helps build a sense of safety and trust. If children feel a positive connection with a parent, the foundation for building healthy trust and a positive self-image begins forming.

Infants also have biological and physiological needs. Those needs include air, food, and shelter; the need for safety, security, and stability; belongingness, affection, and relationships. All of these needs are critical building blocks for an infant's emotional development, not just in infancy but throughout his life. If children are nurtured, feel loved, and have biological and physiological needs met, they are likely to develop trust, security, hope, and optimism regarding the world around them. Conversely, children who do not receive these things have a greater likelihood of becoming insecure and mistrustful of themselves and others.

INTERRUPTIONS IN THE DEVELOPMENTAL PROCESS

So, what happens to a child's brain if needs aren't met? For answers, we'll turn to a biological picture of the chemicals in the brain. Dr. Bruce Perry has extensive knowledge and information on the biological aspects of brain development and what happens chemically to the brain when the developmental needs of a child go unmet.[1] In addition, Dr. Deborah Gray has written a book, *Nurturing Adoptions*, containing easy-to-understand information on brain development.[2] Though this information is available from a variety of sources, these sources are both complete and reader friendly. I will attempt to briefly summarize for you what you would find in Dr. Perry's and Dr. Gray's literature and research.

Children develop a cellular memory of things that happen to them at a preverbal stage. These experiences, although not known or remembered, do affect a child. They are permanently stored in the most primal part of the brain. The brain continues to hold life's experiences, both good and bad.

A child's early life experiences and subsequent life experiences are stored in the brain, and then used as the foundation for the next experience and expression to build upon. This pattern continues to repeat itself throughout an individual's life. You can see why the longer developmental needs are not met, the more your child's brain holds these negative experiences and the more they affect the next developmental milestone. When early developmental milestones have not been met, it affects the way a child thinks, feels, and physically reacts to things, and as a result, a developmental chain reaction is beginning.

As we are aware, our brains release chemicals to regulate our moods and emotions throughout the day. When we have increased stress, specific chemicals increase, and our body responds to these increases through our physical actions. We know one form of this release as "fight or flight mode." In situations where an infant is repeatedly exposed to a stressful environment, an increase in these stress-related chemicals is released. This can physically inhibit his body's growth and immune system development.

The emotional reaction to prolonged periods of overstimulation can look different in children and affect them in different ways. One way is an eventual depletion of these chemicals. As a result, they can be tired, emotionally depressed, and not capable of dealing with stressful events that occur in a day. A child responding this way may show a lack of joy or excitement. The child will seem to have low energy and become easily upset. If stress remains high, the stress-related chemicals can also remain high and will keep children from coming down to a normal range of functioning. A child struggling in this way will appear irritable and often inconsolable. Little things will seem to upset him.

As with many things in life, an individual often experiences one extreme or another. So if you have a child who has been continuously exposed to stress, trauma, or neglect, you may have a child who is hyperalert. On the other hand, you may have a child who has dealt with neglect or loss in such a way that it has led to a withdrawal and a child who appears to be retreating into his own world for safety.

In my own adoption story, I later discovered that as an infant I had four placements in three months: my birthmother, two foster mothers, and then at three months of age, my adoptive parents. Any missed developmental milestones may have been healed based on the relationship with my adoptive parents. However, due to circumstances in my parents' lives, there were difficulties in our ability to bond. The combination of these factors affected me but, though it was difficult for my parents and me, this was used for good by God in my counseling practice as I work with and help other parents and adoptees. This is another example of how everything that happens in our lives can be used by God for good.

KEEPING THE FAITH AMID CHALLENGES

Matthew 17:20 says, "If you have faith as small as a mustard seed, you can say to this mountain, 'Move from here to there' and it will move. Nothing will be impossible for you." You must have the faith of the mustard seed. Believe that all things are possible with Jesus Christ, deal with the fear in your heart, embrace your role as this child's parent, and do what you know will be the most beneficial to your child's development, well-being, and bonding. The list of options is wide and varied. Developmentally, children at this age need to feel the love and security that will help them develop trust, setting them on a course of reprogramming.

Nancy L. Thomas, a foster mother to children with severe Reactive Attachment Disorder (RAD), provides a helpful collection of ideas to utilize as a way to increase bonding and recover from the initial developmental losses. We've seen a few of these ideas in chapter 2, but let's take a closer look:

- Breastfeed if possible
- Always hold the bottle; never prop it up or allow the child to hold it
- Carry the baby in a sling facing Mom or Dad for multiple hours during a day
- Feed milk in Mom's arms with soft eye contact, touch, and a loving voice
- Nap daily resting skin-to-skin on Dad's chest
- Avoid baby carriers; carry the baby in loving arms
- Mom is the only person to feed the baby
- No one holds the baby except for Mom and Dad unless it's less than five minutes a day
- Baby should not be left alone to cry for more than three minutes
- Hold baby close to your heart
- Delay painful medical procedures, if possible until the child is fully bonded
- Play Mozart to soothe the baby
- Respond with joy to your baby's attempts to get your love and attention[3]

Any action that builds a connection is encouraged. There is no reason to believe that simply because your child has encountered circumstances preventing typical developments, the child will be forever damaged. As a parent, you can do numerous things to prepare yourself: Read books, speak with counselors knowledgeable in the field of adoption, research information online pertaining to your circumstances, and meet other parents to learn what they have done. Enlisting the help of a good pediatrician can be invaluable. (Chapter 4 offers more advice on this subject.)

Be proactive about surrounding yourself with those people who will give you wise counsel, not those people who will only offer negative feedback or criticism.

TAKING CARE OF YOUR CHILD, TAKING CARE OF YOU

An extremely important part of a child's well-being is the emotional state of his or her parents. Though adoption is an exciting time and often the fulfillment of a dream, there can be emotions that do not feel positive or exciting. I spent close to eight years working with birth and adoptive families as they moved through their adoption plan. Oftentimes, parents who adopted will feel a sense of sadness for a variety of reasons: grief over their inability to conceive, struggles with the process of adoption, or feeling they were not bonding with their child the way they thought they would. These unresolved issues and unmet expectations often leave parents reporting feelings of depression or an unexpected letdown about their adoption.

In regard to bonding, parents have reported wondering if they will ever love their child the way they thought they would. The short answer is, yes. Just as bonding is a process for your child, so too bonding can be a process for new parents. Even when a parent does not feel the intensity of love or connection he or she anticipated feeling, that parent is still capable of providing a secure and loving environment that will allow the child to flourish.

These acts of love and caring will not only be beneficial for the child, but the parents as well—given they too are learning to love someone new in their life. A delay in the anticipated emotions and bonding is not unique to parents who adopt. It also happens to women who carry and deliver children. They have also reported delays in bonding or a difference in the way they bonded with one child versus the way they bonded with a previous child. Again, bonding is a process and not always experienced immediately.

Addressing concerns within yourself is a critical step in parenting your child. Did you experience abuse that may prevent you from helping your child? Are you afraid of not living up to the expectations of others as it pertains to parenting? Do members of your family look down on adoption or see it as a second choice? How healthy and strong is your marriage? What can you do to nurture and care for your relationship with your spouse right now?

Addressing these and other issues are critical for you to resolve so you're able to be emotionally present for the needs of your child. If you're thinking it's too late because your child is on the way or has already arrived, don't worry. Acknowledging there is a problem is half the battle. Growth and healing are lifelong processes. Know your blind spots; and remember to seek professional help if necessary.

It's imperative as an adoptive parent that you not overlook the importance of your child's first year. Understanding what is necessary for your child's development will enable you to understand her better and to make better choices regarding care, needs, and emotional development. Don't ever believe that because there have been disruptions in your child's developmental milestones, he is beyond help. Adoption is designed by God for children to have opportunities they might not otherwise have had without your love.

■■■

Laura Wassink-Erkeneff, M.A., is a marriage and family therapist specializing in the field of adoption. In addition to her private practice, Laura has worked with adoption agencies, providing counseling to birthparents and adoptive families in the adoption process.

Heart's Echo
by Christine Lindsay

What can a birthmother contribute to a handbook for adoptive families? The first thing I would like to do is go back in time to the morning I relinquished my child. If I could do it all over again, I'd take the hand of Sarah's adoptive mother, look into the eyes of her adoptive father, and give them my blessing: "This is your child. Take comfort and joy and confidence in raising your child." But because of adoption laws back then, I wasn't able to do that, so I say those words now, in love, though we all know adoption is born out of intense loss.

It doesn't seem natural that the emotions of an unmarried pregnant girl would echo those of another woman enduring childlessness. Maybe it was those long nights I spent crying, praying over what was best for my baby, knowing that if I went through with the adoption plan, I'd know the pain of an empty womb. The thought came to me then, *I know what she's feeling—this prospective adoptive mother in the portfolio— how she mourns over her empty womb.* She became as real to me as my baby growing inside my abdomen.

I remember the taxi ride home from the hospital, acutely aware of the empty space within me, milk dripping from my breasts. The maternity ward nurse had told me to press the heel of my hand hard against my breast to stop the milk from flowing. But how does one press, press, press against one's heart and repeat, "Stop being a mother"? I thought of baby Sarah, in the arms of her new mom and dad. They were a complete package, and the only thing that gave me comfort was to love them as a package, but I felt ostracized—a part of the adoption triad that was no longer needed.

When I arrived home from the hospital, I settled into my apartment. And then a florist delivered an anonymous bouquet of pink carnations—so much like the pink pompoms on the little sweater I had dressed Sarah in that morning. The carnations seemed to shout out loud that I had not been forgotten. As the year wore on, I prayed daily for Sarah, and a love for Sarah's mom grew, as though we were sisters born in the same wilderness of loss.

A year after Sarah's birth, a wonderful man came into my life—we married and my empty arms were filled three times over with another daughter and two sons. Life was good. But each year, in the weeks leading up to Sarah's birthday (along with the day itself), I felt the loss of Sarah all over again. I couldn't dismiss our connection even though she wasn't mine. But each year flowers came to me in some form or another, often simple pink flowers on a card from someone who had no idea of the significance of that date, my birthmother status a secret back then; or a friend would unwittingly drop off flowers, pink more often than not—this was a quixotic event that I believe was from God, reminding me that He cared deeply about my loss.

The years crept forward. I quietly celebrated Sarah's nineteenth birthday and started procedures with the private adoption agency to let her know that I was willing to meet her if she was. The fear of rejection was crippling as I wrote my letter to her, but the letter was never delivered to her . . . and so another year slipped by. I told myself it probably wasn't good timing. Maybe Sarah and her family weren't ready for the roller-coaster feelings of a reunion. But the scab of healing over the original loss was ripped off. I felt as I did the day I relinquished her—invisible, silent, tormented by the fear that Sarah's mom would resent my intrusion. Would this proposed reunion bring back the pain of her original empty womb, just like it brought back mine after I relinquished Sarah?

The day of Sarah's twentieth birthday came. At work, coworkers knew I was hurting, but not why. My boss slipped out and came back with a gift for me. It was a plant wrapped in shiny pink paper, profusely dotted with tiny pink flowers that seemed to shout, "I see you! I hear you! I have not forgotten you!"

The letter I had written Sarah was eventually delivered, and we were reunited just months before her wedding. I have Anne, Sarah's mom, to thank for that. As Sarah grew up, Anne never let her forget about me, instilling a love in her daughter's heart for the woman who gave birth to her. Each year they remembered me.

I watched Sarah walk down the aisle but I was in two minds again—overjoyed at being in her life at long last, but the original loss lingered. This beautiful young woman that was born from my womb was not my child. But just like I did during those long nights of prayer during Sarah's gestation, I fancied that I knew what Anne was feeling, thinking, *She's relinquishing Sarah too, letting her daughter go to begin her own life.*

All these years—has it been Anne hearing the echo of my heart, or me hearing hers? Or were Anne's heart and mine knit together by the heartbeat of one child?

Toddlers and Preschoolers
by Alexandra Lutz

*He [Jesus] said to them, "Let the little children come
to me, and do not hinder them, for the kingdom
of God belongs to such as these."*
—MARK 10:14b

All toddlers and preschoolers experience rapid intellectual, social, and emotional changes, in addition to astounding physical development, and they need to progress through all the stages of attachment and separation, no matter what age they were brought home. It's quite an adjustment for anyone involved. And if you recently brought a one- to five-year-old into your home, you have many reasons to be optimistic about the new addition to your family, but that doesn't mean there won't be some extra challenges ahead.

Young children ages one to five make up the single largest group of adoptees from the U.S. foster care system (46 percent) and account for 43 percent of international adoptees. Unfortunately, nearly a third of children in U.S. foster care have severe emotional, behavioral, or developmental problems. They also commonly suffer the effects of low birth weight, prematurity, and drug or alcohol exposure. Children adopted internationally suffer similar hindrances in addition to a variety of medical problems.[1] All of these problems can mean a more challenging adjustment.

At the very least, your toddler or preschooler may grieve the loss of relationships and environment experienced. Though these emotions may not be evident at first, they can emerge as the child learns to trust you.[2]

THE EFFECTS OF ORPHANAGE CARE

Kendra brought Emily home from a Chinese orphanage when her daughter was about nine months old. In many ways, Emily was a perfectly healthy baby. But as toddlerhood advanced, Emily couldn't handle any activity levels outside of her routine. She became increasingly sensitive to sounds and sights to the extent that she seemed unable to function on a physical level. These are signs of sensory processing disorder, a result of lack of stimulation or movement during infancy. Though it may not seem troubling at this age, these disorders, if not addressed, can lead to serious social and academic problems in school.[3]

Feeding presents another common adjustment for children who spent their earliest years in orphanages. Ruling out any medical problems, such children may just be overwhelmed in the first few days following placement, and simply need time to allow their appetite to return. They may be unaccustomed to the flavors and textures of the food being served. Possibly, the children have immature feeding skills and need to be weaned to more age-appropriate foods.[4] Healthy toddlers should be completely bottle weaned by about 15 months of age.

SLEEP DISTURBANCES

Dr. Julian Davies, a clinical assistant professor of pediatrics at the University of Washington, finds that parents who adopt are most concerned with sleep problems during the first three to six months after coming home.

A newly adopted child may sleep soundly for a day or two; this is likely the result of being overwhelmed both physically and emotionally. Once settled at home though, everything about nighttime is likely to be different. New adoptees may have difficulty falling asleep, or going back to sleep after waking. It may be too quiet, too cold or too warm, or just too scary being in a room—and a bed— alone. When you come into the room, your child may be expecting someone else.

Ideally, the parents should develop a soothing routine leading up to bedtime. Soothing activities include listening to music together or reading a book to your child. Don't underestimate the importance of a predictable routine for the final minutes (putting on pajamas, going to the bathroom, brushing teeth, getting tucked into bed, nighttime prayers, warm hug, and a good-night kiss).

Though long-term sleep plans are a matter of intense debate, most professionals knowledgeable of adoption issues do not recommend letting a child cry it out in the short term.[5] Remember, your toddler or preschooler may be a much younger age emotionally, and children with a history of trauma or neglect especially respond poorly to the fear and anxiety of unanswered cries. When you respond to a child's needs and fears you are building trust and nurturing bonding.

Sue had settled in for a little late-night TV after putting Matthew to bed, when he suddenly came racing down the stairs, screaming and frenzied. When she asked him what was wrong, Matthew seemed to not even hear; he didn't even wake up. But after a few minutes, he lay back down on the carpet in peaceful sleep as if nothing had happened. This frightening episode was a night terror—a disturbed, rapid eye movement (REM) state in which children sleepwalk terrified, hysterical, and inconsolable.

Dr. Paul Reisser, primary author of the *Focus on the Family Complete Guide to Baby & Child Care*, recommends that parents protect the child from injuring himself, but otherwise not interfere.[6] Most children will likely fall back to peaceful sleep, just like Matthew, with no memory of the incident. Also frightening to parents is a child who rocks or bangs his head to lull himself to sleep. However, if this behavior began during infancy and ends by age three, many sleep experts or psychologists do not find reason for concern. Still, you should always feel free to seek professional help or advice if you are alarmed.

DEVELOPMENTAL MILESTONES

The toddler and preschool years are full of energy and excitement as your child becomes more physically mobile, and therefore, more independent. Her horizons broaden as she becomes aware of, and engages with, a bigger world. According to the Child Welfare Information Gateway (CWIG), it is normal for children this age to develop new intellectual abilities that can be as frightening as they are exciting.[7]

For example, they can imagine things they have not actually experienced. They imagine unseen monsters under the bed and worry about being lost in the forest. Their verbal skills keep pace with this new information, leading at times to a seemingly endless series of questions. All these new abilities may lead to the realization that Mom and Dad don't know everything—a scary thought for some little guys!

Jacob was perfectly able to sleep alone in his room without fear until he was four. But he suddenly began to ask his parents to check under the bed, in the closet, and behind the curtains. He cried in fear when he was tucked in and would no longer stay in bed, especially if Mom and Dad were downstairs. Jacob had never been scared before, because he had never had the ability to imagine such things as monsters before. And he was not comforted by the fact that his father seemed unable to see the threats that lurked in his room.

It is important to note that children adopted from orphanages typically exhibit developmental delays at the rate of a one-month lag for every three months they spent in an orphanage. Additionally, the Centers for Disease Control and Prevention (CDC) and U.S. Department of Health and Human Services report that rates of developmental delay, learning disabilities, and both physical and mental health issues are higher among adopted children.[8] Always consult your pediatrician if you have concerns or if your child loses previously mastered skills.

LANGUAGE DEVELOPMENT

As with other developmental milestones, language skills vary but have generally consistent patterns in young children. The CDC[9] and Academy of Pediatrics (AAP)[10] offer lists of skills that children should master at varying ages, and the following chart summarizes their warning signs.

By the end of:	2nd year	3rd year	4th year
Consult your pediatrician if he or she does not:	• speak at least 15 words	• use two-word sentences • communicate in phrases	• use sentences of at least three words • use pronouns "me" and "you" correctly

Parents of children adopted internationally should have different expectations. These expectations will vary distinctly depending on the age of adoption, the country of origin, the maintenance of the first native language, and quality of care experienced prior to adoption. Excellent research in this field has been conducted by several people, notably Drs. Sharon Glennen[11] and Boris Gindis,[12] including tables detailing English language milestones for children adopted at various ages. See below some general facts from their research:

- Two types of language skills are needed: communicative and cognitive. Communicative skills emerge almost effortlessly, but cognitive skills— those needed for schoolwork—lag behind, and educational help may be necessary when children enter school.
- To determine how quickly a child should catch up in communicative skills, roughly take the child's age of adoption and double it. In other words, a child adopted at 11 months should catch up by 22 months.

POTTY TRAINING

The AAP suggests that children may be developmentally ready to begin toilet training as early as 18 months or as late as 30 months. Indicators of readiness include dry diapers after naps, predictable bowel movements, and the ability to get to the toilet and undress. But emotional readiness is also important, and a resistant child cannot be forced or punished into using the potty. If your child is under stress such as moving, having a new sibling in the home, or other family challenge, it may be best to wait. Adoption experts also recommend delaying toilet training of a newly adopted toddler or preschooler, perhaps for three or four months.

Generally, children are fully trained during the day by age four. Nighttime success lags behind, but most girls and 75 percent of boys are dry at night by age five. Be aware that bedwetting is hereditary. Your child may be genetically pre-disposed to bedwetting. If you never had to deal with this in your family before, be especially careful not to shame or punish your child for wet sheets. You might consider looking into plastic sheets and other options available for children struggling with this problem.

In a report from the American Academy of Child and Adolescent Psychiatry (AACAP), encopresis—the inability to control the bowels—is rare (about 3 percent), but the rate is higher in sexually abused children and those with cognitive delays.[13] Consult your pediatrician if you have any concerns.

IDENTITY ISSUES

Between the ages of one and five, children begin to figure out who they are in relation to themselves, their peers, their families, and the world. All parents want their children to have a healthy self-image and a secure identity, but parents of adopted children may fret more than others.

As adopted preschoolers move into more complex thinking, they might exhibit behaviors unusual for their personality on important days. Dr. Deborah Borchers, founding member of the American Academy of Pediatrics Section on Adoption and Foster Care, attributes this to their recognition of multiple families. For example, on her birthday, a child may wonder if her birthmother is thinking about her, and whose daughter she is. On Mother's Day she might have several people—birthmother, foster parents, adoptive mother, not to mention grandparents—on her mind and wondering whom to celebrate. Be sensitive during these times. Simplifying the issue—"I'm your real mother now"—doesn't make her feelings go away. Don't feel threatened by her confusion, and don't make her feel as though she has to choose once and for all where her loyalties lie.

Toddlers and preschoolers also begin to identify themselves with their same-sex parent and learn what acceptable behaviors are for a girl or a boy; even children in single-parent homes start making these connections. And as they begin to understand family roles, some children become jealous. Madison's mom thought it was kind of cute when her little girl announced, "Someday, I want to marry Daddy." But when Madison started to become hostile and resentful of her father's affection toward her mother, it was not so endearing. For a while, it seemed like Madison would only challenge her mother. This aggression toward the same-sex parent is a fairly common effect of their new awareness.

TALKING ABOUT ADOPTION

Assuming that a child was brought home as an infant, most experts suggest that she never remembers a time when she didn't know of her adoption, and advocate using the words comfortably at every age. Dr. Reisser adheres to this philosophy, recommending that parents address all questions from children regarding their history in an upbeat, honest, age-appropriate manner.[14] Dr.

Borchers identified age three as the beginning of the "Magic Years" when children delight in hearing their own, fantastic story about being chosen.[15]

Yet other experts promote a different approach. AACAP believes introducing the information to a child who cannot understand it may be threatening and confusing, even traumatic. While acknowledging that young children may ask questions to which they cannot understand the answers, CWIG recommends introducing the concepts of how families are formed, and using that information later—after age six—to discuss your child's adoption.

Of course, toddlers and preschoolers pose many questions, and when he asks, "Mommy, where did I come from?" he may want to know simply in what state he was born (if he met a friend who just moved into the neighborhood from elsewhere), not a thesis on his adoption. He could also be seeking affirmation that he was sent to you by God. Understanding your child's question is a critical step in knowing how to answer.

Remember to use very concrete language and don't expect that saying it once will settle the issue forever. It will take years of intellectual and emotional development for him to understand the story completely. Stay positive and excited— you will have time later to help him process the loss. Tell him how thrilling it was for everyone involved, reinforce how much his birthmother loved and cared about him to make this decision, and let him know that it's okay to ask questions.

Julie, who was adopted at age four, was too shy to ask any questions, even though she remembered her foster families and wanted to know about her birthmother. Now grown, Julie urges parents not to wait for adopted children to bring up the subject. Especially if your child has memories of life before adoption, encourage her to love and think about both of her mommies and daddies. Never make her feel that she is being disloyal to you for her curiosity, and remember: Just because she isn't asking doesn't mean she isn't wondering.

A FINAL REMINDER

Perhaps the most important message to convey to your adopted child at any stage is this: You are God's prized possession (1 Corinthians 6:19–20). A toddler or preschooler certainly understands prized possessions.

But especially at a time when children are piecing together ideas of family and identity, and may be learning about their adoption, parents can use their own family story to introduce the bigger ideas of God's family.

Help him hide God's Word and promises in his heart by reading his very own picture Bible and singing songs together. He can grow up with the assurance that Jesus loves the little children . . . all the children of the world.

■ ■ ■

Alexandra Lutz teaches high school and writes on issues of parenting and education. She wrote one of the first adoption series to appear on Focus on the Family's Web site.

Neti and "NO"
by Tracy Waal

We're at an awkward stage of the language barrier with our two youngest girls, Neti and Meke. We brought them home to Ohio with us from Ethiopia a few weeks ago. They *understand* dozens of English words and phrases, but they don't know how to *respond* in English. Consequently, to the casual observer it might appear that politeness and obedience are out the window. Nothing illustrates this more than Neti's fixation on the word *no*.

Under normal circumstances, a six-year-old has several hundred words to choose from to let Mom and Dad know what's going on in her gray matter. Neti, though, doesn't have that luxury. When Mommy or Daddy ask her to do something and she can't find the proper English response, she has two choices.

Choice #1: Talk with a line of reasoning that makes perfect sense to her but sounds like a string of random, unintelligible syllables and chatter to Mommy and Daddy. (This usually results in her mom or me smiling and saying, "I have no idea what you just said," followed by a repeating of instructions in English.)

Choice #2: Just Say "NO!"

"No" means a lot of things to Neti. When Mom says, "Wash your hands, it's time to eat," "no" can mean, "I will as soon as I go to the bathroom," or "I thought you wanted me to pick up my toys first." It can mean, "I don't like green beans, so please don't put them on my plate," or "Can't we stay up and play a little longer?"

But we're wise to the fact that "no" can also mean, "You're not my boss!" or "Don't tell me what to do!"

So we're faced with paying much more attention to details. We don't want to discipline a child when her no means, "I'm hot. I'd rather sleep without a blanket tonight."

But neither do we want to give a pass to a verbal act of defiance.

Learning a new language can be challenging.

Elementary Age and Middle Childhood

by Rebecca Stahr MacDougall

The goal is to see children come to Christ. And what better place for that to happen than in loving, adoptive families? Jesus took the children in His arms, put His hands on them, and blessed them. Are we ready now to do the same?
—Bishop W. C. Martin, *Small Town, Big Miracle*

"The middle years are highly underrated." So a colleague tenderly told me as my eldest daughter began school. Her words often reverberated through my heart, encouraging me not to take this period of time in our children's lives for granted. Instead, I want to enjoy and invest in this "limited time" opportunity.

What may feel like a lower maintenance time of parenting in comparison to the toddler or adolescent years is a period when more energy is freed for parent and child to develop communication and strengthen their relationship.

It is a time when children, whether adopted as infants or older children, are willing to talk about adoption, the many issues that surround their experience, and the meaning that has in their life.

Few things in life are as delightful as a 10-year-old boy who spends hours on end playing football with neighborhood boys and then, with grass-stained knees, comes looking for the bedtime routine of reading stories and snuggling with Mom or Dad. Equally precious is an 11-year-old girl who spends hours in school or with friends but shares her heart with Mom or Dad from the backseat of the car on the way to a soccer game or a church club.

These years provide an opportunity for you to guide your children through a growing understanding of what it means to be adopted. As their primary support, you are there to navigate them through special identity issues that come with the realization that one was relinquished.

DEVELOPMENTAL TASKS AND MILESTONES

Physically, the elementary-aged child is developing in ways that lay a foundation for emotional, social, and moral development. The brain is maturing in significant ways that move a child from concrete to more logical ways of thinking. As logic develops, children begin to realize that the world does not revolve around them and that others have experiences apart from them.

During this time their fears become less fantasy based (the dark, boogey men, or being alone) and more people related (social rejection, exams, kidnapping). Muscles that control fine and gross motor control are developing, so children can develop skills in sports or playing instruments. And keep in mind that mastery of activities gives your child an opportunity for developing a more defined sense of self and positive self-esteem.

Adopted children develop in all of the same ways that any other child does in the middle years, but the additional layer of adoption is always a part of who they are, sometimes rising to a preeminent position to overlay all other parts of the person, but more often subtly lying below the surface or merging with the other layers of the self.

It's not uncommon for adopted children to feel different, and middle childhood is a good time to expose children to cultural diversity and different types of families. Race and culture add more obvious layers for children who are part of interracial families. (For those families who have adopted transracially, chapter 11 offers more on this important topic.)

A GROWING PERSONAL AWARENESS OF ADOPTION

As the adopted child's reasoning, capacity for empathy, and self-concept develop, the realization of loss of his family of origin dawns in new ways. This may be the time when adoption is first felt as a problem. Brodzinsky, Schechter, and Henig, in their classic book, *Being Adopted,* simply put it this way: "This is when the child, because of his growing capacity for logical thought, begins to realize that there's a flip side to his beloved adoption story—that in order to be 'chosen,' he first had to be given away."[1]

The child begins to tread the waters of ambivalence, maintaining many positive feelings about adoption *and* recognizing more difficult and sometimes confusing feelings. As an older child spins a growing web of social connections and awareness, he may experience a sense of being different and struggle with new attitudes.

It is not uncommon for normally well-adjusted children around age six or seven to exhibit behavior problems, sometimes indicating a period of grief. In open adoptions, a child may exhibit new ambivalence toward his birth family members. Perhaps she begins to understand the lost potential of brother/sister relationships with her birthmother's children.

Several days before a scheduled visit with his birth family, our six-year-old exhibited angry thoughts toward his birthmother's new baby. He hit his fist against his pillow and asked if she loved the baby more than him. We talked about the difference between living with someone every day and loving her, and seeing someone a few times a year and loving her. He was able to verbalize that he loved both his birthmother and me, but it was different because he didn't live with her.

The next morning I suggested that I could call and postpone the visit till sometime when he wanted to go. He replied, "Oh, that's okay, Mom. Today I love everyone. I feel a lot better." Because of the relationship his birthmother and I had, and her desire to be sensitive to his needs, I felt comfortable calling her and letting her know that our son needed to hear a verbal affirmation of her love. When we visited, he displayed no angry feelings but seemed to enjoy the baby. That evening he told me with a smile, "Rachel loves me, Mom. She bent down and whispered 'I love you' in my ear."

During this time, the need to be heard, to ask questions, and to process in an accepting and loving environment is crucial and especially effective.

THE OUTSIDE WORLD'S AWARENESS OF ADOPTION

During the elementary years of school, other children become very interested in the adoption experience and, given the opportunity, openly ask questions. Coach your child so she can "be the expert" and develop a sense of competence about adoption. This way, your child will be able to answer questions from her peers as she chooses. Help her identify what is private information, and encourage her to communicate that boundary to others.

Because our son, Nate, looks different from us, he has been asked many more personal questions about his adoption. I have had strangers ask me questions about my children, in their presence, as if they weren't there, such as:

"How old was the mother?"

"How could she give away such a beautiful child?"

"Is he smart?"

"Does she know her real mother?"

While some questions may seem inappropriate for people to ask you in front of your child, they provide an excellent opportunity for you to model setting boundaries and answering questions. After all, you won't always be there to shield your child.

When the parent answers questions, the child should almost always be asked for permission to share his information. Sometimes our children have brought a friend in and asked me to explain adoption to them because they don't want to do it themselves but they do want the friend to be educated. Have conversations that involve your child and their close friends. Recently our son, Nate, told me that it is good when Kaelen (his neighbor who is older than him and very familiar with our family) is with him because he "explains it all to them."

As a child becomes a "tween" on her way to adolescence, she is working harder to incorporate her physical self (appearance and genetics), her values (usually reflecting her parents' values), the values of her peers and culture, her abilities, and her relationship with God into her total view of herself. The adopted child has at least one more piece to work in as well.

UNDERSTANDING AND TALKING ABOUT ADOPTION

An important and unique task we have, as parents, is to effectively communicate with our children about adoption. Effective communication:

- listens for the questions and concerns being voiced and follows their lead,

- imparts concrete information that may not have been shared before,
- repeats information in an age-appropriate manner (don't assume that if you told them once, they remember),
- frames information in a context that develops a story they can picture (what you don't tell them, they will fabricate in their own minds),
- models appropriate language for relationships (what to call people) and a subject that may not be correctly addressed by anyone else in the child's daily life,
- affords a safe, empathetic environment to explore thoughts and feelings entangled in the topic.

When I receive a call from parents of a school-aged child who are concerned about "adoption issues," I encourage them to first talk through their own feelings and thoughts that might stand in the way of effectively communicating with their child. A healthy awareness of your own feelings can help you avoid dismissive or overreactive responses to your child's feelings, such as, "Well, you were meant to be in our family and we love each other so there is nothing to feel bad about," or "It doesn't matter now." This type of response can immobilize the child from sharing further feelings. Instead, by drawing from your own losses and experiences, you can respond with empathy as your child processes her losses related to adoption.

It is a challenge to acknowledge the role of adoption in your child's life without moving toward either extreme of denying adoption issues or overfocusing, blaming all of a child's issues on adoption. Well-meaning parents can assume that their child is deeply bothered by adoption and suggest counseling or intervention or answer simple questions with very complex answers and more information than the child needs or wants.

Many adoption experts suggest that parents can be too quick to introduce therapy for a child at this age and that the parent is often the best therapist in the middle years. However, counseling can be very useful to parents in providing support and guidance so they, in turn, can be better prepared to address issues with their child. But unresolved problems *can* interfere with a child's development or trigger emotional problems. Consultation with a counselor can be helpful for parents in determining if therapy for their child might help resolve a current problem or provide tools to cope with later life challenges.

The American Academy of Child and Adolescent Psychiatry recommends responding to the following warning signs, indicating that an evaluation might be appropriate:

- Changes in school performance (grades, homework, skipping school)
- Excessive worry or anxiety
- Loss of interest in usual activities
- Change in sleeping habits or frequent nightmares
- Mood changes, including temper tantrums, depression, anger, and aggression
- Dangerous and/or illegal behavior, including use of alcohol, cigarettes, drugs, inappropriate sexual behavior, vandalism, theft, or fighting[2]

Finally, the desire of parents to protect their child and prevent any pain or grief can halt communication just when it could be most effective. You may have to share such difficult information as a birthparent's criminal background or that your child's conception resulted from sexual assault or prostitution. Even the existence of older siblings or children born and parented by the birthparent later can be difficult information to share.

However, difficult information is best shared during the elementary years when the child has time to process it with the help and guidance of his parents. And regardless of the circumstances, birthparents should be given dignity and talked about with respect.

Children who have been adopted need to know their entire stories, not just the good parts. Secrets eventually come out, and keeping a secret may only add a sense of shame. Of course, information needs to be shared in an age-appropriate way. It may be more appropriate for an eight-year-old to be told that his birthfather was very mixed up at the time he was born, that he had gotten in trouble and was in jail and couldn't take care of him. After he learns more about sexuality (when he is closer to 11 or 12 years old) he can be given the details that the father is a registered sex offender, with or without the details of his crime.

Christian families have the blessing of the message of God's grace in all of our stories. Our children need to learn early that God has graciously given us guidelines to live within because He knows what is best for us and longs to protect us, and others, from the consequences of unhealthy choices. It is also our gracious God who, in the midst of those wrong choices, blesses us with good gifts. Your child's birth may be a good gift that came from a terrible situation. Your child also needs to learn that we live in a sinful, fallen world—we are all affected by the decisions and choices that others make. At the same time, talk about your experiences and failures and God's grace in your life.

If immorality was a factor in your child's conception, it is vital to address any perception that an adoption plan was made because something was wrong with your child. As children get closer to adolescence they are less likely to talk to you about sex or their adoption so don't let those middle years slip by without this communication.

Without natural adoption conversation introduced by the parent, the child may not be able to form the words to ask or may deduce that the subject is taboo. Children can easily sense if a parent is uncomfortable with a subject and may even feel disloyal asking about birthparents. Many adults, searching for their birthparents, have told me that as long as they were home, or as long as their parents were alive, they did not feel that they could ask questions or search because it would hurt their parents or they would feel disloyal.

On top of all the other emotions involved, I would not want my child to be worrying about my feelings when she has a need for information. I would hope my child would not wait until I was gone to get answers to questions that she has pondered for years. I want him to seek my assistance and support in seeking the answers he needs.

While you should give your child direct eye contact when she is talking to you, she will often talk most easily about these things in an informal setting when you can't see her, like when you are driving in the car or talking late in the evening with the lights out. Speak naturally and use the same tone you would use for talking about family outings or baseball practice. And if she doesn't ask, introduce the subject in different ways, with an easygoing approach.

Connecting with activities at your adoption agency, other adoptive families, or adoption groups can "normalize" adoption and provide stimulation for communication about adoption. It is a benefit to maintain ties with those who are part of your child's adoption story. Your child's own scrapbook or life storybook is a wonderful starting point for talking. Books or movies featuring adoptive families can also stimulate conversations.

Complimenting your child on a characteristic you appreciate about him and relating it as a gift from a birthparent can let a child know that you are open to talking about his birthparents. Both of our daughters are beautiful creative writers and so is their birthmother. Our son has inherited his birthmother's sweet disposition and sense of humor and his birthfather's tall, athletic body. If you don't have a history for your child, think about who your child is. You may find that you actually do know a lot about the birthparents after all.

Two early questions that children have are, "Who do I look like?" and "Why did my birthmother place me for adoption?" Other questions might include where their birthparents are now and what are they doing. (If you don't know, remind them that God knows where the birthparents are, and He is caring for them.) They often want to know where they were from the time they were born until they came home with you. As you share information, be sure to answer these questions that children may or may not ask: "Will I be all right?" "Will you (the important people in my life) be all right?" "How will this affect my daily life?"

Middle childhood is a key time for children to express, question, and explore their stories and what it means for their identity. They will revisit these issues on different levels throughout their life, and unresolved issues will be carried into adolescence.

When those times arise, you can remind your child of Job 10:8–12: "Your hands shaped me and made me. . . . Did you not pour me out like milk and curdle me like cheese, clothe me with skin and flesh and knit me together with bones and sinews? You gave me life and showed me kindness, and in your providence watched over my spirit."

These words are a beautiful reminder of God's involvement in your child's life before and after his birth—and that He loves him, just the way he is.

■■■

Rebecca Stahr MacDougall is the director of domestic adoption and birthparent services at Sunny Ridge Family Center in the Chicago area. Since 1983, Becky has counseled birthparents and their families, conducted home studies and post-placement services, and educated the community on open adoption and other adoption issues. Becky and her husband are the parents of three children and have personally experienced open and transracial adoption.

Adopting Jake
by Amber Bartell

When our fourth child arrived three days before Christmas, it was a magical time for our family. Seven-year-old Jake was practically perfect in every way. He came down for breakfast every morning dressed and ready to go. I would ask him if he brushed his hair, his teeth, or made his bed, and yes, of course, he already had. He stayed with my husband or me every moment of the day—from the first night on, he even crawled into bed with us.

It was not until later that we realized how scared Jake was. He felt like he needed to be perfect and even worse, he did not feel safe by himself. He would never play outside or in his room unless someone else played with him.

I had always invited one of the kids to go with me whenever I went on an errand so we could have some one-on-one time together. Jake hated it when I went places, but he never wanted to leave home. It took about six months before he realized going with Mom was not so bad, and I often let him choose a treat at the grocery store or took him out to lunch.

A big breakthrough for Jake occurred about two years after he joined our family. He had left a toy out on the patio that needed to be put away. It was already dark outside when I discovered it, so I told him that he could either put the toy in his room until the next day or take the dog and a flashlight with him to put it away in the shed. He sighed loudly and said, "Oh, I'll just go put it away now!" Without the aid of a flashlight or dog, he put the toy in the shed—a huge step!

A few days later, he asked for a sandbox for his birthday, and then spent the rest of the summer playing outside. I would have thought 10 was too old for a sandbox, but before long, the neighborhood kids came over and filled it with army men and pirate ships. That sandbox provided hours of fun for our son, and we watched amazed by how much he had changed since he joined our family.

9

Adolescence

by Patt Wadenpfuhl

Now, with God's help, I shall become myself.
—SOREN KIERKEGAARD

I share life with an emerging adult. Though the words *adolescent* and *teenager* are more technically accurate, I still prefer to think of it in these terms: *emerging adult.* It reminds me what this passage from childhood to adulthood is all about: We are in preparation for launch.

While it is an exhilarating time, it can also be an infuriating, bewildering, excruciating time for child and parent alike. Take it from someone who has been in the trenches, by choice, three times. My Korean daughter, Jennifer, entered our hearts and lives at the age of 16 months. She is now 28 years old and a brilliant chemist with a smile that lights up the room. My 25-year-old German/Irish son, Jacob, is the only child who survived in the midst of our countless miscarriages. He also survived his teen years by the grace of God and is now a multi-talented artist who recently married a spunky, Irish/Italian ballerina. Even as I write this, I pause to thank God for who they have become and for who they are still becoming. It's wonderful to survive the years of broken curfews and slammed doors to become friends and trusted confidants.

But we are not yet finished. When we were in our forties and Jacob and Jen were in their teens, God expanded our family, inserting yet another nationality into the Wadenpfuhl branch of the United Nations. Now my husband and I are steering our third child through the tumultuous waters of adolescence.

I first saw 18-month-old Hana Jun Grace peeking through the second-story railing of an orphanage in Hunan Province, China. That was 11 years ago. Today as I write this, Hana is sprawled on the couch opposite me, intensely lost in a book I bought for her recent 13th birthday: the life story of Condoleezza Rice. Every so often she blurts, "Mom, you *gotta* hear this!" and proceeds to read aloud a passage she finds fascinating. She then follows with a well-thought-out 13-year-old comment about how the government—and the world—should be run. Hana is dogmatic; she *pontificates*—there is no other word for it.

At four years of age she once used the word "cataclysmic" to answer a question. By the age of 10, she sneaked Victor Hugo off her sister's bookshelf and plowed through *Les Miserables*, the unabridged version. Now as I watch her turn a page, her face contorting as she mentally wrestles with new thoughts and concepts, I still see the little girl who suffered months of night terrors when we brought her home from the orphanage. I see the little girl who broke her arm at age three, and starred as a turtle in the school play at age seven. Of course, it is an illusion; she is no longer that child, but she is not yet an adult. And therein lies the rub. Hana raises her head briefly and blurts again, "Parents need to give kids room to breathe. I'm glad you're not controlling." I smile knowingly as she burrows into her book. Give it time, Hana. We're not done yet.

DEVELOPMENTAL MILESTONES

Let's start with the good news: Whether you've recently adopted a teenager or your adopted child is just now reaching those adolescent years, the wild mood swings and self-absorption, the sudden rudeness and emotional meltdowns triggered by heaven-knows-what, are all *utterly normal.* I don't know about you, but I find comfort in the fact that there is a norm for adolescent behavior. To tell us where we are on the journey, experts have identified certain developmental milestones—a set of physical, emotional, social, and cognitive skills—that are commonly reached by all children as they grow up, though not necessarily occurring at the same time.

PHYSICAL DEVELOPMENT

Puberty is a time of unprecedented growth in a child's life. As hormones begin their work, hair sprouts, shoulders widen, voices deepen, and curves appear; girls begin to look like women and boys begin to look like men. Rapid weight and height gains leave boys and girls feeling lanky and awkward or fat and self-conscious. Professor and child development specialist Angela Huebner writes, "If it seems to you that teens' bodies are all arms and legs, then your perception is correct. During this phase of development, body parts don't all grow at the same rate. This can lead to clumsiness as the teen tries to cope with limbs that seem to have grown overnight. Teens can appear gangly and uncoordinated."[1] Well, that explains all the broken dishes.

With so many physical changes, it is understandable that teens become very preoccupied with *body image*. Teens want to fit in; they want to look like their friends. Looking different or feeling out-of-step with their peers causes great anxiety. That's why I don't hassle Hana as she searches for her unique style. As long as it's modest and appropriate for the event, I don't care what she's wearing. I may ask her to leave the Israel Defense Force T-shirt home when we're moving through African airports, or ask her not to wear the ragged jeans to Grandma's house, but when I do, we discuss the reasons and come to an understanding. It gives her some control over her spiraling life and creates trust between us.

As parents of emerging adults, we need to pick our battles carefully. We can enforce our authority and win every skirmish, but we may lose the war—or worse, our child's heart.

COGNITIVE DEVELOPMENT

Meanwhile, the hormones that are shaping their bodies are also shifting their thinking. It's usually not until adolescence that young people begin to wrap their minds around abstract concepts—such as God, or the workings of the wind, for example.

At 13, Hana cares deeply about the environment, politics, and human rights issues ranging from slavery to gender equality. Though she has been exposed to global issues all of her life, this recent activism is directly related to her new cognitive skills. So is her recent self-consciousness and tendency toward high drama. But I don't mean to make light of it. The pain is real; the angst is real. The wild pendulum swing between self-confidence and self-doubt, self-acceptance and self-loathing, is all part of the journey.

Adolescent adoptees face the added task of processing painful and puzzling issues related to their adoption. For instance, adopted teens also have the challenge of looking unlike anyone in their adoptive families. People have often told me that Jacob has my eyes or his father's nose, but, obviously, no one has ever said that about my daughters. It is during the teen years that our children may begin to wonder: *Who do I look like? Exactly whose nose do I have?*

I confess; I often forget that Jen and Hana were grafted into our family tree. They are simply my beloved daughters. But as much as I love my children, their lives did not start with me. They have a history that I do not share. I was not there when they drew their first breaths. I was not there for Jen when, as a newborn, she was left on the steps of a police station. I was not there for Hana when, at 14 months of age, she was left in a field in midwinter with severe burns on her tiny chest. Although we may have no solid answers, it is during adolescence that the big life questions begin to surface more readily.

Of course, each child is unique. My girls happen to be polar opposites. When she was a teenager, Jen asked no questions about her birth family and refused all parental attempts to broach the subject. Although we tried to interest her in Korean culture and language, she would have none of it.

When Jennifer turned 18, we traveled to Korea together to visit the orphanage, and to thank the woman who had cared for her in those early months. The director remembered her and kindly shared stories of her infancy. While I cried many tears, Jen was unmoved and uninterested. Thinking that she might be afraid to speak in front of me, the director took her to a private room to talk. When they emerged from the room 30 minutes later, the director shared Jen's words with me: "I have no interest in finding my birthmother or in any information about my birth family. She either didn't want me or couldn't keep me. Either way, my mother is outside this room and my father and brother are in Cleveland. This is my family."

Jen returned to the U.S. with a new love for all things Korean, but with no answers—because, as she told me, she simply had no questions.

On the other hand, Hana has nothing *but* questions; common questions that teens ask such as, *Am I normal? Does everyone have mood swings like me? Does everyone feel self-conscious?* She also asks the questions common to adopted children, such as, *Why was I abandoned? Why does God let bad things happen? Are my birthparents dead? Will they be in heaven?* Older teens, wondering what lurks in the family bloodline, may worry about the lack of a family medical history. As adolescents practice their new thinking skills, the big "what ifs" begin to surface.

One day Hana asked me, "If you were given a choice between the baby you miscarried and me, who would you choose?" I told her the truth; I would choose her. Most recently she asked if I would be willing to help her find her birthparents when she gets older . . . if she decides she wants to look for them. I told her the truth again—yes, I will, if that is what she truly wants. I've learned not to be threatened by questions like this. It's not personal. It's not even about *me*.

I've also learned that while we don't always have the answers our children seek, we can give them a safe place to ask the tough questions. We can listen to them as they try to find out who they are and where they fit in the world. Most importantly, we can love them—no matter what. But this confusing and painful search for personal identity will test even the strongest love.

IDENTITY DEVELOPMENT

While the experts don't agree on whether there is a noteworthy difference between adopted children and birth children on the issue of identity formation, they do agree that it is the primary task of adolescence. In order for young people to become fully-functioning healthy adults, they must first find out who they are as distinct individuals, separate from their parents.

They may, in the process, try on different personalities for size. Teens may imitate celebrities or their friends, but the personalities they don't want to assume are their parents'. As they attempt to pull away and distinguish themselves from Mom and Dad, they may become critical—even disrespectful.

Using their new mental skills, they begin to grapple with their own beliefs, philosophies, and values. Sometimes they embrace those of their parents; other times they discard them. Jennifer never shared identical anything with me as a teen. She was, in a word, contrary.

From the very beginning she fought me for control of her life. She defined herself as whatever was the opposite of Mom. For Jen it was dangerous to agree with me, so she didn't. If I chose red, Jen chose blue; if I said yes, Jen said no. We pushed and pulled our way through her adolescence. And like all others her age,

Jen flipped back and forth between the need for independence and the need to depend on us as she learned to make her own choices and stand on her own two feet.

Identity formation is more complex for adopted teens, for a variety of reasons. As we've already discussed, there are the physical differences and unanswered questions about their beginnings. Then, there is the fear of rejection and abandonment. They've already lost one set of parents; if they begin to disagree with the parents who have loved and raised them, will they lose another?

Some teens may be afraid to express contrary opinions or beliefs for fear of being rejected. Other teens test their parents' love and commitment by pushing against them and acting out. They may grow hostile, or they may cling tightly. They may fantasize about their birthparents and create a romantic version of their history to deal with what they suspect is a painful truth. They may disagree with everything the parent says, or they may be completely compliant—too compliant.

The root of rejection and deep fear of abandonment at the very core of their lives influences their behavior and decisions—whether they are aware of it or not. When I recently remarked to Hana that we had about five years left together, a look of panic crossed her face. She snuggled closer and assured me that she wasn't leaving home—ever. The next day she announced that she had narrowed her college choices to Harvard, Oxford, or maybe a university in South Africa. I expected that; and I expect that she will flip-flop on this for a while. My goal is for Hana to be so secure in her sense of self that she is ready to fly when it's the right time for her.

Of course, there are still other unique issues that adopted teens face as they grow up. If the child is of a different ethnic identity than her adoptive family, she will need to integrate that into her sense of self. Unfortunately, she will also face racism in one form or another and this often comes in ways we do not expect. For instance, because the stereotypical Asian is seen to be self-disciplined and brilliant, especially in mathematics, science, and the arts, Asian children can feel a pressure to perform.

When we were still in China waiting for Hana's visa we would often take walks through the city with our adoption group. I can't tell you how many strangers came up to us, poked Hana in the head, and said, "Big head, smart baby." Well, she *is* smart, but she struggles with perfectionism. I wonder how much of it is her desire to excel and how much of it is an unspoken need to live up to the expectations of others. Keep in mind that your teenager, like mine, will have unique pressures, triumphs, and sorrows as she grows to be herself.

It is important for us as parents to stay above the emotional fray during these unpredictable years if we are going to see and think clearly. Try to spot the high hurdles from a distance and anticipate what your adolescent will need to get over them. For instance, be proactive in your conversations. For years, Hana and I have talked about issues that are unique to adoptive teens. But we have also already discussed common topics such as eating disorders, drug abuse, and sexual purity.

A friend of mine who is a single adoptive parent saw clearly that her preteen African son would eventually need a male mentor to help guide him through the adolescent passage. Instead of waiting until the storm hit, she contacted a local university and found willing mentors through an African-American fraternity. Through the years, other men from her local church have also played an important role in this young man's life—but this was by invitation. My friend anticipated her son's need and acted to meet it.

There are times, however, when a conversation or a cultural mentor/friend is not enough, when even loving parents are not enough. If your emerging adult begins to act out in dangerous ways, or withdraw into isolation and depression, it is time to reach beyond your immediate family circle. Again, be proactive and pay attention to the signs. Notice, for instance, if your teen begins to spend too much time alone, struggles in school, or loses interest in his usual activities, hobbies, and friends.

Your teen is unique, so these behaviors do not necessarily mean there *is* a serious problem. But if you determine that the scope of your child's problems goes beyond your ability to cope, don't hesitate to find professional help.

Consult your family doctor or pastor; ask him or her to recommend a good counseling program. Or call Focus on the Family and ask the staff to recommend, from their nationwide network, counseling services available in your region. The yellow pages of your phone book will yield contact information for crisis intervention, social service programs, community youth organizations, and adoption support networks.

Don't be afraid or embarrassed—the important thing is to *act* in the best interest of the child and family you love. Keep the two-way lines of communication wide open, even when you think your teen isn't listening.

Understanding and Talking about Adoption

In talking about adoption, it is important to understand the power of words. Words can cut a person to the heart. The Bible tells us that the tongue has the power of life and death (Proverbs 18:21). So as we talk about adoption with our teenagers, it's important to reexamine our words and make sure they are communicating life. Are we being critical; are our words speaking death to their hopes, dreams, or even their sense of belonging?

For example, I do not introduce Jen and Hana as my *adopted* daughters. They *were* adopted; that's how they entered the family. Now that they are *in* the family, *adopted* is no longer a part of their title or identity.

When well-meaning people say our daughters are blessed because they were rescued, my response is that we are *all* blessed and we have *all* been rescued. When someone asks, "Do you have any daughters of your own?" the answer is simply "yes."

As our children hear us speaking naturally and positively about adoption, they see themselves in a positive light. For instance, instead of using words like *abandoned,* which means *forsaken* or *deserted*—we have found words like *relinquished*, which implies *regret* or *reluctance* to let someone go.[2] While I can't answer Hana's questions, "Why was I abandoned?" or "Are my birthparents alive?" she and I have tearfully prayed together for her birthparents.

The other day she told me, "I have been loved twice. Just the fact that my birthparents left me where I would be found is an act of love. They took a risk; they could have been arrested if they got caught abandoning a child. They could have just killed me like so many other baby girls, but they wanted to give me a better life." You might think she is making up a story, but where no facts exist, sometimes a well-deduced story is enough to settle a child's heart.

Stories have the power to shape thinking. Hana never tires of hearing how I carried her referral picture in a locket next to my heart for months before we met. Jen never tires of hearing how I slept with her referral picture on my pillow every night. Both of them love to hear the stories of how they were chosen by God and born in our hearts. They love to hear about the miracles God worked to bring us together as a family. We tell and retell the stories of their childhood, sharing how deeply loved they were before we even knew their names.

The other day I asked Hana if she ever wondered what her given birth name was. She said, "No, because God named me 10 years before I was born." And she's right. In 1984, 10 years before her birth, God spoke a word to my heart. He told me that I would have a daughter and her name was Hana Grace. A story like this gives a sense of divine destiny to any life.

When Hana first came from China, I used to rock her every night as she took her bedtime bottle. Like every other mother, I was determined that "mama" would be her first English word. So night after night, as she stared up into my eyes, I would ask, "Who am I?" and I would answer my own question: ma-ma. This continued for some nights; then finally she decided to speak. Not really expecting an answer, I asked her again, "Who am I?" To my surprise, Hana took the bottle out of her mouth, looked straight into my eyes, and said clearly, "*Mine.*"

For those of us who are privileged to steward and love these wonderful emerging adults, I pray that God would give us not only His wisdom, but also His merciful heart.

■■■

Patt Wadenpfuhl is the president and founder of WorldView International (WVI), a not-for-profit organization that exists to incite compassionate action and ignite hope in a hurting world. She focuses on WVI's work with orphans and the neediest children in the African nations of Malawi and Madagascar. The Wadenpfuhls' story of their journey to China to adopt 18-month-old Hana Jun has been broadcast on *Focus on the Family* and shared in various venues throughout the world.

My Adoption Story
by Carissa Woodwyk

I used to always begin telling my "adoption" story by saying, "I was born in Korea and, at the age of five months, I was adopted into a pastor's home in Michigan." But over the past eight years, I've come to realize that there's much more to the beginning of my story.

I was conceived in South Korea to birthparents still unknown to me. I don't have the details surrounding my conception, my parents' relationship, or why I was relinquished at such a young age, but I do know that my adoption papers report that I was abandoned at a Korean orphanage. After that, I spent time in a foster home before arriving in the United States where I was adopted by a pastor and his wife.

Growing up in America with my adoptive family seemed the perfect situation—shouldn't every baby be grateful she was adopted? What kind of life would I have had in Korea? As I grew older, I had a quiet understanding that I should be grateful for the life I led in America. You could even say that I was a "good" adoptee, but I was secretly grieving my losses.

We want so much to believe that there is little or no effect on a child when he or she is adopted, but the effect is *so* significant! There are emotional consequences that affect an adoptee's heart. They begin when a birthmother contemplates giving up her baby and linger throughout the child's adult life. Questions surface, most of which can't be answered.

As I grew up, I realized that there were many unknown and missing pieces of my history, pieces that no one seemed to care about, even me. I didn't know any better! I wasn't aware that there were pieces of me left in Korea, pieces that had the ability to bring meaning and definition to who I was.

Without realizing the significant effect of being relinquished, nor knowing I needed to grieve what I had lost, I became a fighter. My identity was already distorted by the lies that Satan had been throwing at me from very early on. He inundated my mind from the very beginning with lies about who I was as a person, which became deeply embedded in my heart and mind. I began to believe things like, "You're too much," "No one is going to fight for you, so you better fight for yourself," "You don't need anyone," and "No one wants you."

When I was born, I didn't receive what all babies *need*—bonding, attachment, and love from the two people who gave them life. My first life-lesson was that I didn't deserve to be loved. What a lie!

I've had to wrestle with these ingrained lies my whole life. It's hard to remember that these messages are, in fact, untruths. But I know that my heavenly Father delights in me, just the way I am. He sees my heart and He loves me unconditionally. There's such comfort, assurance, and peace in knowing and believing this truth.

My parents were good, faithful, wise, diligent, and protective. They loved me the best ways they knew how. They instilled many great things into my life—a strong foundation of faith, what it means to be a woman, how to interact with people, how to be a successfully functioning person in today's society—so many invaluable lessons! But, even though I looked good externally, even though my accomplishments were great and I seemed to have it all together, my heart was still wounded from being relinquished, and it desperately needed healing. I'd learned to find my identity in being a "good" person and "doing" rather than "being."

After an increasing awareness of the effects of being relinquished, I began exploring who I was as a relinquished baby *and* as an adopted daughter. God drew me into a healing journey, taking me back to the "beginning," helping me see the painful parts of my history. I had to be honest about what my experiences had done to my tender heart, grieving what I had lost, including the missing pieces that I might never know. The parts of me that I had silenced so many years before had to be reawakened. There would be no healing in my life if I didn't take an honest look at what I'd done with my grief, my pain, and my wounds.

I found myself facing a choice—would I receive God's love and forgiveness or would I believe the lie that my heart was not worth fighting for?

I chose to fight for my heart. Over the past 10 years, I've explored who I am in Christ. I'm still learning what it means to live without being driven by what others think of me. I'm learning to love *me* so that I can love my husband, my family, my friends, and others around me. And I'm still learning that it's not about eliminating the past, but that God wants me to use what happened—the good *and* the bad—for His glory.

The truth is, those early lies still creep into my head in the most random and sneaky ways, triggering my old wounds, but now I have God's truth as a standard to which I compare and identify those lies that Satan throws at me. I am endlessly pursuing God's best for me, and along the way I hear His gentle voice reminding me, "*I* created you."

So, maybe my life began in a way that God would never have intended for a baby to start her life, but now I have the opportunity to partner with Him to make something beautiful out of my life—and all the glory goes to Him! I love knowing that the story of my heart matters.

Part III
Unique Identity Issues

10

Loss and Grief

by Ron Nydam

*How long must I wrestle with my thoughts
and every day have sorrow in my heart?*
—Psalm 13:2

One of the biggest challenges that parents face, a task that may mean shedding tears, is that of helping their adopted children grieve. The emotional pain that adoptees must deal with very early in life has been a subject of debate through the years in much of adoption literature. It was once thought that the exchange of birthparents for adoptive parents could be a relatively seamless, painless transition, certainly not a process that could cause emotional injury. People believed that the less relinquished children knew about their birth stories and birth families, the better.

The goal then was to get on with life *as if* relinquishment—whether done willingly by the birthparents or demanded by the state authority—never mattered. This view of things was driven by concern about avoiding shame for all triad members. Birthmothers, often sent hundreds of miles away for secret baby deliveries at homes for unwed mothers, could avoid the shame of nonmarital pregnancy. Adoptive parents, often wounded by the pain and embarrassment of infertility, could enjoy parenting. And adoptees could be relieved of their unwanted child status if no one knew their truth. But the experts of the day were wrong; relinquishment has its price.

There is part of the adoptee's heart that can never be adopted; the part forever connected to birthparents and birth history. The loss has its own pain, and parents who adopt are therefore summoned to journey with their children through the sadness and even the anger that loss creates.

THE REALITY OF ADOPTEE SUFFERING

In 1993, in her book *The Primal Wound,* adoptive mother and social worker Nancy Verrier broke new ground by identifying and describing the pain that she intuitively sensed in her relinquished and adopted daughter's heart.[1] She argues that a baby experiences, even prenatally, an important bonding with his birthmother, and that with relinquishment, this first break in attachment is an injury, a wound of some sort to the heart of the child.[2] (See chapter 2 for more information on bonding and attachment.)

Relinquishment has to do with breaking this connection and adoption has to do with introducing an infant or young child to strangers who seek to become her new mother and new father.

At age 18, Allan began to cause serious problems for his parents. Relinquished as an infant in the Philippines, Allan spent three months in foster care in Manila and then came to the United States as the adopted son of white Christian parents. The bonding that Allan accomplished to his new parents was strong and their attachment to him was good by all reports. His childhood was filled with lots of smiles, happy play, success in school, and good living in general. But then, when as a high school senior, Allan met a young woman whose skin was mellow brown, the only thing that suddenly mattered to him was her presence and her affection. He fell deeply in love with so much intensity that other relationships, especially those with parents, family members, and friends, fell off his radar.

Allan's parents lamented that they felt as if they had lost their son. His new love had filled the hole in his heart. Though he could not see it, *it was as if she were indeed the birthmother whom he had never grieved.* When she moved away to another city with her parents, he was angry and devastated. Once again, he had lost his first love.

Unacknowledged grief does not go away by itself. Grief that lay dormant, below the awareness of his daily life experience, overtook Allan with great force. Now at age 18, the time had come to be both sad and mad; his parents wondered and puzzled at the depth of his pain. This left them asking what they might have done earlier in his life to mitigate this present suffering. How could they have prepared better to manage this sadness in his heart?

RELINQUISHMENT AND ADOPTION ARE DIFFERENT FROM ONE ANOTHER

Many consider "relinquishment" and "adoption" simply as legal moments in time when birthparental rights end and adoptive parental rights begin. In adoptee reality, however, they are better understood as lifelong processes that inform and affect each other in complex ways. One very thoughtful adoptee, openly acknowledging her plight, put it this way: "I love my adoption, but I hate my relinquishment." She honored the good relationship that she enjoyed with her adoptive parents *and* she mourned the absence of any relationship with her birthparents. She lost her birthmother early in life and a birthfather who refused to acknowledge her very existence when she knocked on his apartment door.

Relinquishment and adoption play against each other in what is called the catch-22 of adoptive development—the dilemma relinquished children face as they turn to their new parents for nurture and care. To whatever degree losing birthparents, even at birth, causes injury, there may be a compromise, a limited ability to bond to new/strange parents. Yet the new/strange parents are precisely the resource that the relinquished child needs in order to face sadness, grieve losses, and form new life-giving attachments.

LOSSES ALONG THE WAY

One young boy, adopted from Russia at age two, surprised his parents when they asked him what he would like for Christmas. He had already spent several years in the United States, playing catch-up with motor skills, language difficulty, and sensory integration in a loving Christian home. Yet he told his father that he would like a tractor so that he could send it to Russia to his birthfather. There was an indelible place in his young, still-broken heart for his parents across the ocean.

Every young adoptee begins life with significant losses. We may forever speculate about the nature of the disruption that occurs when even a baby is handed to new parents. For some, this may be a relatively smooth transition; for others it may be a traumatic event. We just don't know exactly what occurs nor how to predict which children will experience lifelong struggles and which ones will sail through seemingly without effect.

What is critical to note here is that the child's ability to bond to new parents depends directly on how well this transition is negotiated. For example, parents sometimes report the powerful protest of newly adopted infants who arch their tiny backs and actively fight the embrace of their new parents. They are absolutely refusing to accept the loss of their original caregivers and first environments.

As the adopted child develops, his cognitive awareness dawns at a variety of points along the way. He realizes in pieces that something is different and that someone is missing. It hurts to be relinquished, and, if not facilitated, grieving sets up developmental risk, even for an infant. If living hurts, we anesthetize nerves to our own hearts so that we can survive. If too many such emotional nerves are numbed, children are left with difficulties with attachment, with poor eye contact, or even with compromised conscience. Too much is at stake to simply ignore the issues of grief and loss.

With the newer practice of open adoption, the intensity of the loss experience may be minimized as birthparents are known and/or more available for contact and care. But a sense of difference, a puzzling awareness of loss, is always a part of relinquishment, be it open or closed. Whether their parents are known in reality or sensed as "ghost parents,"[3] adoptees know sadness and hurt when they figure these things out.

At age eight, young Travis was happily involved with his friends at a local AIDS benefit concert, sitting in the front row with his own soda and popcorn in hand. But when one of the singers dedicated a song to "all the boys and girls in the world who don't have moms and dads," intending to mean the thousands of African children whose parents died from HIV infection, Travis melted down. Leaving his refreshments on the floor, he ran, weeping, to the back of the concert hall. Finding his mother, he crawled in her lap and bleated, "Mom, I miss my birthmom." Wisely, she hugged him tight and responded, "I know you do. I'm sorry it makes you so sad."

When second, third, or fourth graders start to figure out what relinquishment, even abandonment, really means, they are usually touched by their own grief. They are mourning the loss of wished for, often fantasized—even perhaps known—birthparents who, for whatever reason, did not keep them. In an important, painful manner, they wonder why. *Why didn't she keep me, love me, and care about me?* They may even ask, "What was wrong with me that I was given away? Why was I not good enough to be kept?" These are the stinging questions of

A Few Steps Back by Tracy Waal

For the first two full weeks we were home from Ethiopia with our adopted girls, Neti and Meke, things went much better than we could have expected. But, suddenly, bedtime became something entirely different. No longer did Neti find rest quickly. Instead, she would lie on her side, eyes glassy, sleep elusive. Meke eventually stopped sleeping, too. She began to toss and turn, waking herself up all sweaty and crying. One night she actually fell out of bed.

Grief had finally caught up to our little girls.

What were they grieving? Did they miss their old country, with its bustling streets? The food, or maybe their friends at the orphanage? What about the smells? Teachers? Language? Culture? They'd lost all those things in a very short amount of time.

But when the sun comes up, things appear nearly normal. Happy Neti and bouncy Meke attack the day with the intensity of children. During the day, no one would know that something heavy had been taking place inside their little heads over night.

Grief is a normal part of the process, but, with things going so well, we thought that we had somehow leapfrogged the inevitable. Don't interpret this as a complaint or as a disappointment. It's just our reality. We expected this—this is what we signed up to do when we became parents to Neti and Meke.

being abandoned, no matter what the real reason, that haunt the hearts of adoptees.

During adolescence, that now-expanded period of development from puberty to young adulthood, more sorrow ensues. It is often presented in the form of anger and irritation. There are times when teens who are relinquished and adopted "go off like bombs" with deeply felt frustration and confusion. Anger is part of grief even if it looks so different from sadness. Many times anger is driven by the hurt underneath, the hurt that loss keeps alive.

Early and middle teens sort out questions of identity. When you have four parents instead of two, constructing a sense of self is that much more of a challenge. And when birthparents and birth story and birth family history are unknown, adopted teens are left to invent themselves, not just discover themselves. It is no wonder that they vent frustration when they have little knowledge of where they came from, no medical history to access in times of illness—and sometimes, knowledge of birthparents who have been invisible, belittled, judged, or feared.

Many children will not display this loss or grief in obvious ways. Yet, at some point in the growing-up years, these issues will be a part of their experience—perhaps expressed only on rare occasions, or only as a subconscious foundation to other experiences. Understanding the reality of loss and grief, no matter how it looks in your child's life, will allow you to parent more wisely and compassionately.

THE CHALLENGE OF RESOLVING THE LOSSES OF RELINQUISHMENT

When grief is shared, managed with a supportive mother and father, adoptee grieving becomes more doable, less of an impossibility that "just hurts too much." The *healthy* adoptee is a child who can feel her heart and be connected to the wide range of her emotions. She is able to experience sorrow and joy, anger and peace, shame and relief, rather than being someone who simply manipulates life in order to survive. As odd as it may therefore sound, helpful parents will invite whatever sorrow and anger sit heavy in the hearts of their children and lead the way to resolving the necessary mourning set in motion by relinquishment. Here are some important steps for parents to follow:

Step 1: Face Your Own Sorrow

It may well be that one of the biggest obstacles to effective adoptive parenting is that of doing your own grieving to whatever degree necessary. You cannot visit your child's suffering if you cannot visit your own. For example, if sorrow about infertility is a challenge, it must be faced head-on by the parents. Adoption does not solve the hurt of nonconception. This is a grief of its own. If this loss is avoided, adopted children become replacements for lost or never-conceived daughters and sons by birth—something an adoptee never wants.

If avoided, parents will not be open to conversations about relinquishment sorrow and will inevitably send the message to their children that certain things are not to be discussed. This leaves relinquished children with no place to go with their sadness and anger. As a result, the child's relinquishment, sorrow, and grief will be denied or lead to general malaise.

If you carry unacknowledged pain, now is the time to deal with those issues. Don't be afraid to seek professional help if necessary.

Step 2: Lead the Conversation

Inviting a conversation about the well-being of a child's birthparents is always a gift to that child. "I wonder how your birthmom is doing" opens up the right channels for adoptive development. Even if the child brushes off the conversation or does not engage in the wondering, the child nevertheless learns something critically important—that it's okay to talk about such things. Understandably, parents who have adopted hesitate for a variety of reasons to lead the conversation about birthparents, birth story, and birth family history and culture—all things their child has lost. But avoiding the conversation sends an unhelpful message and may in fact cut the child off from the part of the adoptive parent *most needed* for the grieving to be accomplished.

Step 3: Ask Questions About Sorrow

It is not difficult to imagine that a relinquished child would have mixed feelings about celebrating Mother's Day or Father's Day when such an event brings up tender questions about his or her loss.

And of course, birthday celebrations bring the adoptee precisely back to the primitive moment when life beyond the womb meant loss. On such occasions, wise and sensitive parents will not insist on celebrating anything, but invite conversation about the sorrow and ambivalence that may be part of the mix for the adoptee. Of course, every child is different, so you might follow your child's leading in these areas. The helpful adoptive parent is the mother or father who can be truly "with" his or her child in terms of the entire range of emotional responses to whatever occasion, comment, or experience brings loss into focus. Using these events to invite the grief that may be there is good adoptive parenting. Both joy and sorrow are usually part of the adoptee story.

Step 4: Honor Birthparents, Birth Story, Birth Culture

One of the insensitivities that adoptees often endure is that of hearing comments that are negative and disparaging about their birthparents. This is both tragic and unnecessary, but it often happens. Adopted children take in a sense of self from every comment made about their parents of birth, and when these lost parents are portrayed in a negative light, the effect on the self-image of the adoptee is direct and painful.

Unfortunately, birthparents are sometimes seen as threats to adoption plans and adoptive parenting instead of as partners in the formation of families. But casting birthparents and birth stories and birth cultures in a negative way always has a price in adoptive development. Our children usually know what we really think, and they internalize our attitudes. They may form negative opinions of themselves as the bad seed of birthparents unable to parent. Taking care in this regard is critical. Even the parent who was abusive was a human being with some positive quality. His or her addiction or sin is not the full picture of who he or she is as a person created in God's image.

Honoring the reality, person, and voice of the birthparent, by way of contrast, offers the adoptee the opportunity to take in good (and realistic) ideas about self, history, and culture. Homeland visits, if adoptions occur from overseas, are wonderful opportunities to take seriously the value of other people, and other cultures, all part of the diversity of many adoptive families.

Step 5: Practice Openness in Adoption

Some adoptive parents fear that relating more openly to birthparents may be anxiety producing for them as well as confusing for their adopted children. Most often, however, adoptive parents who know and even enjoy real relationships with birthparents actually parent more calmly. Adoptive parents change in the process and do better parenting. Openness is an attitude toward adoptive parenting that engages the various realities of birthparents and birth stories that lets things be what they really are.

By this way of thinking and behaving, negative fantasies and fears about birthparents abate, and adoptive parents and adoptees themselves have more freedom to face whatever may be tragic and painful in the stories of relinquishment. The grieving gets done. Birthparents themselves can be resources in conversations with adoptees about their beginnings and the reasons they were relinquished for adoption. Facing reality, whatever form it may take, however painful it may be, is always a better option than living in fantasy and darkness about one's story.

Step 6: Join the Sadness and the Anger

To empathically join hands and hearts with your hurt child is perhaps the most difficult task, but also the most important. Spreading the pain makes the load lighter. A tear in a father's eye about the sadness his son faces as he learns that his birthfather took no interest in him is the glue of good adoptive fathering. Sharing the anger and consternation of her Korean-born daughter because it is shame, not law, that keeps the records closed in Seoul, builds a bond between parent and child as part of good adoptive mothering. "Honey, I am sorry that this hurts" is one thing to say—a good thing. But how much better to comment, "It hurts me, too, wondering if your brother in Romania is okay." Remember, when we bear each other's burdens (Galatians 6:2), we fulfill the law of Christ, especially with our children.

Step 7: Be Ready to Seek Professional Help

While there may be an understandable resistance to seeking out the assistance of a counselor, it can greatly assist you in two critical ways. First, a well-qualified professional can help you identify and understand certain behaviors that suggest struggles with attachment. Second, a good counselor will work with you and your child to develop therapeutic attachment and increase the emotional support for the developmental challenges the adoptee faces.

When withdrawal is significant or when negative behavior is out of control, counseling of some sort is necessary. Sometimes, without intervention, families become held hostage by one child—in battles for control that the parents can't win. Certainly, in such cases, qualified help is needed. But counselors need to be informed about the dynamics of relinquishment and adoption. Because the culture has historically not taken note of these concerns, not all counselors are aware of or trained to recognize them. Check with adoption support agencies or fellow parents for referrals. You can also see the Resources Guide at the end of this book for more suggested reading materials.

God's Message to Those Who Grieve Loss and Relinquishment

So often, the Christian faith is presented as primarily a means of forgiveness for sin, and the other themes in the Christ-story may not be clearly heard or appreciated. Some adoptees don't feel very guilty or very much in need of anyone's forgiveness. If anything, they feel that they were wronged in the first place and that someone out there ought to apologize to them for a hard start in life. For these persons the words from the cross, "Father, forgive them for they know not what they do," have little traction.

And yet forgiveness is part of the challenge of adoptive development, a task that adoptive parents can help to facilitate. In the adoptee's case, it sometimes has to do with forgiving birthparents for the choice to relinquish them, as difficult and necessary as that decision may have been. We are to forgive as God forgives us (Matthew 6:14–15). And not forgiving—not grieving and letting go of hurt and its corresponding anger—leaves us bitter, and the poison of that bitterness can move us far away from God.

Bringing closure to injury, including the injury of the adoptee's relinquishment, demands the strength and the grace to face truth, no matter how painful it is. Though it may take a long time and increasing maturity to do this forgiving, the adoptee is not free to live life fully (John 10:10b) unless the forgiveness gets done. This is a long road that you, as parents, will need to walk with your child.

However, there are other words from Scripture that adoptees usually do understand. "My God, my God, why have You forsaken me?" are words that ring true to the adoptive experience. When Jesus cried out these words on the cross, He expressed His grief in agony and tears. Adopted children get that. Jesus understands their experience.

Our Lord knows the heart of every relinquished child. And parenting that heart becomes the great honor of bringing restoration and redemption.

■■■

Dr. Ron Nydam teaches pastoral care classes at Calvin Theological Seminary in order to equip seminarians for the challenge of pastoral ministry. He is the author of *Adoptees Come of Age: Living within Two Families*, and has a special interest in the study of relinquishment and adoption.

A Birthfather's Perspective
by Woody Shoemaker

I lived through the turbulent 1960s with the Vietnam War, student protests, the civil rights movement, and a rock and roll culture that changed an entire generation. Our parents' definition of success and their values were out; the new era of love and understanding was in.

My girlfriend and I were very much like other couples whose parents allowed them a lot of time together. The longer we went together the more time we were allowed to be alone. This, of course, led to greater familiarity and more physical contact. Though our families had provided us good moral teaching, intimacy became unavoidable.

In 1968 we had a baby daughter together. We were both 19 years old, very immature, and very unprepared for marriage, to say nothing of raising a child. I was quite unaware of the treasure of a baby, being a thoroughly self-absorbed young man, so the relationship didn't work out. My girlfriend felt that it would be selfish of her to keep the baby and that the best thing to do was to give the baby up to a complete family through adoption.

I went off to the military and served with the Navy SEAL team in Vietnam in 1971 engaged in guerilla warfare. After returning to the States, I began doing a good bit of soul searching. It was at this season that I experienced a life-changing encounter with the Lord Jesus Christ. I sensed that I was loved and accepted, and that God was willing to forgive me if I would only give my life to Him that moment early in 1972. I did, and things have never been the same since.

It was this change and the decision to make things right with God and others that led me to resolve that if my child ever found me I would be open to her and do what I could to help and encourage her. Though I experienced wonderful freedom in my new life with Christ, I still thought of her occasionally as the years went by. From time to time, upon noticing a small girl about my girl's age, I would wonder about her and even go so far as to question if that little girl could be mine.

I never felt the liberty to actually search for her. She belonged to others now and had a new family—her true family—and I had no right to intrude or even to inquire. I was taught that adoptions are final and that they should remain closed to birthparents—that was the price of relinquishment. I was not aware of the possible benefits of "reunions"—meetings between children and their birthparents.

But in October of 1999, at the age of 31, my daughter contacted her birthmother, who called me and said, "Guess who I just heard from?" I knew instantly who it was!

I was immediately glad and drawn to her, and within an hour I had fallen in love with a child I had never seen, or touched, or spoken to. I have three other daughters and three sons, and I can say that my love for her is just as strong as my love for the others. I had not as yet even seen a picture of her nor heard her voice. It was only that she asked her birthmom of me, "Do you know where my father is? Would he be open to contact?" It didn't matter what she looked like and it didn't even matter what she was like, or her lifestyle. Here she was—bone of my bone and flesh of my flesh—and I loved her. I am aware that those who have not been touched by adoption might have difficulty with my feelings and awakened interest, but those who are members of the adoption community probably do understand.

I realize now that I always loved her and that she lived somewhere in my heart. While I am not proud of the sins of my youth, I realize that children are always a gift from God and I am very proud of this one.

My wife, Gail, has always known about my life before becoming a Christian. She has been wonderfully understanding and supportive of my interest in this child.

In August of 2001 I arranged to meet the daughter I had never seen before. It was a wonderful encounter for me and, I hope, helpful for her as well. She is happy and whole, having had a good upbringing by her wonderful family. She is a productive citizen, working in public service. It was very good to be found by her, to know that she is fine, and to have had a chance to ask her to forgive me. She, her birthmom, and I have been lastingly affected by decisions I made as a young person, yet there is a God of love who enjoys writing last chapters.

I hope that my experience might encourage anyone looking for resolve over past failures. Each of us can be a model of a life restored if we will allow Christ to work in us. No matter what the past, there is a bright future for those who respond to the offer of forgiveness and renewal.

Editor's Note: This article first appeared in Sherrie Eldridge's ministry newsletter at Sherrieeldridge.com. Reprinted by permission.

11

Ethnic Identity

by Kurt and Margaret Birky

From one man he [God] made every nation of men, that
they should inhabit the whole earth; and he determined
the times set for them and the exact places where they
should live. God did this so that men would seek him
and perhaps reach out for him and find him,
though he is not far from each one of us.
—ACTS 17:26–27

They say that the apple doesn't fall far from the tree. Well, sometimes the apple falls from the tree, rolls down a hill, and comes to rest beneath an orange tree. That can be a great blessing, but also a bit unnerving for both the orange tree and the apple.

Adopted children will face many challenges as they strive to find their place in the world. When these children have an ethnic background that is different from that of their parents, the dynamics get that much more complex. Can transracial adoption be done successfully? Of course. But it isn't an easy journey. Then again, parenting never is.

Ethnicity is a powerful link for adopted children that can help them develop a positive sense of self. Parents who adopt, therefore, have a great responsibility to pass on a heritage that may not be their own. This may seem like an overwhelming task, but remember, race is only one aspect of who we are. Our true identity is bestowed upon us by the Creator of the universe and can only be found through a right relationship with our Lord, Jesus Christ. But while our identity in Christ is paramount, for better or worse, racial identity still plays a pivotal role in society. The first step toward a successful transracial adoption is to take an honest look at how this adoption will affect those involved.

WILL YOUR CHILD'S ETHNICITY BE AN ISSUE?

Regardless of how *you* feel about your child's ethnicity, it is important to consider how culture views it.

Racism. Few words in the English language evoke such deep emotion as racism. It is an ugly word that instantly frustrates, scares, and angers us.

Our family is composed of two white parents, three black kids, and three white kids. We have seen racism from all angles. We have heard racist comments and jokes from white friends and coworkers who don't understand why they are offensive. We have encountered hostility and disgust from white families who dislike us because we dare to be a transracial family.

We've seen African Americans who seem angry that we would attempt to raise black kids. One of our social workers told us that she wouldn't place black kids with white parents if the law didn't require her to. Regardless, we are a multiethnic family, and we take great pride in it. We are your run-of-the-mill German-Scottish-Norwegian-African-Ethiopian family (or Gerscottnorafriopian for short).

Regardless of your perceptions on the state of racism in our culture today, one thing cannot be denied: We live in a culture that is acutely aware of race. Individuals can be color blind, but as a society we are not. A quick review of major news stories from the last decade will demonstrate that, though we are nearly 50 years removed from the birth of the civil rights movement, racial equality is still a hotly debated and divisive topic.

Racism in all forms is wrong. Even subtle stereotyping is a destructive force, especially to a transracial family. It is not enough to only fight against racism directed at your family members' ethnic background(s). Transracial families must demonstrate love, respect, and acceptance for all ethnicities, not just those represented within their family unit.

Your Feelings

The fact that you are open to the idea of raising a child of another race is a step in the right direction. A number of things move people to transracial adoption:

- For those who come from a diverse family background, the idea of a transracial family is not only preferable, but they couldn't imagine it any other way.
- For many, affinity for a certain ethnic group makes them open to adopting a child from that background. Perhaps a mission trip to another country or living in another community has sparked a deep love for the people there.
- For others, it is as straightforward as wanting to adopt a child in need, regardless of color or gender, simply to provide a forever home for a child. What that child "looks like" is of little importance to them.

Ultimately, there are many good reasons for adopting transracially. But whatever your reason, it is helpful to unpack your motivations to make sure there are no red flags.

It is important that parents strive to understand what it means to be a transracial family. Too many parents enter into a transracial adoption with the intention of becoming a "white family with an Asian child" or a "black family with a Latino child." Once you adopt transracially, your family has been forever changed. A new branch has been grafted onto your family tree, and it has changed the makeup of the entire tree. You are a new family with a shared ethnic identity.

Later in this chapter we will look at some suggestions that will help you and your child successfully transition together. But for those pre-adoptive families, take the time now to discuss and pray about the challenges your family may face. Ask yourself if you are willing to put in the hard work that it will take to build a strong transracial family.

Most adoption agencies will have good resources to help you evaluate this decision. They may have a questionnaire, workbook, or self-guided CD; or they may simply provide talking points to help you understand your thoughts on adopting transracially. Even for those families who have already adopted, these resources can help your thinking and planning as a multiracial family.

YOUR SUPPORT SYSTEM

After you have evaluated your feelings about transracial adoption, you will need to turn your attention to those who support your family. While, ultimately, the decision to adopt is yours and yours alone, it will affect those in your sphere of influence. Have open and honest discussion with the people you will rely on in the months and years ahead to play an active role in the life of your child.

The intention is not to change your decision to adopt. You simply need to understand their feelings and make sure you have the support necessary to help raise and care for your child.

There is always the possibility that you will uncover opposition to your desire to adopt transracially. Sometimes that opposition comes out of practical concerns, but occasionally it may have darker roots. When faced with bigoted opposition, many prospective parents deepen their resolve to adopt a child from another ethnicity. They will not be intimidated by the prejudiced opinions of their friends or family. To take a stand against racism is certainly to be applauded, but never underestimate the challenges that your adopted child may face (see chapter 3 for more help on dealing with extended family relationships).

And remember that as role models in a transracial family, parents must set an uncompromising standard with regard to bigoted attitudes.

YOUR ADOPTED CHILD

Your child's experience all through life will be vastly different from yours. No matter how close you are to your children, you will never truly know what it feels like to be them. With that in mind, how can you try to understand what they will experience as your son or daughter with regard to race? Do some role-playing. This is not the kind of role-playing that you did in drama class or in a therapy session. It can be as simple as going through your normal weekly routine but imagining what the world would look like through the eyes of a child of another ethnicity.

Walk through your home and take a visual inventory of your house. In all of your artwork, collectibles, coffee table books, or the cluster of family photos on the mantel, are there other faces that look like your child's?

Try viewing your neighborhood the same way. When your child goes out to play, will he see anyone who looks like him? Next week at church, take a moment to scan the pews and take note of how ethnically diverse the congregation is. To get a rough understanding of that experience from your child's perspective, why not visit a church where the congregation is predominantly made up of people

Family Photos by the Birkys

We never really took the time to see the world through our son's eyes until we attended a family reunion. And this was one of the big reunions, with several generations and hundreds of cousins present. At the time, Damond was the only African American in our family of five. A week or so after the reunion, we had our film from the trip developed. As we flipped through photo after photo, it dawned on us that there was only one black face in the whole lot. For the first time, we began to understand how challenging it might be for our son to understand how he belongs.

It wasn't long after that we got a phone call from Margaret's brother, Brian. The reunion was the first time that Brian's three children had met Damond. The cousins became fast friends as they spent the weekend playing together.

Brian called to recount a conversation he had with his five-year-old daughter, Hannah. Evidently their family had been talking about adoption. Hannah, however, was having a hard time understanding the concept behind adoption. Knowing that she had just met Damond and spent the better part of the reunion tossing rocks into a river with him, Brian tried to explain adoption by saying, "Adoption, you know—like Uncle Kurt and Aunt Margaret adopted Damond."

Full of shock, she quickly replied, "Damond's adopted?"

Could it be that sometimes grownups make too big a deal of race—especially as it is seen through the eyes of a child?

of your child's race? Then consider, were you uneasy in that situation? Why or why not? Take note of your feelings—they may help underscore your child's need to become comfortable with his environment.

What Are You Willing to Do?

Once you have some understanding of the thoughts and feelings of the main parties involved in this adoption, you may be facing a whole new set of challenges.

How far *are* you willing to go to become a transracial family? Can you create an environment in which everyone in your family feels valued, loved, and accepted?

Most likely, you'll be able to identify areas in your current lifestyle where some changes can take place. It could be as simple as framing new art or finding racially diverse toys and books for your family. Or you may be facing bigger decisions: Perhaps you'll feel the need to relocate to a more diverse community, or change churches, or look into another school.

Whatever you come up with, your decisions should be centered on your desire to truly become a transracial family. Develop a plan of action and be prepared to take the deliberate steps that are necessary.

How Do We Affirm Our Child's Unique Heritage While Building a Common Family Identity?

So what does it really mean to be a transracial family? All children respond differently to the idea of "heritage." What works for one family may not work for yours. Simply stated, you'll need to develop a shared heritage. And just as it is with marriage, two will become one. In a transracial family, two (or more) races combine into one family unit. Many of the traits of the individual cultures are still present in the family, but they'll have merged together to form a new heritage that is shared by each member of the family.

This doesn't mean that a family with a Chinese daughter needs to order out for Kung Pao Chicken three times a week. But you should look for natural ways to incorporate all aspects of your family's combined heritage. This may not feel natural at first, but over time it will. Many parents, especially those of European descent, fail to see the value of embracing and instilling their heritage. For many, heritage or ancestry is nothing more than an interesting conversation starter. For some, it is critically important. For others, it may not matter at all. Whether or not heritage is important to you, do not underestimate the importance that heritage can play to an adopted child.

Attempting to mold an adopted child completely and solely into your existing culture will ultimately fail. It is natural to want to celebrate one's own culture. For many children, it is the only link they have to their birth family and blood heritage—and an answer to that ever-present "who am I" question.

UNDERSTAND YOUR CHILD'S NEED TO AFFILIATE WITH HER RACIAL GROUP

Parents with children of other ethnicities need to understand that they cannot be the sole transmitter of their child's culture. You are going to need help. Learning as much as possible about your child's ethnicity is an important journey to embark upon, though the road maps may be lacking.

You can be deliberate in seeking out and building relationships with those of your child's race. As a parent, the role you play in your child's life is still the most important. So don't feel threatened by the need to bring ethnic role models into your child's life.

No matter how hard a father tries, no matter how many books he reads or how many relationships he builds—a white father will never truly know what it is like for his adopted son to grow up a black man in America. Minorities need to develop unique skills to succeed in this culture. There is much that parents can do to help their child build these skills. Ultimately, positive relationships with those of the same race will help your child develop a healthy self-image and equip him for his unique life challenges.

So how do you go about enlisting the help of others in transmitting your child's heritage? First, consider the people around you. Does a family at your school or church whom you would like to get to know better happen to share your child's ethnicity? Why not invite them over for dinner or a play date? It may sound a bit odd, but who couldn't use more friends? And if they can provide some tips for caring for an unruly afro or getting steamed rice to clump, consider that a bonus!

Join an online forum (the moderated kind that requires you to join and sign in to participate) that allows for some pretty personal discussion as you navigate sensitive topics related to your transracial adoption. This will provide insights without making you feel inadequate or inept.

Network through your church, employment, local community center, or adoption agency to find a similar adoption group and make a point of going to their gatherings. (If they aren't that organized, consider volunteering.) Visit, develop friendships, and try to get together with those individuals on a frequent basis.

As transracially adopted children work to understand their identity, it is natural that they would want to affiliate with their own racial group in some way. This may mean an interest in the culture or an intense desire to form relationships with people of their race. Do not be intimidated or hurt by this desire. This exploration is not only normal, it is healthy to the development of your child.

Your child's activities provide one way you can be deliberate about finding role models that are not the same race as you. When you sign up for sports, dance, tutoring, music, drama, and so on, look for chances to have a member of your child's race fill that role in his/her life. It will feel awkward, and it may get you into a few conversations that you'd rather not be in, but your child needs those interactions more than you need to feel comfortable. Our children are very active in youth sports. When Damond got hooked up with a great, positive, African-American football coach, we made sure we were on his team next season.

BALANCE RACIAL DIVERSITY WITH CELEBRATING SIMILARITIES

If you have a mixture of adopted children and birth children, the entire family should engage in cross-cultural activities. Simply put, the activities need to become a part of your family's DNA, not merely "mandatory diversity training activities."

Seeking out ways to diversify your family is not just for the benefit of the adopted child. Your entire family is now transracial, and all races are equally important in shaping your family's experience. If the activities that you seek are seen as "for the adopted child," they will do more damage than good. For children struggling to find their place in the world and the family, these activities will further demonstrate how different they are and how they fail to "fit in" with the rest of the family.

Adopted children also need to see the positives of the culture that they are being adopted into. They need to have positive feelings about their own race, but they also need to see the wonderful attributes of their parents' cultures.

At the same time, they need to know they "belong" to your family. For small children, this may mean pointing out things like having the same number of hands, toes, eyes, and ears. For older children, it's acknowledging similar interests or habits with a parent or sibling.

As they adjust to being in a transracial family, they will no doubt be looking for ways that they belong. They may look physically different, but they will be excited to discover other commonalities that they have with their parents. For example, my son Damond was thrilled when he discovered that he had raging seasonal allergies like his dad. It didn't matter that we were both miserable all through the spring. The itching, bloodshot eyes, uncontrollable sneezing, and scratchy throat were, for Damond, a positive connection that he shared with his dad.

CELEBRATING YOUR CHILD'S ETHNICITY

Celebrations of culture such as dance troupes, music presentations, and holidays should be accessed regularly to be a really transracial family. Encourage your family to become absorbed in these things so they can become the norm.

While she may be the minority within their own family, you can strengthen your child's sense of pride and belonging in many small but important ways. Here are a few simple tips:

Environment: Make sure your home has items that depict and celebrate your child's heritage.

Food: In an international adoption, learn to make a few dishes specific to your child's heritage (though they may take some practice to cook).

Toys: Kids love to imitate and role-play. Make a point of buying ethnically diverse dolls, action figures, Legos—just about any toy that depicts people of color. You don't need to give each child a doll of his or her own skin color. The point is not that kids have to play exclusively with toys that look like them. The point is that the home is full of multiracial cues for all family members.

Books: Make sure you have a selection of children's books that both address and illustrate the variety of God's creation. Seek out books that feature main characters of your child's race but that aren't about race and color, that are just about life.

Media: Again, make it a point to search out age-appropriate media, TV, and music that provide a link to their culture. Many movies deal with orphans, adoption, and transracial families. This is another way to reinforce that transracial families are normal. Each family should have its own safeguards with regard to media consumption, so don't expose your kids to anything that you feel is inappropriate. But with even a quick scan of movie titles, you can come up with good options, including *Cinderella, Snow Dogs, Lilo and Stitch, The Prince of Egypt,* any Nativity story, and the list goes on.

When we were looking for a way to discuss racism with our son, we came across the movie *Remember the Titans.* This film depicted racism, but with little violence and language, so it was a great conversation starter for our family. It is gut-wrenching to tell your kids about oppression, slavery, and violence, but it is better for us to be uncomfortable than for them to be uninformed about the past and unprepared for their futures.

Heritage camps: Heritage camps are growing in popularity. A quick Internet search can provide you with numerous camps in any given state that celebrate a variety of different cultural backgrounds. These allow for intense immersion in many aspects of your child's culture at once. An added benefit is that your children get to see you fully engaged in their culture, learning so many pieces of where they come from alongside them. Many attendees say that the most important part to them is to simply be around so many other kids that look like them. Not just having the same physical look, but also mirroring that "mixed" family culture. Prices can vary and, for obvious reasons, proximity to home plays a big part; but these camps can be great "mortar" as you build your family.

WHAT TO DO WHEN YOUR CHILD'S ETHNICITY IS UNKNOWN

Take your cues from the child. He will most likely be curious and will be attracted to something in another culture as he grows. Nurture those quests as best you can. Chances are, you have some basic information or ideas about your child's ethnic background. Certainly this is true in an international adoption, although there are often several different people groups within any given country. Or perhaps you are in a domestic adoption with a mixed-race child. Just start building into your lives some possibilities from the cultures you and your child are drawn to, based on what you do know of your child's story.

WHAT TO DO WHEN A CHILD IS UNINTERESTED IN HIS OR HER ETHNIC BACKGROUND

Children are all individuals—but you knew that already. Some children adopted internationally (especially older children) may refuse to even speak their native language. They seemingly want no part of their culture. They want to be fully American as quickly as possible.

Even if your child appears uninterested in his ethnic background, look for "low-intensity" encounters, such as a Cinco de Mayo parade, or a Chinese New Year celebration, where you and your child are merely observers.

If, later in life, your child struggles with her ethnicity, then at least you have laid a positive foundation upon which she can build her personal ethnic identity. Even if your child never takes an interest in his background, it still has been good for your family to have learned about that culture. We need to take our cues from our kids, and the only way to do that is to be engaged in their lives, talking to them, offering up opportunities for experiences in their native culture—but being sensitive to what level of emotional investment they are willing to make at any given time.

EXPLORING GOD'S PERSPECTIVE ON ETHNIC IDENTITY

What does God, through His Word, tell us about this idea of ethnic identity? Interestingly, not a whole lot. The Bible is not overflowing with passages that demand racial equality. Why? Perhaps it is because God knows that all people share a common ancestry. There really is only one race in the purest sense. Acts 17:26a (NKJV) clearly makes this point: "And He has made from one blood every nation of men to dwell on all the face of the earth."

Throughout the Old Testament, God is clear that He intended for His chosen people, the nation of Israel, to remain separate from neighboring cultures. Was this a form of racism? It seems clear that God did not want the Old Testament Jews to mix with other cultures.

A clear understanding of the history of the Jewish nation and a careful examination of the text will reveal that God demanded that they remain separate so that the Jewish people and their God-given heritage would not be corrupted by the pagans. God chose the nation of Israel to be the carriers of His divine plan. The Jews were His chosen people. However, never does Scripture say that a Jewish life was more valuable than a Gentile life. According to His purpose, God identified Abraham's descendants as His own. And as we read in Ephesians 2:19, we discover that the Gentiles are also welcomed to become His own people: "Consequently, you are no longer foreigners and aliens, but fellow citizens with God's people and members of God's household."

Scripture is clear that His people are not limited to one race or one color. The people of God are not determined by the color of their skin, the language they speak, or the land in which they live. In his letter to the church in Corinth, Paul, under the inspiration of the Holy Spirit, wrote this passage: "For we were all baptized by one Spirit into one body—whether Jews or Greeks, slave or free—and we were all given the one Spirit to drink" (1 Corinthians 12:13).

In that passage, Paul clearly communicates that our identity is based on our spiritual standing alone. Followers of Christ have a new, holy, and redeemed identity, an identity that is not determined by race or social standing. All believers in Jesus Christ are adopted into the Lord's family. We are grafted onto His family tree (Romans 11:17–24). We are heirs to His blessings, as we read in Galatians 3:29: "If you belong to Christ, then you are Abraham's seed, and heirs according to the promise."

The idea of racial equality isn't mentioned much in Scripture because there really shouldn't be any misunderstanding about it. While God created all varieties of wonderful people, their spiritual identity is much more important than their ethnic identity. We were bought at a price, and we must never lose sight of the identity that our Heavenly Father has lovingly provided for us.

This idea of ethnic identity is a fairly simple concept: All races, all peoples, are of immeasurable value, regardless of ethnicity, because we are all created in the image of God; and He sent His Son to die for *all* peoples.

■■■

Kurt Birky is creative director for Focus on the Family, joining the ministry in 2003 after nine years working in the creative department for Universal Studios Hollywood.

Margaret Birky is a busy stay-at-home mom for their six wonderful children: Christian, Emma, Damond, Carter Habtamu, Bronwyn, and Cooper Fekadu.

My Adoption Story
by Alyssa Hoekman

For as long as I can remember, I have always stood out in a crowd when all I really wanted to do was blend in. Born in India but growing up in the Pacific Northwest, I was not surrounded by very much ethnic diversity, and as a result I often felt alone in an ocean of predominantly white faces.

At the age of three, when most kids are learning shapes, colors, numbers, and the alphabet, I struggled with my obvious difference in appearance not only from my mom but from everyone else.

When I was five, I noticed a group of neighbor girls sunbathing on the lawn. I told my mom that I should join them so I could turn white too. All I wanted was to fit in.

To anyone who might be considering adopting a child from an ethnicity other than their own, it is important that you are aware of what it might be like for your daughter or son to grow up as a societal minority.

As I grew older, most of my cross-ethnic struggles became internalized. Well-meaning friends and acquaintances often asked, "Do you know who your *real* parents are? Do you want to go back to India someday to better understand your cultural heritage?"

Like many internationally adopted children, my adoptive mother was not provided with any documentation about my biological parents. So in addition to feeling alienated from my birth family, I frequently felt as if I was unable to identify with my adoptive family. There was a continual personal identity struggle growing up in Western culture as an American but believing that I *should* want to return to my native roots.

There are no easy answers for adopted children who might be grappling with developing their own ethnic identity. Even now, as a graduate student, I find myself feeling isolated and keenly aware of the fact that I am the only person of color in a class of 20. Moments like these continually challenge me to cope and acclimate to ethnic differences.

As an adoptee, I will probably always struggle with knowing that I am different and at times do not fit in. Yet knowing that my adoptive family is aware of my feelings even if they cannot empathize is comforting. And as a result, I do not have to be embarrassed by the fact that I am learning to accept ambiguities as they relate to my own personal development and ethnic identity.

And yes, 21 years later I now know that sunbathing will not turn me white!

Part IV
Special
Challenges

12

Early Childhood Trauma

by Therese McGee and David Anderson

He will have compassion on the poor and needy,
And the lives of the needy he will save.
He will rescue their life from oppression and violence,
And their blood will be precious in his sight.
—Psalm 72:13–14 (nasb)

Every child has her own unique story. Certainly all stories are not so troubling, but sadly, some children have been deeply traumatized by severe neglect, by terrible physical abuse, and even by sexual assault. As Christians, we know that God is the Healer and no child is beyond His power. We know that healing is possible, yet our experience as psychologists shows that healing can take a long time. This chapter is about the aftermath of trauma and what caring adults can do to help a child along the path of healing.

What Trauma Does to a Child

When a child is exposed to very stressful circumstances, when a child is physically abused, when a child is neglected, when a child is sexually assaulted, or when a child is abandoned, he will have a stress response. This is a physiological response in which the body gathers all its resources to deal with the stress. Stress hormones are generated. Heart rate and blood pressure change. Other functions, such as development, take a backseat for that moment and survival becomes the top priority. Sadly, the traumatic event may not just be one time, or even a few times. Some children live in traumatic and very stressful environments for years before any action is taken.

These children can experience biological changes that significantly affect them for many years. During those critical early years, when the child should have been developing emotional control and good thought processes, she was in a state of stress and crisis, trying to survive. Later, the child may have immaturities of emotions and thinking. That is, as you talk to her or try to teach her, you may have the sense that you are dealing with a much younger child. You know that she is 10 years old, but somehow you feel as if you are talking to a seven-year-old. When such a child is stressed, she may revert to an even more immature state, throwing tantrums like a two-year-old. When she is sad, she may need nurturing like a toddler.

Because a young child has immature control mechanisms for her emotions and her thinking, severe trauma can cause the child to experience extremely intense emotions. She is too young to understand or cope, and the emotions overwhelm her. The abuse can elicit fear, rage, defeat, resignation, shame, betrayal, and even guilt. The child may fear for her very life. She may be very angry at the hurt she has experienced. She may feel betrayed that she is being so hurt by the very people who are supposed to love and care for her.

Continued abuse may cause the child to accept the abuse as "normal," and she may become resigned to her situation and hopeless that change will happen. The abuser may tell the child that it is the child's own fault that she is being abused. "You were bad, so I had to hit you." "You came on to me, so I molested you." Sometimes the child may be seduced into sexual abuse, and she later thinks that she was a willing participant. The result is that the child feels shame and guilt, as well as hurt and fear. One 13-year-old girl that we worked with was stunned when the therapist told her "it was not your fault." She had been sexually assaulted repeatedly over many months when she was eight years old, but the abuser had convinced her that she *wanted* him to hurt her.

Years after the trauma, the child may continue to have a "physiological dysregulation." The control mechanisms that should have developed in his young body seem to have gone awry. The body seems to run too fast or at times too slow. When the body runs too fast, the heart rate and blood pressure stay high, and the child appears hyperactive and even manic.

Emotions swing widely. The child overreacts to simple stimuli. Small slights may be perceived as threats. A fire drill may be exciting for other children, but this child becomes hysterical and is fearful even hours later. When everyone comes in from the playground, the other children calm down in a few minutes, but this child can't calm down and continues to run around and disrupt the classroom. If the child happens to encounter a situation or a stimulus that reminds him of the trauma, he may hyperreact, suddenly becoming extremely anxious, fearful, or even angry and aggressive.

Other children may have a body response that is chronically too slow. A girl may have a heart rate and blood pressure that stay too low. She is withdrawn, frozen, and afraid, even in circumstances that seem safe to everyone else. She sees herself as helpless, and the world as a hopeless place. She wants to stay emotionally numb. Such a child may appear cooperative, but her lack of response may cause people to think that she is of low intelligence or "spacey."

Whether the body is running too fast or too slow, thinking and logical processes are often disrupted. The child cannot focus and pay attention. He cannot cope with new stresses, and he has trouble adjusting to new situations. He has trouble figuring things out, and he may become unreasonably frustrated or angry when he is faced with a problem. Often this is misdiagnosed as Attention Deficit Hyperactivity Disorder, but the child does not respond to the usual treatments for ADHD. He does not have ADHD; he is traumatized, and his lack of focus is born out of anxiety and other unresolved emotions.

Many traumatized children have trouble sleeping. Especially when children were abused at bedtime, they may be very anxious in the evening and have trouble falling asleep. Others may experience nightmares or bedwetting. Some have digestive problems from the continuing anxiety. Others overeat to comfort themselves. Some children complain of odd aches—headaches or muscle aches, as if the chronic tension of their anxieties is being carried in their muscles.

WHAT IS NEEDED

At this point, you as a parent may be getting a bit overwhelmed by the magnitude of the problem, so let's talk a bit about what is often done to help such children. What can caring adults do to help a traumatized child? The first step is to provide, as much as possible, an environment in which the child can heal. The environment needs to be one that is safe, where the stress response will not be actively triggered, and where the child will not be further damaged. We'll talk more about this a little later.

Let's consider a few other ways to help a traumatized child.

Do We Need a Professional?

If you suspect that your child has experienced significant trauma and you are seeing characteristics such as those mentioned in the above sections, seek help from mental health professionals. They can provide information and guide you as to whether formal therapy is needed. Keep in mind that any therapists should be experienced with traumatized children.

Also, we prefer that the therapy plan include the parents. Parents struggle with knowing how to relate to the child and how to provide a home that will help the child to heal. The parents must manage the day-to-day ups and downs of a child whose emotions swing and whose fears interfere with daily living. The parents need advice specific to their child, and they themselves may need to talk about the difficulties they are experiencing.

Can We Talk about It?

When adults are traumatized, therapy can take the form of talking about the trauma and the person's subsequent feelings. Issues that trouble the person such as "How could this happen?" or "I am so angry" can be discussed. Talking about it can help the person to dissipate some of the emotions and bring a sense of perspective.

Children face similar issues as they deal with the aftermath of trauma—but talking about it doesn't happen automatically. Still, being able to "talk about it" is usually a breakthrough moment that allows the child to make progress in dealing with the trauma. A therapist who is skilled in helping a child to express herself may be the person that the child talks to, but it has been our experience that a child is just as likely to talk to an adult caretaker—the adoptive parent or even a foster parent—who makes the child feel safe, who will patiently listen, and who will be supportive of the child. The key is, when the child opens up, listen patiently. Tell the child that you are very sorry that the abuse happened. Remind her that you are here with her now to help keep her safe.

It takes courage and strength to listen to a painful story from a child, to face the reality that such sinful things could happen to a child. It takes strength to share the terrible burden that the child is carrying. As you listen, you will likely feel sad or angry. After all, you are sharing not just the facts of the abuse but also the emotions that the child experiences. Take to heart the words of Scripture: "Be strong and courageous! Do not tremble or be dismayed, for the LORD your God is with you wherever you go" (Joshua 1:9 NASB). As you listen, you must trust God to help you bear this burden with the child, and to give you the wisdom to respond with kindness and compassion.

What about the child who seems to be traumatized but doesn't talk about it? Often a child does not know how to describe what he is thinking, feeling, or remembering. Especially if the trauma happened when he was very young, he may not have the words to describe what happened. Therapists use play therapy or other expressive therapies, such as art, to help a child express what happened. In a home setting, the child may spontaneously start playing out the scenes that he experienced. If this is what you are seeing, you need a therapist's help to sort out the child's behavior. If his play is violent or sexual, you need professional advice on how to respond and how to keep him safe. (See chapters 5 and 13 for more information on dealing with sexually abused children.)

Fear and confusion may keep a child from talking about the trauma. The scenes may be too frightening to face. He may have been threatened that if he tells, bad things will happen to him. The child may not know how or may be afraid to talk about the emotions that he experienced. When his emotions swing, he cannot explain why. The memories may not make logical sense. He may have vivid scenes of stimuli or events, but he cannot tell the sequence of what happened, or he may misperceive the actual events. As you patiently listen to what he does have to say, you can try to help him make sense of it and reassure him that you will help him face the memories.

Tommy, a 12-year-old boy, told us that his father shot him in the foot with a gun when he was three years old. He was greatly disturbed by the memory. He had all his toes and his foot looked all right, so it was hard for us to tell if the memory was real. Eventually, in family therapy, Tommy worked up the nerve to ask his mother. His mother revealed that the father shot him in the foot not with a real gun, but with a BB gun, which at the time had bruised his foot badly. She also told the boy, "That's why I left him. He was so irresponsible. Who shoots a little boy with a BB gun?" Tommy was greatly comforted that the memory had a basis in reality, and that his mother agreed that his father was wrong.

Carl was a 13-year-old boy who had lived in the Chicago public housing projects. Although he had been removed from his home at just four years of age, he had very disturbing memories of violent things that he had seen there. A woman minister who had grown up in a similar housing project was able to help Carl sort out his memories. As he described the details, she could affirm the reality of those scenes and also affirm his feelings about the memories. As he put words to the memories and the feelings, the fears began to dissipate, and his anxieties began to ease.

WHO'S IN CONTROL?

People who work with traumatized children are often frustrated by how defiant and oppositional the children can be. They are trying to help the child, but all they get is resistance, anger, and arguing. Where does this come from?

Abuse victims later report that one of the really terrifying things about abuse is how helpless they were when they were victimized. They don't ever want to feel like that again. Here is a child who was badly hurt in a situation in which someone else was in control. He doesn't want it to happen again. He is afraid that if you have power, you may hurt him. If he has control, he can keep from getting hurt. So he resists authority. If you try to take control, he becomes oppositional, even aggressive. Given his past hurts, he may be desperate—far more desperate than you are—to have control of the situation.

The desire to resist and control is a reflection of a lack of trust of adults. The child learned, the hard way, that adults cannot be trusted. Adults are dangerous people who hurt children. Manipulation is part of this same lack of trust. Tell the adult what he wants to hear, because that is the only way to get what you need. Honesty is at best irrelevant, at worst dangerous. The child may feel that outright lies are necessary to avoid getting hurt.

So what should you do? Here are some pointers:

- Avoid power struggles. Try to work with, rather than overpower, the child.
- It is good to stand firm, but keep control of your emotions. Do not operate out of anger.
- Use fewer words. State your position simply; then maintain a firm, silent presence. The child may have a lot to say, but as you stand there, silent but firm, the child will run out of steam.
- Give the child time to calm down.
- When the child is calm, you likely can work with her to resolve the issue.
- Try to give the child a sense of control by giving her choices in her daily life. For example, she can choose to sweep the floor *or* load the dishwasher; he can wear the blue shirt *or* the brown one.

Because trust is an issue, it is important to continue to be a safe, trustworthy adult, even when you feel frustrated by the defiance. It may take considerable time to establish the level of safety and trust that is needed to dissolve an oppositional and defiant stance. After a year of living at Lydia Home, 11-year-old Emily told us that she had finally realized that we were not going to physically abuse her. This was a rather startling statement, as she had never mentioned that she was afraid of being hit. She went on to reveal, in disturbing detail, how she had been abused before she had come to live at Lydia. She had assumed that we would hurt her as well.

The point is, hang in there. As you provide a place that is caring and safe, every day you are building the trusting relationship that the child needs.

HELPING THE CHILD TO DEVELOP PHYSIOLOGICAL AND EMOTIONAL CONTROL

Although therapy may directly address the trauma, there remain the issues of developmental delays and dysregulation that are the aftermath of trauma. Interestingly, some of the common activities that children enjoy can greatly help to counteract physiological dysregulation. Dance, music, exercise, and sports promote brain development and the regulation of emotions and energy. Such activities help children to develop control of their bodies and, in turn, control of their emotions.

Also of great help are positive one-on-one personal interactions that are repeated and predictable. That is, children really do learn from those one-on-one conversations where you sort out what just happened and what went wrong. These are teaching moments that help a child do better next time. It may be a social interaction. It may be an issue of resolving a conflict with a friend.

As for those wild swings of emotion, children need calming and soothing to bring their physiological states into mid-range. With smaller children, holding and rocking (as you would a baby) can soothe jangled emotions and calm distress. For both younger and older children, a calm tone of voice, a patient word, and a reassuring presence on the part of the adult will go a long way to helping a child understand that the adult will handle the situation and the child is safe.

Physical Safety and Healing

Over and over, we have said that children need an environment that is safe, but what do we mean by safe? Certainly, the home must be physically safe. No child will heal if he is being hurt or threatened with physical harm. The caring parents must also take responsibility for protecting their child from adults who think threats or hitting are the way to "handle" children, and also from the violence of other children. This can be especially difficult (but necessary) if the abused child has developed a pattern of being physically aggressive. Her tendency to interpret small slights as threats can make her prone to getting into fights. She may have a pugnacious attitude and provoke other children. The adult may have to invest considerable time in teaching the child how to deal with conflicts, how to problem-solve, and how to avoid violence.

Likewise, the child who has been sexually abused may have poor boundaries, making the child vulnerable to others who would draw him into further sexual activity. He may even seek out opportunities to sexually act out. Despite what his intentions and desires appear to be, it is important for the adult to realize that these experiences only result in further trauma and keep the child from healing. Acting out keeps the child from learning how to have healthy relationships with appropriate boundaries. Parents must be aware of potentially harmful situations and be proactive about establishing boundaries and protecting the child—even from his or her own behavior.

EMOTIONAL SAFETY AND HEALING

Another type of safety that is needed is emotional and psychological safety. When a child has experienced so much emotional turmoil, she needs adults who are stable, predictable, and honest in their emotions. The child needs to be able to learn how to appropriately respond to the adult. The more consistent the adult is, the easier it will be for the child to learn what is appropriate. To overcome the child's very negative outlook, a great number of positives are needed in that learning process: love, nurturing, kindness, compassion, empathy, and encouragement are essential. But this is not to say that adults should let the child "get away" with doing wrong. Rather, right and wrong need to be made clear, but with patience and consistency, rather than with anger and abuse.

MORAL SAFETY AND HEALING

The third type of safety that is required is moral safety. Many families have tried diligently to protect their children from exposure to sin in the culture and the society. They screen movies and television shows; they monitor the Internet; they even homeschool their children. Protecting children from such influences is good and necessary. Yet we have found that it is the close-up sins that seem to affect children more, the sins of the people that they see every day. If we want our children to be better, we need to watch ourselves and be careful of sin in our own lives.

So often we try to rationalize and understand what happened in psychological terms. We set aside morality and try to be intellectual and "professional." But we have found that children think more clearly than that. I [Dr. McGee] was sitting with a group of 11- and 12-year-old boys in a discussion group, and one boy said, "What I hate about women is that they stick you in hot water and then beat you with an electrical cord." The others nodded in understanding. One after the other, they let out little pieces of what had happened to them. I was deeply grieved by their stories.

Finally I said, "What happened to you is sin." It was a simple statement, but it had an amazing effect. The boys visibly relaxed. They sat back in their chairs. That was it. What had happened to them was morally wrong. They wanted it named. It was sin. They were glad someone had finally said so.

We cannot protect an abused child from the knowledge of sin. He already knows all too well about sin. What we can do is clearly say what is right and wrong, with no excuses and no rationalizations. It is such a relief for the child to hear someone say what she has known all along.

Once we say aloud that it is sin, there is no avoiding the next step: At this point, most children will ask for justice. Someone is guilty and ought to pay for the sin. Otherwise there is no justice and the world is not right. Now it gets complicated. We can condemn the abuser and say that he must pay, but what if the abuser is someone the child loves? What if the child has in turn abused others? The call for justice is offset with the fear that justice will be done.

We cannot avoid the fact that *all* have sinned and come short of the glory of God. The abuser has sinned, but so have we. The child may be angry at the abuser's sin, but the child also may be keenly aware that he himself has done wrong. What do we tell the child?

We have come to the basic tenets of our faith—that Jesus Christ died for the sins of all of us. We all ought to pay, but instead we thank God that Jesus paid. The only answer is to throw ourselves at the feet of Jesus and ask forgiveness for ourselves. What about forgiveness for the abuser? I have heard counselors talk about the need for the victim to forgive the abuser, but without justice, forgiveness feels wrong, as if the victim has been robbed of what was due.

The only path to forgiveness is to trust God for the justice. To trust that God will take care of the payment, that He will punish who needs to be punished, or extend grace to whom He will give grace.

So how do we provide moral safety? We protect the child as best we can. We work with the child to be clear about right and wrong. We face the issue of justice and repayment for sin. We help the child to trust God, who is the only One who can resolve the issue of bringing about justice. Only then can we help the child to seek forgiveness and to forgive. Ultimately, the only guarantee of moral safety is that God is in control.

TEACH MANAGEMENT OF EMOTIONS

Children with dysregulated emotions need to be actively taught how to manage their fears, their anger, and their sadness. The adult may have to explain strategies for coping with emotions that inexplicably rise up in the child. A child who is frightened may need to be shown how to play and enjoy playtime. A tense child has to develop the capacity to relax and be happy. We expect that children will "naturally" just go play, but a traumatized child may need for the adult to plan and provide healthy, nurturing emotional and relational experiences.

TEACH NEW COGNITIVE SKILLS

Likewise, in the midst of a conflict, the adult may have to step in and explain how to resolve the issue. She may have to patiently discuss and brainstorm with the child how to solve relational problems. Step by step, she may have to help the child to think situations through to understand what happened and why. Eventually, the emotional and cognitive teaching will give the child new insights and skills. Over time, you will see that he can manage situations that he could not handle before, and he will become competent, just as other children are.

In short, what the child needs from adults is:
- Kindness (but not always sympathy)
- Patience
- Insight
- Encouragement
- Reassurance
- Genuine caring
- Good judgment
- Controlled emotions

In order to provide these things, the adult has to have good emotional control himself. The adult cannot just respond on a whim. He has to think about how to handle the current situation. Out-of-control adults do not help children to be under control. Rather, out-of-control adults further traumatize children.

It can be difficult, in the moment, to be aware of and manage your own feelings, but it really is necessary. The adult needs a support system where she can sort things out and discuss how best to deal with the child's problems. That is, as parents, you need other adults who can be encouraging and insightful and who will pray for you through this process. Get connected in a support group. And don't hesitate to seek out professional help when dealing with these difficult issues.

True Healing

Sin against a child does physical, emotional, and spiritual damage. The loss of hope and trust is spiritual damage. The sense that "I cannot be loved" is fundamentally a loss of connection to God, who loves us unconditionally. As much as possible, caring adults need to work with the child to rebuild trust through relationships that are loving, healthy, and consistent. We adults have had our own traumas. There are times when we look into a child's eyes and we understand. But often that understanding has only come because of our own experiences. We all want to know Christ in the glory of His resurrection, but sometimes it is in the fellowship of His suffering that our deepest connections are made.

The biblical book of Joel begins with a description of the devastation of a locust invasion. The people are called to weep and mourn the loss of their land. But then there is that wonderful promise: "So I will restore to you the years that the swarming locust has eaten" (Joel 2:25a NKJV). Just like that land stripped by locusts, the abused child is devastated. Someone ought to mourn and grieve what has happened to this child. But ahead is the promise that God will restore this child! We have to have confidence in that.

Whether or not we think that the child can heal, we have to trust that God is able to bring wholeness to him, a restoration of all that was lost.

■■■

Dr. Therese McGee is a licensed clinical psychologist who directs the Lydia Home residential therapeutic program. The program provides a healing environment for 41 children with severe emotional and behavioral issues.

Dr. David Anderson is a licensed clinical psychologist and the executive director of Lydia Home Association, a Christian child welfare agency based in Chicago, Illinois.

Ghosts of an Infant's Past
by Dawn Gasser

The ghosts in my adopted daughter's past revealed themselves very early on in our relationship with her, during our first night in the hotel room in China, in fact. She was terrified and exhausted from suddenly being thrust into a stranger's arms. That night she didn't want us to hold her, so we put her in the crib beside our bed; she rolled away from us and fell asleep, letting her subconscious deal with the pain and confusion of the day. It was then that her mind betrayed her and she began to cry in her sleep.

She wept pitifully, making sounds like a severely wounded animal—muted, persistent, and undeniably painful to listen to. She was fast asleep and grieving deeply. When I woke her up, I saw that she had become even more frightened at the sight of me and my husband, but then her steely resolve kicked in—she turned her back on us again and fell back to sleep. We were left just staring at her curled up all alone in her crib, and we cried right along with her.

Enter the Ghost of Grieving.

Like many children cared for in institutions, she didn't cry when she was hurt, either physically or emotionally. One night while my husband and I were out, we called home to check in on her with the babysitter. The babysitter said that she was "fussy" and didn't want to play. Also, she wasn't putting weight on her left leg. Most parents would say that isn't much to get excited about, but we knew that she was hard to read; our parental instinct kicked in, telling us that something was very wrong and needed our immediate attention.

We met the babysitter and our daughter at the hospital, where we waited for over eight hours to be seen in the emergency room. She sat willingly in my lap while we waited. It was the first time she had actually sat still in my lap and let me hold her. Although I loved the opportunity, it told me that she was going through something horrible. Even though her outward appearance didn't indicate that she was afraid or in much pain, I knew differently.

However, I wasn't able to convey that effectively to the triage nurse who let many people see the doctor ahead of us. In the end, the doctor wanted us to see a specialist in another town. He acknowledged that she should've been seen much earlier; he feared compartmentalized swelling in her leg, a serious condition.

It was an additional two hours before we were seen by the doctor at the children's hospital. As they put the cast up past her mid-thigh, we learned that she had broken her tibia and fibula while playing on a trampoline. The only ones to shed tears were us, her mom and dad.

Enter the Ghost of Denied Pain.

Growing up, she has never been able to hide the fact that she didn't always have enough to eat in the institution. When she was very little, she always had to have food in her mouth and in both of her fists at meal times. If there was a specific food that was on someone else's plate and not on hers, she loudly let us know.

When she was a little older and accustomed to the fact that food was available, she began to share. To this day, when she's sure that she's been offered a chance to have some of everything on the table, she picks someone with whom to share her food. Even if she's earned a special treat for good behavior, she'll try to share. There are no exceptions, no matter how hard she had to work to earn her treat.

Her survival instinct is always present; when food enters the picture, however, unexpected compassion takes over in her. When she was still in China, someone must have shared a portion of their food with her and it must have happened at a time when she was in great need.

Enter the Ghost of Hunger.

Our daughter's night terrors happened many nights during the first six months after we returned home from China. She was unable to wake herself up or calm herself down. When she was a little older, she began to speak English, which enabled her to explain her fear to me one night after a nightmare: She had heard "the train, Momma . . . the train."

I didn't think much of this until she began to wake up terrified at four A.M. every night.

After a few nights of this, my body must have become conditioned and, one night, I actually woke up before she started screaming; it was then that I heard the train for myself. Suddenly everything began to make sense.

There's a train that passes through our town at four A.M. every night. It's quite far away, but you can hear it in the distance. As I listened, I was strongly reminded of the train tracks that we followed on the three-hour bus ride to her orphanage in China. I'm sure she'd been frightened by the train whistles at night, especially with no one to comfort her. Her night terrors were a visceral memory that her body would not let her dismiss, even though she couldn't verbalize her fears to me and probably didn't understand them herself. She is four and a half now and frightened by train whistles to this day.

Enter the Ghost of Trains.

These were the first ghosts we identified. We've discovered many more since then, and we know that our daughter still has some fears that we haven't been able to identify yet.

But on my brave days, I take a purposeful stance. I look back on where we began and take time to consider where we are now. I continue to pray for the strength and wisdom to see the big picture in the small details of parenting this special child with her unique needs. My goal and duty as her parent is to assist her in reframing these ghosts so that they don't define who she will become, but rather who she was before love changed them into tools and resources upon which to build a strong, compassionate character.

Recently we were watching a movie as a family, all cuddled up together on the couch—it wasn't that long ago that my daughter had not wanted to sit close to anyone. But here we were, my daughter cradled in my husband's lap, both of them intently staring at the TV. I had victory in my heart. Just then I *know* I heard the silent flutter of a ghost exiting my daughter's future.

We've come a *very* long way together.

13

Sexual Abuse

by Sharen E. Ford and Constance Vigil

*For he chose us in him before the creation of the world to be
holy and blameless in his sight. In love he predestined us to
be adopted as his sons through Jesus Christ, in accordance with
his pleasure and will—to the praise of his glorious grace,
which he has freely given us in the One he loves.*
—EPHESIANS 1:4–6

It had been three years since George's third grade teacher had gone to the principal to inquire about his problem. You see, it was the third time that week that George had soiled his clothing toward the end of the school day. The first two times Mrs. Parker asked George if there was a problem and tried to help get him to the school bus without too much of a fuss. She noted the incident in her records and attempted to reach his parents. She had left messages for them without a response and had asked the school social worker to follow up.

This time Mrs. Parker asked George to meet with her and the school counselor. George just sat there. He couldn't tell them what was going on. The school counselor called social services while Mrs. Parker asked to have George's sister, Samantha, a fourth grader, join her in the principal's office. After that, everything happened so fast.

The children were placed in foster care for their safety while social services and law enforcement completed their investigation. The judge decided that the children could not be safely returned home. The agency learned that both children had suffered physical and sexual abuse at the hands of a third party individual who had been staying in the family home over the last 30 days. The children's parents had separated six months before. Their mom hadn't been taking her medication and was not providing appropriate supervision for the children since taking in a new roommate to help pay the bills. The social services agency provided therapy to the children to help them process their emotions while they were placed in a foster family. There were so many adjustments to be made.

After 90 days, the children moved to a more permanent foster home. Samantha was very protective of George and often challenged her new foster mother's ability to care for him. George trusted Samantha; after all, it was she who told the principal and the school social worker what "really happened."

Both of the children acted out. That placement lasted eight months. They didn't know whom they could trust. After 20 months of working with the children's family, the court determined that it would be in the best interest to terminate the parents' rights. The agency would have to find a forever family for them.

The children had moved twice since they lived with the first foster family. Each time starting over was harder than before. Their worker came to continue her discussion with them about being adopted. Samantha remembers that it was on a Tuesday in late January. They were scared. Their worker said that she had been searching for an adoptive family and thought she had found one and asked if they wanted to meet them. George and Samantha longed for a family of their own. They didn't tell anyone that they considered themselves "spoiled goods." What they didn't know is that their very first foster parents had seen their picture in the Heart Gallery and asked to speak with their worker. The children hadn't seen the couple in three years. So much had happened since then—could they make this work? These children had been through so much—was there hope?

It wasn't easy. But the original foster parents were committed to adopting George and Samantha. At first, Samantha had her doubts. Since she would have to consent to her adoption, it was decided to delay the finalization of the adoption. Everyone wanted Samantha to be sure. The family was willing to let her work through her fears. It would be a year after placement before Samantha would decide that she could make the commitment to be adopted. In total,

George and Samantha were in foster care for almost five years before their adoption was finalized. But there was, indeed, hope. These children found their forever family.

How Sexual Abuse Affects Development

A child who has been sexually abused has been subjected to sexual assault, has been molested, or has been sexually exploited or prostituted. Both boys and girls, at any age, can be victims of sexual assault. The vast majority of sexually abused children have no injuries that can be observed by anyone, including a health care provider. However, there are often internal scars that may affect your child emotionally.

No matter when the sexual abuse occurs, it affects the child for the rest of her life. Very often, the child's emotional or psychological development stops at the age when the abuse took place. If sexual abuse occurs preverbally, it is very possible that the child's caseworker or other caretakers have no knowledge of any incidents or may only suspect that abuse occurred. These children have no words to explain what happened to them. Their cry is a cry that is waiting to be heard.

Outcomes of childhood sexual abuse include, but are not limited to, impairments in learning and problem-solving, concentration, self-esteem, problems with interpersonal relationships, impulse control, and reality testing. The psychological damage to the child's development can cause serious interruption in the attachment process.

Recognizing the Effects of Sexual Abuse

Children who experience developmental delays as a result of sexual abuse may tend to behave in ways that elicit further maltreatment and, in effect, double their victimization. Adolescents often place themselves in dangerous situations, increasing the risk of significant impairments and failures in developing and maintaining interpersonal relationships and accomplishing emancipation tasks.

Some other indicators of sexual abuse might include the following:
- Somatic problems, particularly stomachaches and headaches
- Excessive fear of being approached or touched

- Imitates sexual behavior when playing with dolls
- Seductiveness
- Sexual behaviors or references that are bizarre or unusual for the child's age
- Sexual knowledge that is too sophisticated for the child's age

Some parents may suspect that their child has suffered sexual abuse—maybe even preverbally—but are unsure because of limited knowledge of their child's past or because their child is acting out in nonsexualized ways. If you feel that your child is having problems that are not the "typical" problems a child his or her age might be exhibiting, it is time to consult with a therapist or your child's pediatrician. If appropriate, you might also consult with the agency that placed your child for adoption. Re-review any information about the history of abuse or potential abuse experienced by your child. Rely on teachers, other parents, or day care providers for your child to assist you in deciding whether the behaviors are something about which you should be concerned.

Keep in mind that some children seem to be able to overcome and thrive despite their history of sexual abuse due to their tolerance for pain, their intelligence, extroversion, psychological constitution, or other characteristics, which have a genetic basis. And with your help and involvement, you can make a difference in your child's life despite the difficult circumstances.

DEALING WITH SEXUALLY ACTING-OUT BEHAVIORS

All children are unique, and depending on the age of the child, all act out differently. Some children act out without "acting out" at all (withdrawing from everyone and all of his or her activities). Others might act aggressive, provocative, sad, angry, hyperactive, or defiant.

What might this look like for a child who has been sexually abused? Specific behaviors could include, as mentioned, acting older and sexually inappropriately with adults or other children, running away, becoming violent with others, crying inconsolably, having emotional outbursts, masturbating, refusing to obey, and many more actions. In whatever way your child acted that made him or her feel safe previously—that is how he or she will continue to act until those behaviors no longer make him or her feel safe.

Many things that happen in a child's day-to-day life can trigger memories of trauma. The memories will cause your child to act the way he or she has acted before so that he or she can feel safe again. Emotional and punitive responses from you (such as yelling or sending your child away) will, most likely, create a stressful response from your child and are apt to exacerbate the state of affairs. Depending on the age (and maturity level) of your child, give verbal and non-verbal cues to him that the behavior is not acceptable. (See chapter 5 for more information on dealing with discipline issues.) *Gentle* reminders should continue as long as required and the behavior persists.

Help your child to replace the unacceptable behavior with other behaviors. She is counting on you to teach her new behaviors. If she is old enough to understand, have her select the replacement behavior. These new behaviors will also depend on your child and his or her age, personality, and the behavior that is being replaced. If your child runs away when she is under stress, you might sit down and talk with her about where she would feel safe without having to go far away—her bedroom, the basement, the garage, the backyard. Make an agreement with your child that whenever she feels like running away, she will always go to the same place so that you know she is safe and where she is. If your child masturbates frequently, perhaps he would like to draw pictures, write a story, or play a musical instrument instead. Your child will need to be reminded, at first, to replace the unacceptable behavior with the one that you and the child have identified. Remember to use gentle reminders.

If she has a therapist, that therapist will be very helpful in providing the resources for helping your child to extinguish the behaviors. It is possible that the therapist and your child have already done much work in this area and your child will be very aware of when she is acting out (or about to) and can be easily stopped with verbal or nonverbal cues.

It is quite natural that you will also experience anger and sadness because your child was hurt by someone in this way. It's okay to tell your child of your feelings. It will be an ideal way for you to show and model replacement behaviors for your child. Talk to him about how, why, and what you do when you feel sad or angry. Remind your child that these feelings are part of the way God made us.

PROTECTING YOUR CHILD FROM FURTHER SEXUAL ABUSE

All parents worry about protecting their children from sexual abuse, regardless of a history of victimization. There are many tactics that parents use when attempting to protect their children:

- Help your child understand "good touch" and "bad touch."
- Help your child protect herself by making sure that she gets the appropriate therapeutic intervention:
  - Therapy
  - Education
- Get to know your child's friends and his friends' families.
- Make sure that you are involved in every part of your child's life, especially when she is young.
  - Volunteer in her classroom.
  - Coach or assist with his or her athletic, academic, or other extracurricular activities.
- As often as possible, attend your child's activities, practices, and performances, and make sure that teachers and coaches know who you are and that you are always available.
- Teach your child that there are no secrets in your family.
- Help your child understand that he is a good person; that he is loved unconditionally; and that he does not have to do things to make people like him.

CREATING A SAFE ENVIRONMENT

The same rules and circumstances apply in this section as the previous section. There are some additions that are helpful in providing for the safety of your child and those around her.

- It is important that you are fully aware of how the long-term effects have manifested in your child so that you are prepared for conditions that might arise.

- It is also important that you understand how your child was abused:
  - Who the perpetrator(s) were.
  - What the circumstance(s) were in which the abuse occurred.

You may or may not have all the information available to you. But even if there are pieces of your child's story that you don't know or that he has been unable to tell you, by having thorough knowledge of all areas of your child's life, activities, and history, you will be more likely to prevent further abuse and create safety all around your child.

As the parent, it is necessary to make sure that your child is not put in situations where there is a chance for her to re-create the sexual abuse by being a perpetrator or victim.

Ongoing therapy will be very important in order to give your child and your family the weapons, the strength, and the education to avoid unsafe circumstances and environments. The understanding that therapy establishes will allow you as the parent(s) to continue to assist your child to grow into a healthier, secure, and stable individual. If your child had a therapist with whom she was working before coming to your home, ideally, she should continue this relationship. If that's not possible, there are several things to consider when choosing a therapist.

It is necessary to find someone who has experience working with victims of sexual abuse as well as an understanding of adoption issues. Start looking by contacting local adoption resources—your caseworker, a leader in your faith community, adoption support groups, post-adoption organizations, and so on—for referrals or lists of nearby therapists. Do not limit yourself to psychologists or psychiatrists. Social workers, marriage and family therapists, licensed Christian counselors, and pastoral counselors can also be possible resources for your child and your family.

Be sure to interview any individual whom you are considering. Here are some questions to consider:

- What is his/her experience with adoption in general and, more specifically, with the issues that are particular to your family, including grief and loss?
- How long has he/she been in practice and what degrees, licenses, or certifications does he/she have?

- What clinical training does he/she have on adoption issues as well as sexual abuse of children?
- Does he/she include parents and other family members in the therapeutic process? If so, how? What does this look like?
- Request and/or state your expectations that the therapist provide regular reports to you.
- Can he/she estimate a time frame for the course of treatment?
- What are his/her arrangements for coverage when he/she is not available, especially in the event of an emergency?
- Is he/she willing or does he/she have experience to work collaboratively with school personnel?

The key to working with any mental health therapist is feeling comfortable enough to be able to talk to that person openly and honestly. If your child is not responding to the chosen professional or does not want to talk to her at all, this is probably not the person on whom you should rely to help your child heal from her subconscious wounds. Most young children will look to their parents for guidance. If the parents feel comfortable with a therapist, it is most likely that the child will also feel comfortable and will, eventually, open up to this person because she is trustworthy and nonjudgmental. Be sure to choose a therapist who is willing to work with the whole family, not just the child. Remember, therapists are available to give guidance, direction, and information, but it is the parents who must build an ongoing, stable relationship of trust with their child.

After selecting a therapist, reevaluate your decision on a regular basis. Make sure that everyone is comfortable with the choice and that everyone is seeing improvement.

"What if" is a great tool for all children (and adults) in facing new situations. Before embarking on a new activity or going to a new place, help your child to think about what might happen while he is there, what people he might meet, what he might say, and so on. This is a very easy way to prepare him, and he will be more apt to avoid uncomfortable and potentially dangerous occasions, if something unexpected were to happen.

You, as a caring parent, should also make sure that other adults who are responsible for your child's safety will be made aware of your child's history. It is not necessary (or appropriate) for every person to know about your child's abuse. However, your child's therapist can be very helpful in making the decisions about who to tell, when, and how much information is absolutely necessary.

Gently educate your child to avoid potentially dangerous situations for her. As every parent knows, however, you need to remind her that the world is a good place, but there are dangerous people. Help your child to understand that you love her no matter what, and that you want to help her be safe in any circumstance.

SHARING ABOUT ABUSE

As mentioned above, a therapist, caseworker, and others knowledgeable about your child and his needs will help you make the right decision about whether to speak of your child's past abuse. There will be times when nothing needs to be said, but there will also be times when some (or all) of your child's history must be told in order to provide the most optimum conditions for your child. These times must be decided daily, on a case-by-case basis.

As you get to know your child, you will become more comfortable in making these decisions. Most often it is important to tell (to some degree) other adults who will be around your child frequently—teachers, Sunday school teachers, and immediate family.

Whether or not you tell parents of your child's friends depends on the parents. You want responsible adults to be alert to keeping your child safe, but you don't want to give information to people who will not treat your child and his private information with respect and confidentiality.

If your child is participating in overnight activities, it will be important to develop a safety plan with the adults providing supervision and make sure your child understands what appropriate behaviors are and what she needs to do if she is feeling unsafe. In this situation, giving your child a cell phone to call home if necessary can be beneficial. With proper planning, sleepovers and camping experiences can be a part of your child's activities.

Remember that this history is very painful for your child. It is possible that bringing up this history might create anxiety, stress, and the prospect that your child might revert to previous behaviors or have flashbacks of the abuse. However, it also can help the people around him to understand him better and assist him to grow and thrive.

HELPING YOUR CHILD HEAL FROM SEXUAL ABUSE

- Your child needs to be able to express both negative and positive feelings. Hiding socially condemned feelings and behaviors will not resolve them.
- Your child needs to know that he is loved, understood, and respected even if his related behaviors are not condoned.
- Your child needs to feel that this new family is committed to creating and maintaining a "forever" relationship.
- Your child needs to feel accepted, worthy of love and having inherent dignity, regardless of behavior.
- Your child needs to feel that he is not being judged or condemned for his behavior and history.
- Your child needs to know that her history will be kept confidential from people who do not have a compelling need to know.
- You need to build a trusting relationship with your child:
  - Pay attention to verbal and nonverbal cues.
  - Communicate an understanding of your child's feelings, fears, and beliefs.
  - Show a desire to understand everything that is significant to your child.
  - Discuss what is important to your child.
  - Do not argue or debate with your child. If there are differences of opinion, ask questions and affirm him, then suggest "what if" scenarios.
  - Look for and acknowledge your child's past successes, no matter how small.

God has planted your child into your home and says, "Provide for those who grieve in Zion—to bestow on them a crown of *beauty* instead of *ashes*, the oil of gladness instead of mourning, and a garment of praise instead of a spirit of despair. They will be called oaks of righteousness, a planting of the LORD for the display of his splendor" (Isaiah 61:3, italics added).

Praying a hedge of protection around your child and sharing the message of the heavenly Father's love will be key to your parenting. Consistently pray for God to give you the strength and endurance to not give up on your child and trust Him to indeed give your child beauty for ashes.

■■■

Sharen Ford has been involved in child welfare services in the state of Colorado for more than 20 years. Her areas of expertise include special needs adoption, concurrent planning, adolescent issues, adoption medical assistance, and mental health issues.

Constance Vigil is the adoption program specialist for the Colorado State Department of Human Services. Prior to coming to the state department she served as an adoption supervisor in Denver County Department of Human Services.

Protecting the Broken
by Julia Campbell

Some pretty shocking things had come out of Christy's little three-year-old mouth. More shocking, however, were the foster mother's reports and the professional evaluation done regarding our daughter-to-be's sexually acting out behaviors.

True, my husband, Steve, and I had received training about the ramifications of sexual abuse and had walked through the healing journey with several adult friends. Still, we would come to experience the very different day-to-day reality of raising a child who has been hurt in such profound ways.

We had no factual record of what kind of abuse had occurred in the first three years of Christy's life, but the reality of the abuse was apparent. Friends and family who were trained in the counseling field instantly recognized her gregarious lack of boundaries as indicating something more than just an outgoing personality. Some were highly concerned that Christy would act out in a way that hurt other children or make false accusations against my husband or our teenage son. I wanted to be full of hope—and I was—but I couldn't ignore the pressing reality, either. Along with the hope, we had to establish safeguards for everyone in our family.

Even though it felt unfair to a bubbly little girl who just longed to be loved, we set very firm boundaries in our family in regard to modesty, physical affection, and supervision.

Suddenly, there was no roughhousing or wrestling allowed in our household. We did not have our children snuggle in bed with us either, even on a Saturday morning. Even though Christy was still a preschooler, dressing by all members of the family took place behind closed doors.

Our teenage son knew that he did not have to hug or hold Christy unless he chose to do so. We rarely asked him to babysit his younger siblings—and only if Christy was already in bed.

When friends came over, I had to keep Christy within sight and sound at all times. I couldn't let her go to play at the house of a friend, even people we trusted, unless we felt completely comfortable asking them to supervise vigilantly. We didn't know if or when Christy would say something inappropriate or attempt to touch another child in a sexual manner.

Steve sometimes felt frustrated when his little daughter would gaze up at him like a lovesick teenager. He remained firm with her: "Christy, I'm not your prince. I'm your daddy." Whether she got the message from the words he said or the day in, day out demonstration of his deep love and steadfast authority, we began to see her sexualized responses to him fade.

While Steve did not do any of Christy's personal physical care, he always dried her hair after she had bathed and put on her pajamas. He used this opportunity to affirm her—complimenting her on her pretty hair, caring for her needs—in an appropriate way.

I felt barricaded by the structures we had to maintain. Whether it was in public or visiting with friends, I had to always be on the alert. Christy had no stranger awareness and few personal boundaries. We had to enforce rules about staying by my side, asking permission before hugging anyone (even family members), and keeping her hands to herself.

I also felt sad that our preschool daughter, through no fault of her own, had no opportunity to experience a season of innocence. Her girl cousins of the same age could run through their house in their underwear or dress in front of their dad, and none of them thought anything of it. But even if Christy had no motive to her flirtatious actions, her actions and reactions were not the same as a child who had not been sexually abused. When Christy was exposed to sexual activity and sexually abused as a small child, she was harmed in ways she doesn't realize. Besides damaging her psyche, a "switch" was flipped that should have been left alone for 10 to 12 more years. Christy was sexualized so that she has responses typical of a girl well into her teens.

When Christy came home and told me that a boy in her first grade class said he wanted to kiss her "privates," I had to talk with the teacher. I didn't know if this boy had really said this (maybe he was from an abusive situation too), or if Christy had made it up. She lived in an imaginary world already, and lying was both an unconscious habit and a means of disobeying. Either way, I had to address it with the teacher and ask that she monitor Christy carefully as well as discourage any boyfriend-girlfriend talk.

The teacher was gracious and helpful, but when I spoke to the teacher the next year about certain structures and boundaries, I think it created a sense of reluctance and anxiety in his relationship with Christy. Even careful sharing about Christy's background can hamper her relationships.

We keep Christy's environment as minimally stimulated as possible. We are careful about what books and television shows and movies we allow her to watch. Particular toys—such as certain dolls or other toys that seem at all provocative—are completely off-limits. I've worked hard to make sure that her wardrobe is more than appropriate. It's still not fair. Lots of little girls wear spaghetti strap tops without any sexual effect. That's just not an option for Christy, and I can't always explain it to her.

The past few years we have seen great strides in Christy's responses and her behaviors. We continue to keep our home structured and safe. We address attitudes and behaviors that aren't appropriate. We talk about sexuality in an honest and age-appropriate way. Steve and I model a loving and affectionate marriage relationship, but we're careful not to be too physically affectionate in front of Christy. That fascination is still there.

I used to be more fearful about parenting a child who has been sexually abused. How can I ever help her? When should I tell her what I know about her history? I want to make sure that I provide all the resources and help that she needs, but I don't want to push her before it's the right time. I know what the healing journey is like for a person who was sexually abused as a child. It's a worthwhile—but long and difficult—road.

Thankfully, I know that my daughter is not facing this journey alone. As a child, she has trusted Jesus Christ and the Holy Spirit lives within her. I commit her often to God's care and healing work. Specifically, I ask the Lord to "rewire" Christy's heart and mind in a way that no parent or therapist could ever accomplish. And Steve and I will continue to watch over and protect her as long as we can.

14

Drug and Alcohol Effects

by Dr. Steven Gray

*Yet to all who received him [Jesus Christ], to those who
believed in his name, he gave the right to become children
of God—children born not of natural descent, nor of human
decision or a husband's will, but born of God.*
—JOHN 1:12–13

Having been in the neuroscience field spanning four decades, I am amazed by all the complexity and acronyms. To this day, I feverishly attempt to translate neuropsychological code-speak into everyday English. Allow me to start off as resident code-breaker for the three primary acronyms regarding gestational alcohol/drug effects.

FAS (Fetal Alcohol Syndrome): the most severe form of in utero drug/alcohol effects, almost always showing the presence of facial characteristics, stunted growth, and/or mental retardation

FAE (Fetal Alcohol Effects): a lesser severity of FAS, often with no outward physical manifestations or mental retardation

FASD (Fetal Alcohol Spectrum Disorder): a catch-all category encompassing both FAS and FAE, on a continuum

Because of an inability of clinicians to agree completely on the definition of FAE, two other terms have come into use in recent years:

ARND (Alcohol-Related Neurodevelopmental Disorder): refers to cognitive and/or behavioral problems associated with fetal alcohol exposure, whether or not physical manifestations are present

ARBD (Alcohol-Related Birth Defects): a term encompassing problems with physical structures, including the heart, kidneys, and bones

While you may hear these last two terms, FAE is still widely used and is the term I will use in this chapter. In addition, throughout this chapter I will primarily use the term FASD; in so doing, I am not making a distinction between the *severity* of effects suffered by a child who was exposed in the womb to drugs and/or alcohol—unless I directly allude to FAS or FAE.

Moreover, please don't be misled by the word "alcohol" in the above distinctions. "Drugs" are implied in these acronyms as well. Unfortunately, experience has shown that when a pregnant mother consumes alcohol, the odds are high that she is also using at least one form of an illicit drug.

RECOGNIZING FETAL ALCOHOL AND DRUG EFFECTS

FASD children more often than not reveal drug- or alcohol-related brain compromise by way of cognitive and emotional disruption. If FASD only affected a child's facial features and physical stature, there would be only minimal effect upon the quality of his life and the custodial family's life.

But, for children suffering FAS, what *are* some of the common physical manifestations?

- Smaller physical stature (below the tenth percentile for age and race)
- Microcephalus (smaller brain size)
- Eyelid ptosis (drooping of the upper eyelids)
- Vermilion border (very thin upper lip)
- Flat philtrum (flatness of the typical groove above the upper lip)
- Narrow palpebral fissure (narrowing of the inner/outer corners of the eyes)
- "Hockey stick" palmar crease (upper crease in the hand's palm shaped like a hockey stick)
- Clinodactyly (permanent curving of the fifth finger, inward toward fourth finger)
- "Railroad track" ears (top curve of the ear folded over, and parallel to the curve beneath it, giving the appearance of a railroad track)

Yet, as I've already stated, the lion's share of struggles faced by youth with FASD are cognitive and emotional in nature. The most commonly cited FASD-related cognitive feature is impaired attention and concentration. Thus, Attention Deficit Hyperactivity Disorder (ADHD) is almost always an FASD spin-off diagnosis. Moreover, ADHD then dominoes a child into emotionally related fallout. If a child struggles paying attention in school, what is the typical result? His emotions are affected. He begins acting out in class due to frustration with keeping up with the teacher, or he may become the class clown.

FASD is also notorious for producing the following: impulsivity, poor judgment, faulty cause-and-effect thinking, flawed self-evaluation skills, impaired gratification delay, weak planning and sequencing abilities, along with hair-trigger ballistic episodes.

Another common result of FASD is a harmful effect on intelligence. In utero drug- and alcohol-affected youth, according to research, do not as a group perform as well on IQ tests as do children born from a non-toxic pregnancy.

EFFECTS OF PRENATAL ALCOHOL/DRUG EXPOSURE ON CHILD DEVELOPMENT

I liken the effect of FASD on the developing child in two ways. First, many children—those with FAE—frequently show developmental *delays*. They might be slower to walk, talk, ride a bike, or read. It's not that they cannot achieve these skills; they just take longer to emerge. And it may be necessary to provide the child with a regimen of specialized help for a period of time—for example, speech therapy over the course of a year or two for a child with articulation struggles.

Second, amid the more severe side of the FASD continuum—children with FAS—certain developmental arrests will occur. For example, children who suffer from mental retardation (MR) may not develop higher-level academic skills, the ability to fully grasp cause-effect thinking, or engage in mature judgment or decision-making. Due to the severity of FAS, brain integrity has been affected such that certain areas of development simply cannot occur.

Developmental Expectations for Children with FASD

Once again, the range is vast in terms of rates of development of children exposed to toxins during pregnancy. With FAS, there may be mental retardation (MR)—usually of mild or moderate severity, with IQs anywhere from 50 to 69. Such a cognitive impairment will then make special education at school imperative. In some states, this is called a "developmental skills" classroom. Equipped with a low teacher-student ratio, these classrooms have a very tight structure. And "structure" is the key word here. Moreover, academic subjects are understandably less challenging.

As youth with FAS/MR progress into young adulthood, they frequently require some form of structure within their living environments. This could range from a halfway house setting to a relatively independent lifestyle supplemented by intermittent supervision via a caseworker.

The same holds true vocationally for FAS/MR. Here again, there is wide variability regarding worksite complexity. While an adult with moderate severity MR may require the repetition and structure of, say, an assembly line job, other higher-functioning persons with FAS/MR often do well as valued assistants to persons working in skilled trades such as construction, plumbing, or technical repair. In fact, some of these youth turn out to be especially *gifted* within various spheres of the workforce.

With the milder severity FAE, developmental expectations are much broader. For example, IQ impairment can range from the so-called borderline range (70–79), to the low average range—sometimes referred to as the "slow learner" range (80–89), up to the solid average range (90–109).

A wider choice of school options is also reasonable with FAE. Among most such children, there is a need for special education. But unlike FAS where a developmental skills classroom is most appropriate, a child with FAE does not usually need such intensive structure.

School options for FAE usually include two different possibilities. One would be a Resource (or "Lab") classroom (teacher-student ratio of approximately 1:10, replete with a modified curriculum and special accommodations, such as the allowance of more time to take tests). The other educational option would be Content Mastery (a hybrid, if you will, between a regular/mainstreamed classroom and a Resource classroom). With either Content Mastery or Resource, a child can spend 20 percent of her day in one or both, 30 percent in one or both, and so on—depending upon the educational needs of a given child.

Vocationally, FAE options are much broader than with FAS/MR. Many children with FAE grow up to graduate from community college or four-year institutions and do quite well for themselves in all sorts of jobs, such as skilled trades (landscape design, food service industry, construction supervisors, sales, etc.).

EFFECTS OF FETAL ALCOHOL AND DRUG EXPOSURE ON ATTACHMENT AND BONDING

Tragically, FASD and the capacity for interpersonal attachment are inextricably linked. Why? Because a child's ability to bond with Mom and Dad is made possible by the integrity of certain brain structures. So, if prenatal exposure to drugs and alcohol compromises brain structures, it makes logical sense that an affected child's ability to interpersonally attach becomes compromised.

Increasingly, we are learning that fear is the common denominator to all or most forms of psychopathology. As such, all too many adopted children receive a double body-slam to their brains as a result of FASD *plus* early postnatal trauma. If a child's brain is in perpetual overdrive from fear, how then can bonding and attachment to another human being take place? It often cannot. That is why the technology of neurofeedback (discussed a little later) is so vital to these children.

THE BLAME GAME AND FASD

The first and foremost point I need to make here is that adoptive parents of children with FASD should bear no guilt or responsibility for their child's struggles. After all, it was not the adoptive mom who carried this child in her womb and chose to consume drugs and alcohol during all or part of nine months. Regardless, one of the most common sentiments I hear among adoptive moms and dads is that their child's behavior is somehow the fault of the adoptive parents! Unfortunately, our society is all too quick to cast blame upon good parents—be they adoptive or biological—for *whatever* ails their child.

My message to you as an adoptive parent who has lovingly opened your home to a special needs child is, "God bless you; may your tribe increase!" Do *not* get sucked into society's need to play the blame game with you. Not only should there be no shame in your marvelous endeavor, but you are to be roundly applauded.

EMPHASIZING THE POTENTIAL OF A CHILD WITH FASD

Please know that children struggling with FASD have strengths. Just as is the case with all children and youth, it is our job as parents, educators, and allied health care providers to help the child discover what her God-given strengths are. Despite life's daily challenges and pitfalls, God has a unique plan for every life. Discovering your child's strengths helps guide her to the unique plan God has for her life.

EFFECTS OF AN ALCOHOL- OR DRUG-AFFECTED HOME ENVIRONMENT ON CHILDREN

Much has been written concerning how a child is affected by residing in an alcoholic home. Some children appear to be remarkably resilient. Others are not as fortunate. Depression, anxiety, shame, anger, and resentment can linger for years.

Let's take a moment to look at two major types of alcoholic or drug-infested homes: 1) the abusive parent(s); and 2) the neglectful parent(s).

For many parents, drug and alcohol abuse turns them into monsters within the home. They do and say things to their spouses and children that they would never do while sober. The repeated bouts of this type of chaos then become, to the child, a series of traumatic experiences. The child's home life is spent in perpetual fight or flight mode. Biochemically, there is frequent release of stress hormones such as cortisol and adrenaline, which highjack the child's central nervous system—sending it into almost perpetual overdrive.

The second type of drug and alcohol-infested home instead has the neglectful parent. In this situation, the child may not have a fear of Mom "going off again." Rather, the child must now constantly deal with getting his needs met on his own. *Will there be enough food in the house? Am I going to spend another night alone at home? Who's going to help me with my homework? Will I have any decent clothes to wear to school tomorrow? Does anyone love me?* This is the ongoing trauma of neglect rather than the trauma of abuse.

Regardless of which of the two trauma scenarios a child faces, she suffers. Common among such youth are: depression, anxiety/nervousness, low self-esteem, sleep disturbance, poor attention at school, bedwetting, fighting with peers, and oppositionalism toward teachers. Without professional help, many of these youth grow up to carry their trauma issues into their marriage and/or job. They can also become very bitter toward God.

HELPING YOUR CHILD OVERCOME THE ENVIRONMENTAL ALCOHOL OR DRUG EXPOSURE

Many adopted children hailing from a chaotic birth home go through an initial honeymoon phase. It's as if they're thinking: *I know what "home" has been like for me in the past. Will it be any different here? I sure hope so. I better be on my best behavior because I don't want to get sent back. I better just lie low and test the waters for a while.*

After a few weeks or months, however, the adopted traumatized child begins to feel a comfort level in your home. *Wow. This is certainly different from what I had before! These people actually show me love and respect. How's that possible? After all, my birthparents treated me with contempt and neglect. I don't think I deserve to be treated this well. Being given love and kindness makes me feel, well . . . kind of weird. In fact, it's downright awkward to be treated this well! Better hurry up and do something bad—to get in trouble and be punished—so I can feel "normal" again.*

Consider the honeymoon now over.

But how do we help a child who has spent extended time in the drug- or alcohol-affected home? Well, the first step, and a crucial one, is simply getting the child out of his old home. This alone is huge! For older children, another helpful resource is Alateen. This is an organization that helps children of alcoholics. Based upon the philosophy of the Alcoholics Anonymous Twelve Step Recovery Program, Alateen equips children and teens to understand that they are not responsible for an alcoholic parent's drinking/drugging and that their own recovery is in no way dependent upon the alcoholic's recovery. (Inclusion of this reference does not necessarily constitute endorsement of material, content, or organizational viewpoint by Focus on the Family.)

Professional Christian counseling is another important lifeline for children of alcoholics. Here, attendance to a child's emotional condition can be assessed and addressed. Is the child suffering from clinical depression, Post-Traumatic Stress Disorder (PTSD), shame, false guilt, or possibly an eating disorder? If so, treatment can be instituted.

The astute school counselor can also be an effective ally to a child who has dealt with family alcoholism. Although expertise varies greatly across the country in terms of the unique dynamics of the adoptive child, school counselors can be hugely helpful. For one thing, they can provide a much-needed conduit between parents and teachers. This ensures that the child cannot engage in the art form of "triangulation," otherwise known as "playing the parents against the teacher."

School counselors are also vital members of the child's educational support system—offering emotional support as well as consulting with teachers and administrators in setting up the most optimal classroom and curriculum accommodations.

Helping Your Child with FASD

First, enlist the prayer and practical-needs support from family and friends. Don't be afraid to ask for help. The next step is obtaining a thorough physical examination of the child. This should include lab studies analyzing blood and urine. A portion of children with FASD and its comorbidities (also known as "running buddies") will have endocrine (hormonal) anomalies.

The classic example is hypothyroidism, an underproduction of thyroid hormone. Among many other potential symptoms of this disorder, hypothyroidism can cause an organic form of childhood depression. This type of depression does *not* respond to counseling; medical treatment is needed. The polar opposite of hypothyroidism is hyperthyroidism, an overproduction of thyroid hormone. This can cause anxiety or nervousness for the child, as if his central nervous system is on constant red alert. Again, we can *counsel* the anxiety produced by hyperthyroidism until all the cows in Kansas come home, but to no avail without appropriate medical care.

The Neuropsychological Exam

Once a thorough physical examination is completed, it is now time to conduct a neuropsychological (NP) evaluation. An NP exam is a series of procedures designed to identify irregularities in the child's brain function. Think of the NP evaluation as a series of mental gymnastics, with each task geared at measuring a particular area of the brain. For example, an NP exam asks the child to perform various tasks, such as: (1) constructing colored blocks to simulate geometric shapes, (2) listening to various tape-recorded audio vignettes, (3) monitoring a computer that flashes a series of numbers, (4) recalling a list of words, and so on.

Each of the various mental gymnastics listed above taps into different brain regions. In this way, the child's brain function is thoroughly analyzed. Then, a tailored treatment plan can be devised for the child (discussed below). But without a thorough NP evaluation, parents, teachers, and counselors are forced to wander in the wilderness, searching out the underlying root causes for a given child. For example, does FASD exist for the child? If so, what else could be co-occurring for her? ADHD? Obsessive-Compulsive Disorder (OCD)? Pediatric Bipolar Disorder (PBD)? A Borderline Psychosis of Childhood (BPC)?

Tragically, all too many adopted children never have the benefit of a comprehensive NP exam. And, for those children who have had such an evaluation, it came years *after* adoption, following much frustration by the parents and the child. Once the NP exam has been conducted and results revealed, the most frequent comment I hear from parents is, "Oh, if we had only had this done years ago." The sooner the diagnosis is made, the sooner a correct treatment can be applied.

Medication Considerations

One thing a thorough adoption-specific NP exam can identify is medication options. Would a psychostimulant (Ritalin, Adderal, Concerta, etc.) help this child? What about a low-dose antidepressant such as Prozac or Zoloft? How about something to stabilize the child's maddening fluctuating moods?

Okay, I know what you're thinking. *What if I, as a parent, am dead-set against treating my children with psychotropic medications? In fact, come to think of it, I'd rather be tarred and feathered on downtown Main Street than give my kids drugs!*

I hear you. In my experience, parental attitudes concerning the issue of children and psychoactive meds fit into three classes: (1) Anti-medication, (2) Pro-medication, and (3) Ambivalent—"I'm torn both ways!" In my own practice, I first find out to which of the three groups a parent belongs. Then we talk over the pros and cons.

Sometimes a parent may have developed a legitimate or an irrational fear about children and medications. Another parent may be too quick to pull the trigger in using meds, based upon unrealistic expectations. This is where unrushed dialogue between a specialist and parent comes in.

Psychotherapy

What about counseling to help my child? Unfortunately, the term "counseling" these days has about as much specificity as the term "car." And in truth, most forms of counseling, or "therapy," are inappropriate for a special needs child with FASD and companion issues. So, what *is* a Christian parent to do?

Number one, we need a Christian clinician, or, at the least, a clinician who is supportive (not just tolerant) of your family's Christian faith and values. But then what? The next litmus test is: Does this counselor have a thorough grounding in the unique dynamics of special needs children? Is he familiar with FASD? With attachment issues? With the discernment of "psychotherapeutic timing" that is so crucial to working with traumatized youth? With the effects on brain function for a child with FASD?

Does the clinician working with your child possess the requisite education and training unique to adoptive youth? A great resource in terms of finding a specialized therapist in your area of the country is www.attach.org. This is the Web site of the Association for Treatment and Training in the Attachment of Children (ATTACh). And many of the clinicians registered with ATTACh are Christians.

So, what is the bottom line when it comes to choosing a therapist? Make sure the individual is an experienced, well-trained clinician who eschews any techniques that are physically coercive to a child. Again, the ATTACh Web site can help you find such a person.

Neurofeedback

A cutting-edge approach for directly influencing and repairing damaged brain function is neurofeedback, at times referred to as EEG biofeedback. Think of neurofeedback as brain training, brain training that can affect millions of simultaneous *sparking* electrical impulses.

Brain cells communicate with one another in two ways, through: (1) tiny squirts of chemicals (neurotransmitters), and (2) tiny electrical bursts. Medications work on the former; neurofeedback works on the latter. In the case of neurofeedback, however, the brain is actually taught how to produce, permanently in most cases, optimal electrical activity. In turn, many children have been able to learn how to normalize abnormal electrical activity corresponding with FASD and many of its common running buddies (ADHD, PBD, impaired pre-frontal lobe dysfunction causing impulsivity, poor judgment, raging, weak cause-effect thinking, etc.).

How does neurofeedback work? Think of two computers linked together. One computer houses the EEG (measuring brain electrical activity). The other computer houses a series of computer games (e.g., Pac-Man). In order for Pac-Man to keep moving around the mazes eating dots, the child's brain electrical firing must achieve a healthy mode. When the electrical activity lapses back into its old ways, Pac-Man stops. Thus the child receives real-time feedback as to how to optimize his own brain function. With repetition, the brain clings for dear life on to *healthy* brain electrical states—thus working the child out of impaired neurological function that underlies FASD and its malevolent sidekicks.

Wait. It gets better. Neurofeedback is incredibly easy to learn. Most persons learn how to make the video game "go" in a matter of a couple of minutes. It is the repetition over time that allows the brain's newfound electrical signatures to lock in. Thus, neurofeedback is not something the child must engage in over the lifespan because it quickly becomes natural. Also, most children enjoy the video games, there is no pain involved, and the EEG is not putting any sort of electrical activity into the child's brain. EEG is in no way kin to electroconvulsive treatment (ECT).

Moreover neurofeedback technology is constantly getting better, and more research on it is published virtually every month. The field has advanced light years since I was first trained in the procedure back in the early 1990s. A wonderful and informative Web site to learn more about neurofeedback is hosted by EEG Spectrum International (www.eegspectrum.com).

Sensory Integration Training

Another promising treatment is Sensory Integration Training (SIT). Performed by a specially trained occupational therapist (OT), SIT's objective is to link together, or integrate, various sensory modalities such as the visual, auditory, tactile (touch), proprioception (balance/equilibrium)—all of which are housed, if you will, in the brain. A percentage of children with FASD struggle with a disjointed sensory system. That is, they are averse to the texture of certain foods, certain fabrics or tags in shirts are highly uncomfortable, and so on. Examples of SIT exercises with the children might include playing catch while sitting on a large beach ball, listening to tape-recorded stimuli while putting together complex blocks, and so on.

Parenting Style and Discipline

Tweaking discipline by parents is an essential help to youth with FASD. A counselor specializing in adoption dynamics can be especially helpful when it comes to this subject. Some parents, out of a sense of pity for the child, may allow her to become abusive to Mom or Dad. "Well, after all, Sharon *has* had a very tough life up to this point . . ." Thus, the child now has way too much power in the home. Setting firm yet loving boundaries is vital. No parent should have to put up with verbal or physical abuse.

On the other hand, some parents respond to their adopted child's behavioral mayhem by going too far in the other direction—that is, becoming stern and rigid. This often leads to endless power struggles. Similarly, the stern or rigid parent often has not learned how to laugh and play with the child. Maybe Sharon *is* seemingly in constant trouble, thus making levity and recreation difficult at best. Nevertheless, laughing and frolic are crucial with these children. And the reality is that, initially, the rigid or stern parent may have to play-act at having fun, until the cycle of Sharon getting in trouble followed by parental discipline, over and over, is abandoned.

The School

Next, school intervention for youth with FASD is huge. As a parent, what is your line of work? Medicine, law, business? Well, for a child, *school* is her job. We all know if things aren't percolating well at work, our lives can be pretty miserable. Hence, regular education or "mainstreaming" at school with FASD isn't likely to work. As mentioned above in the "Developmental Expectations" section, youth with FASD as well as other common adopted-child syndromes almost always require at least some degree of special education intervention. By federal law, schools must provide an effective learning environment for your child. As such, an Individual Education Plan (IEP) must be constructed by the school.

An IEP involves IQ and academic skills testing in order to produce a blueprint for which special ed services are appropriate for your child. And, it's not unusual for the school and parents to disagree upon what components need to be included in the IEP. A special, small classroom? Test-taking accommodations? Reduced homework? A personal aide? In the face of an impasse, there are attorneys who specialize solely in school law, to ensure that a school district acts responsibly on behalf of your child's special needs. A local bar association or Juvenile Rights Project firm would be a good place to start, but you will want to get recommendations concerning the reputation and integrity of any attorney you hire.

Family Counseling

Family counseling is another often-helpful modality. Let's suppose that we have a family with two typically developing children and one high-maintenance adopted child. Constant home strife and emotional disruption can take a toll on siblings. Family counseling can assist in making sure that the typically developing siblings' needs are recognized and addressed.

Parent Education

A sometimes overlooked yet vital help to children with FASD and special needs adoptive issues is bibliotherapy. Bibliotherapy is psychobabble for "reading everything you can get your hands on!"

How many parents have I met over the years who have become self-educated experts in adoption dynamics? Way too many to count! In fact, a common statement I hear among savvy adoptive parents is: "We went to see Dr. Doe regarding our son, and we knew more about what was going on with Jimmy than he did!" Check out the Resources Guide at the back of this book and those listed at www.attach.org. Do, however, be careful about pulling up just anything on the

Internet. Contact your local adoption agency for recommended Web sites or printed material. Talk to other parents who have been through similar situations.

HOPE FOR PARENTS OF CHILDREN HURT BY SUBSTANCE ABUSE

As Christians, we know God fervently desires relationship with His children. What might this look like for a family struggling with the effects of FASD?

I believe it is loving God despite our pain, reveling in the times when we feel His presence, trusting Him when we don't, obedience in raising the children He has loaned us, trusting Him to provide for our needs, forgiving our child's birthmother for drinking or using drugs during pregnancy, forgiving our children as they excruciatingly test us, forgiving ourselves when our parenting misses the mark, persisting when parenting seems futile, waiting on Him though submerged in discouragement, bombarding Him with requests for wisdom. And finding comfort and strength in His promises:

> Yet those who wait for the LORD
> Will gain new strength;
> They will mount up with wings like eagles,
> They will run and not get tired,
> They will walk and not become weary.
> (Isaiah 40:31 NASB)

Seems God doesn't need acronyms or complexity!

■ ■ ■

Dr. Steven Gray is a board-certified pediatric neuropsychologist. His specialty is working with complex special needs children, many of whom have a history of early maltreatment. He also works with bright academic underachievers, some of whom suffer from accompanying emotional disorders of one type or another. Dr. Gray has written two books: *The Maltreated Child: Finding What Lurks Beneath*, and *Motivating Marvin: Helping Your Bright Underachiever Succeed in School.*

Caring for Katie
by Amber Bartell

When Katie was two years old, she hit the ground running, literally! When she was ready to climb out of her crib, she flung herself out with no regard to how she landed. She did not cry when she landed, either, no matter how hard she fell.

Our daughter suffered from Attention Deficit Hyperactivity Disorder (ADHD). We could not read even a single word-to-a-page book to Katie without her hopping off our laps. She was not able to sit still even temporarily. We took her to a specialist and the appointment took nearly an hour. I knew I would not be able to handle her on my own so my husband came too.

Dave chased Katie around the tiny room, removing her hands from the blinds, and picking her up off the items she climbed. All while I tried to listen to the doctor explain her obvious diagnosis, ADHD. The doctor explained that ADHD is a common diagnosis for children exposed to drugs in utero. Our other children—Michael and Katie's sister, Amy—also suffered from ADHD. Michael's mom abused meth, and Amy and Katie's mom abused cocaine, heroin, and alcohol.

In 1989, when Michael was born, very little was known about the effects of prenatal drug exposure. We were warned by caseworkers to be aware of this possibility, but not given specifics about what to expect. When we began to struggle, keeping up with three little ones, two of whom had challenging behavioral patterns, I started doing some research.

One day I stumbled upon a book about fetal alcohol syndrome (FAS) in our public library. As I read, I began to recognize the symptoms. FAS is not new; it has been well studied and documented. I had been told about the drugs, but I had never considered what goes along with drugs: alcohol! The thin upper lip, the wide-spaced eyes, the flat forehead . . . characteristics of my little girls!

From the time they were ages three, two, and one we took our children camping, to the zoo, to the beach, and to the children's museum, but it was not easy. We counted to three a lot, keeping track of where they went and holding hands near every street or parking lot. Temper tantrums, short attention spans, and a fearless stunt child whom God protected from major catastrophes complicated everything.

Looking back, I am thankful that Katie was kept safe even though she ran off at every opportunity. On many occasions, one of us carried Amy to the car when rage overtook her. I could hardly carry her when she was having a fit and often had to put her up over my shoulder to carry her out of a store. Humiliation was becoming familiar.

Once, at a grocery store, Amy was missing for 15–20 minutes until we finally found her in the back room. Everyone in the store was looking for her and I was nearly ready to call the police.

That is when I decided never to let my embarrassment keep me from finding my kids; I did just what I would do at home. I took a deep breath and called their name loudly in my come-here-now voice. It worked. I broke out in a sweat and was a deep shade of red every time I did it, but I never lost a child for more than a minute or two again.

It took time and patience, but eventually I learned to anticipate when Katie would act up and that really was the key to managing her every day in every way. I needed to be in tune to how she was feeling and to know when to intervene.

15

Physical Disabilities

by Jorie Kincaid

*For you created my inmost being; you knit me together
in my mother's womb. I praise you because I am
fearfully and wonderfully made.*
—PSALM 139:13–14a

"This is the reason this child was placed for international adoption," the pediatric developmental specialist emphatically declared after evaluating our seven-month-old daughter and diagnosing her with cerebral palsy. "No, it isn't!" my emotions silently screamed in protest to the accusation and unwanted declaration that our precious Erikaa, adopted from Vietnam three months before, was not normal.

I, as a mother, was heartbroken. I fiercely wrapped my arms around my tiny Asian beauty. I stared into her dark, expressive eyes and wept, imagining the fields she would never run through, the waves she might never jump in, and the cartwheels she would never turn. I wanted to somehow insulate her from the taunts and teasing she would receive because she was not like other children. I wept because I couldn't.

Once the diagnosis was declared and recorded in Erikaa's medical records, I could no longer rationalize, as I had for several months before, that my baby would outgrow her condition and everything would be normal. I was angry with the doctor who stole my imaginary world.

"Do you think her nanny could have rolled over on her arm at night when Erikaa was in the orphanage?" I had asked my husband as I cuddled our daughter several months after bringing her home. I had noticed that her left arm seemed limp soon after receiving her and my mom-sensors had been on high alert. Though she was our ninth child, our joy in having Erikaa in our family was immense, yet I, her mom, had been nagged by the growing fear that something was wrong with her.

In those early weeks I mentally reassured myself that her alternating rigidity and floppiness was merely fatigue or the result of living in an orphanage. I promised myself that she would catch up in time, or that her arm might have been damaged during nights of rooming with her caregiver and her head was weak because no one had ever placed her on her tummy. I asked friends in the medical field about nerve damage and read about effects of institutional living in my efforts to declare Erikaa healthy and normal. But it was not to be. At seven months, when Erikaa was diagnosed with cerebral palsy, our entire family was devastated.

ADJUSTING TO UNEXPECTED HANDICAPS

A physical disability is any condition that permanently prevents normal body movement and/or control. The main ones include muscular dystrophies, brain and spinal injuries, spina bifida, and cerebral palsy. While spina bifida is obvious at birth, cerebral palsy is often not diagnosed until a child is more than a year, unless it is very severe or is the result of a birth injury. Muscular dystrophy may not be diagnosed until after age five.

Some families feel uniquely prepared by God to love and parent children with physical disabilities and have knowingly chosen to adopt a child who is physically handicapped. To be honest, ours did not. Families who choose to adopt children with physical disabilities usually approach their adoption with energy and excitement, knowing they are emotionally prepared. Other families, like ours, who expected to adopt a healthy child later diagnosed with a physical disability, often face great adjustment to unexpected handicaps because they are not emotionally prepared.

We know that no reputable agency would knowingly try to place a child with disabilities as a healthy child. This is why adoptive families receive medical reports on prospective children, and should ask for them in their original language, not just an English version, to make sure nothing was lost or misinterpreted in the translation. But sometimes an accurate diagnosis of physical disability is not possible in a developing country, or symptoms have not yet appeared when a child is placed into a family. Some families, like ours, will unwittingly receive a child with physical disabilities. All prospective families are wise to be aware of this possibility.

We adjusted to being parents of a child with physical disabilities because we needed to, for Erikaa. We discovered that it's necessary to grieve for your child's losses. I had envisioned early morning walks together on the beach sharing secrets and girl talk. I grieved for those unmet expectations. If you adopt a child with physical disabilities, there may be dreams for which you need to grieve as well.

We needed to accept Erikaa as the child that God, in His goodness, planned for us. There were days when I wondered what was to become of Erikaa and us, what our family recreation and holidays would be like in years to come. I even wondered, at times, if God had made a terrible mistake, though in my deepest soul I knew He had not. Maybe this has been your experience as well.

The truth is that God knew, before Erikaa was born and before she was placed, exactly what her circumstances were, and He knew that our family was the right one for her. For Erikaa, it was a big advantage to have multiple siblings who could work with her in a variety of ways. Though none of her siblings do actual therapy with her, one is more concerned about her speech, while another worked to help her learn to hold a pencil, and still another helped her navigate the stairs without falling. We also learned that Erikaa helped us as much as, or more than, we helped her. We are confident that she has brought out sensitivity in each of us that we never would have seen otherwise.

PREPARING FOR TAUNTS AND TEASING

We instinctively knew that Erikaa could become the object of ridicule at every level from people who do not have experience or knowledge of individuals with physical disabilities. We wanted to address this issue right away as a family. Parents with children with physical disabilities need to prepare their family for taunts and teasing their children may encounter. First, we recognized that we are the family who can best help her become the person that God intends for her to be.

We vowed to never introduce our daughter with an apology, such as, "This is our daughter with cerebral palsy," as if we needed to give others an explanation for her uniqueness. After all, no one introduces me, saying, "This is Jorie with reading glasses!" We always want to introduce her without any disclaimers regarding her physical disabilities.

If we are not apologetic about our child's physical disabilities, others often won't be, either. They will take their cues regarding our children from us. In the same way, if we approach our child's physical disability with the attitude that this is the way God created her, just as He created everyone else with their uniqueness and special abilities, there is nothing to tease. We are all unique and we are all special. My child may have cerebral palsy; your child may have a hearing loss or have been born with her spinal cord outside of her body. These are obvious physical disabilities. But everyone has a physical feature that is less than perfect, no matter how small. If our children understand that God loved us enough to give us life, loved us enough to die for us, and longs to adopt us as His children, they will understand how incredibly valuable they are.

Then, if they are taunted for being in a wheelchair or walking with braces on the school playground, they will be a little better able to handle it because they know that in God's eyes, they are immensely valuable. We want Erikaa to understand the truth that God loves her even more than we do. She is a daughter of the King. Every little girl longs to be a princess and ours is no exception. We want to make sure that every day when she goes to school she remembers who she is, a princess. If your special needs child realizes that he is infinitely valuable to God, it will help taunts and teasing deflect off him, too.

PLANNING YOUR LIFE WITH A CHILD WITH PHYSICAL HANDICAPS

We needed to readjust our family's goals and values to include every member of the family, seriously evaluate our family finances, investigate all legal issues pertaining to parenting a child with physical disabilities, and understand government benefits available to us in our situation. It is wise to make long-term plans for your family with consideration for your child's physical limitations.

First, we tweaked our family goals and values to incorporate a family member with physical disabilities. We want to make sure each of our family members, with his or her unique needs, is nurtured as best we can. Simply stated, we want all of our children to reach their full potential and become independent, productive adults. This may look somewhat different for Erikaa, but our greatest desire is independence for her, too. We want all our children to view themselves in the same way that God views them, that they are valuable because the God of the universe created them.

We are an athletic and active family, and we want Erikaa to be included in everything she can do. For everything a child may not be able to do physically, there is something else he or she can do. Erikaa may not be able to jump rope like her sisters who perform in jump rope competitions, but she can step back and forth across a rope set on the ground and tell us "I won" with great delight. She is not able to snowshoe with our family, but she has been able to go with us riding in a sled we take turns pulling.

We also want to make sure every other family member feels important and that we are not neglecting their needs by overemphasizing disabilities.

Second, in proactively planning for life with a child with physical limitations, we seriously evaluated our family's finances, including anticipated expenses, savings and investments, and insurance. Many children with physical disabilities require costly therapy and equipment, and it is important to know and understand the coverage and services your health insurance provides.

If your child needs ongoing physical, speech, or occupational therapy, surgeries, or equipment, as ours does, it will be important to know how many sessions, and what percentage of surgeries and equipment, are covered by your insurance. It is possible to request a personal case manager to advocate for your child so that you have one person with whom to communicate when many services are needed. This person is independent from the insurance company, so he or she should not have a conflict of interest over payment for services, but is paid for by your insurance to coordinate all aspects of your benefits.

If your child needs additional therapy, surgery, or equipment beyond that which insurance covers, your family will need a plan to meet these expenses. Will your family be capable of paying out of pocket, or will you need to find additional funding through grants or private organizations that serve families with children with disabilities, like Shriners Hospitals, Scottish Rite Hospitals, and United Cerebral Palsy? These private services are available to families of children with disabilities and deserve consideration to make sure family resources are not depleted, causing the whole family to suffer.

Third, planning for life with a child with physical disabilities requires you to consider legal factors, including your will, guardianship needs, and consideration of creating a Special Needs Trust to ensure your child's future. It is especially important to plan for your child's guardianship in the case of your untimely death and to reflect this in your will. If, before adopting, you already had a guardian for your children in the event of your death, you may need to revisit that decision. Is that person willing to be the guardian for additional children? Children with special needs?

It is important to provide funding for this child's care in your will in the event that you die. In most cases, a person with physical disabilities does not qualify for state or federal disability money if he inherits money left in a will written in the usual way, until those funds are depleted to total assets of $2,000.

A Special Needs Trust, however, enables a person under the age of 65 with a physical disability to have an unlimited amount of assets held in trust for his or her benefit, and those assets are not considered countable assets for qualifications for benefits like Supplemental Security Income (SSI), Medicaid, vocational rehabilitation, or subsidized housing, all things to consider in long-term family planning for your child. A Special Needs Trust is usually its own document, and has its own Employer ID number issued by the IRS, rather than being registered under your child's social security number. If you're considering creating a Special Needs Trust, consult a lawyer who specializes in this area.

Fourth, it is also important for family plans to include understanding of government assistance for residential services, day care, and respite care through tax deductions and credits. All families of adopted children with physical disabilities should consult tax specialists or enrolled agents who are licensed by the IRS to represent taxpayers for tax counseling. Tax laws are complex, and families are at risk of losing benefits worth thousands of dollars in unclaimed tax benefits if they are unaware.

Though it will take time and energy, doing the research and planning ahead for your family's future is necessary for all involved. Look to professionals and others who have walked the same road for help and advice. Remember that the purpose is to be proactive and prepared when it comes to taking care of your family.

ACCESSING SUPPORT FOR THE CHILD WITH PHYSICAL DISABILITIES

All parents of children with physical disabilities need to know about three federal laws as they access support available to their child:
- The Individuals with Disabilities Education Act (IDEA) (1975)
- Section 504 of the Rehabilitation Act of 1973
- The Americans with Disabilities Act (ADA) (1990)

IDEA is a federal law that governs all special education services for children in the United States. This law is what enables a child with physical disabilities to be eligible for special education services.

Section 504 is a civil rights statute that prevents schools from discriminating against children with disabilities, and it requires them to provide reasonable accommodations for their education including extra time for taking tests, adjusted homework, sitting in the front of the classroom if necessary, and other extra services. It is wise for parents to request a copy of their school district's Section 504 plan.

The ADA law requires all educational facilities and transportation services to meet the needs of children with disabilities. In addition, each state has separate criteria for eligibility for state services, and parents need to be aware of their state regulations.

In order to access services, parents of children with physical disabilities should request an evaluation of their child to determine his or her needs for special services. If your child is in school, this request may be made directly with his or her teacher. If your child is not in school, you should contact your local school district and ask where to send your request for a special education evaluation for your child. It is important to follow up all queries in writing, including your child's name, birth date, address, description of why you are asking for the evaluation, and the date of your query. It is also important to keep a file with copies of all communications regarding your child's special education.

After an evaluation is completed, if your child is eligible for special services, an Individualized Education Program (IEP) will be developed. You as parents will be notified of the date and are able to participate in the IEP meeting. The other people you may expect to see at a meeting will be a regular classroom teacher, a special education teacher, an administrator who has authority to make decisions and commit funding, and perhaps appropriate therapists, aides, or other personnel involved with your child.

The written IEP should identify educational goals and how those goals will be evaluated. If you as a parent are not in agreement with the IEP, it is possible to appeal. Educational services are available from birth to three years and three to five through Early Intervention Programs and throughout the public school years.

SECURING FUNDING FOR YOUR CHILD'S CARE

In securing funding for your child's care, it is important to consider both public and private sources. It will be necessary to obtain a social security number for your child for all funding sources. In addition to the adoption tax credit and the Child Tax Credit for each dependent child, many families will qualify for the Child and Dependent Care Tax Credit that offsets part of the cost of paying for care for a disabled dependent while you work. This includes after-school programs and day camp.

Under medical expense deductions, the IRS will allow tuition costs for special schools and boarding schools with programs for children with learning disabilities and amounts paid for children's tutoring by a teacher specially trained and qualified to deal with severe learning disabilities. Special instruction or therapy is also deductible. Generally, to qualify for these deductions, your child's doctor must recommend the school, therapy, or tutor and declare the specific diagnosis. Transportation to these special services is also an allowable deduction. When parents choose to attend conferences to obtain medical information for treatment and care of their children, some of the costs related to these may also be deductible.

Costs can mount quickly for children with special needs. Families need to plan together for therapy that is affordable with their circumstances. In addition to the free state and federal programs and tax credits, there are free private programs as well. Scottish Rite Hospitals and Shriners Hospitals are two of those that take children with physical handicaps at no cost to the families. They are privately funded and provide exceptional services to children with physical disabilities. Both have an application process and are accessible by all families.

Your child needs you to be an active, persistent advocate in his life. Be proactive in finding solutions, financial or otherwise, for your family. Talk with other parents, research different options, and remember to seek professional advice when necessary.

An Important Reminder

Psalm 139:13–16 can help each of us understand the delight that God takes in each child with physical disabilities:

> For you created my inmost being; you knit me together in my mother's womb. I praise you because I am fearfully and wonderfully made; your works are wonderful, I know that full well. My frame was not hidden from you when I was made in the secret place. When I was woven together in the depths of the earth, your eyes saw my unformed body. All the days ordained for me were written in your book before one of them came to be.

God's message to all of us is clear. Each of us is fearfully and wonderfully made by God Himself. There are no mistakes. God loved each of us enough to give us life; He loved each of us enough to die for us. And that is what gives each child value, regardless of his or her issues or circumstances in life.

Children with physical disabilities are precious to God. Had we been given the choice as to whether our family would take a child with physical disabilities, we would have said a polite, "No, thank you." But we did not know what we would have been missing, and we have received so much more than we have given. One of my children recently said, "I think God wants every family to have a child with disabilities." Maybe she's right!

■ ■ ■

Jorie Kincaid was adopted as an infant and is the parent of nine children, five of whom are adopted, one domestically and four internationally. She lives with her husband, pastor of Sunset Presbyterian Church, and her large, multicultural, multiracial family in Portland, Oregon. She is the author of three books, including *Adopting for Good: A Guide for People Considering Adoption*.

L'histoire de Fleur-Ange
by Jonathan Godfrey

It all started with a prayer and a phone call. We were at a pastor's conference in Ottawa and one of the men in our group got a cell phone call from a family asking if he knew anyone who wanted to adopt a little three-month-old Vietnamese girl with a scar on her cheek.

My wife, Sylvie, had been praying for 14 years that the Lord would send us a child with special needs. We had considered adoptions, but the opportunity had not materialized. We even contacted an adoption agency, only to be told that adoption was for those families that did not have children (at that time we had four children). We also knew that we did not have sufficient funds to afford adoption, so we trusted the Lord to send us a child of His choice. And we continued to pray.

From the time of the initial call, Sylvie had told me that for some reason she had felt that this little girl was her answer to prayer and that the Lord would end up getting her to us somehow. For the next 11 months we tried to get the little girl out of Vietnam. We had many hurdles to overcome. We were contacted by Canadian officials in international adoptions and told not to get involved because all adoptions with Vietnam had been stopped and there was no agreement between Canada and Vietnam, making the process extremely uncertain. We were also told that we would not have access to the Medicare system to treat her injuries. We asked our family what they thought of the idea—they feared that we might get attached to the child and then not be able to adopt her.

We had a decision to make: Would we allow our fears to dictate whether or not we would get involved, or would we step out by faith and trust the Lord? Could we tell God that we would only get involved if He gave us solid assurances that we would be able to adopt this little girl? We finally decided that we would get involved—not because we were without fears, but because we were convinced that this was what the Lord was leading us to do. We certainly did not have a clear idea of all that was on the road ahead.

We found out that our baby, Fleur-Ange, had more than just a scar on her cheek. She had been attacked and had lost half her face. In a jealous rage, her father, convinced that his wife had been unfaithful and that this child was not his, took a machete to her face, then threw her outside. The neighbors found her and took her to the hospital and left her on the steps to die—but she survived.

We found out about an organization called "Fresh Start" in California which provides operations free of charge on children who are disfigured and don't have access to insurance. They agreed immediately to provide the surgery that Fleur-Ange needed. They wrote a letter and it was translated into Vietnamese to be sent to the Vietnamese authorities. Because of this letter, Vietnam allowed Fleur-Ange to come.

Our adventure went into high gear. We saw very quickly that she was suffering from serious medical conditions that needed immediate attention. She weighed only 14 pounds and was 14 months old. She was somewhat dehydrated and malnourished. She was suffering from scabies, ear infections, and sinus infections, and she was showing signs of depression and institutional neglect. We were told that she had never seen the sun and had never had a bath. She did not want to eat. It was as if she had given up.

That first week was very difficult, and we shed a lot of tears. When we put her into her crib to sleep, she would get on her hands and knees and begin to rock herself and bang her head against the bars of the crib. From that point on, we took her into our arms 24 hours a day for the next 30 days. Dad had the night shift and Mom had the day shift. Only after 30 days did she show interest in getting down from our arms to begin to explore. At night I could only put her down if she was sleeping deeply. We found ourselves adjusting continually to new challenges as we discovered more about her condition.

Fleur-Ange began to grow by leaps and bounds. In three months she grew three inches and put on 10 pounds. In most cases this would be a positive thing, but for Fleur-Ange her facial scar tissue began to put pressure on her skull, deforming her head and tearing at the corner of her mouth, causing it to tear and bleed. She had to have an operation as quickly as possible. It turned out to be the first of many.

We had always wondered if Fleur-Ange would suffer long-term trauma from the initial attack and all the distress associated with her multiple medical treatments. For the first couple of years she would have nightmares and unexplainable fits of fear from what seemed to be harmless objects, such as a picture of a monkey in a children's book. We could not explain what triggered these episodes or why. But time and lots of love have made a way through all of this.

We have other long-term concerns for Fleur-Ange. The one that we feel most deeply is the question of how she will deal with the forgiveness issue toward the man that did this terrible thing to her. We have decided to be honest with her as we have always been. We are not sure when or how to begin, but we are confident that the Lord will show us as He always has. With our birth children, there were many times we felt we needed to have a heart-to-heart talk, so we would ask the Lord to provide an opportunity through some event or circumstance and He always did. We believe that He will again guide us with Fleur-Ange.

Learning Disabilities

by Michael Safko

All children can succeed, but they need our love,
our support, and most of all, our belief that they are more
than the sum of their disabilities. We need to envision
their success and help them see it too.
—SHARI RUSCH FURNSTAHL,
FROM STUMBLING BLOCKS TO STEPPING STONES

According to the National Center for Education Statistics, between 5 and 12 percent of children enrolled in public education are receiving special education services.[1] The disabilities that require individualized interventions range from pervasive developmental disabilities to specific learning disabilities. Although adopted children represent 2.5 percent of school-age children,[2] they account for an estimated 4 to 7 percent of children in special education classes. In 1996, the Barker Foundation conducted a survey with parents of five hundred adopted children. Thirty percent of these children are reported to have had some type of learning or attention problem.[3]

Previous chapters of this book have helped to identify some of the environmental, developmental, and physiological factors that contribute to the number of adopted children placed in special education classes due to a learning disability. The focus of this chapter is to assist parents with information that may help them to identify, understand, and intervene with disabilities that may be present in their child.

Categories of Learning Disabilities

A learning disability can be defined as a cognitive, developmental, neurological, or psychological factor that interferes with the child's ability to learn at a level consistent with his or her intellectual ability. The Individuals with Disabilities Education Act identifies 11 disability categories.[4] These are:

1. Mental retardation: an IQ below 70 and a deficit of adaptive functioning.
2. Hearing impairments: when a permanent or temporary hearing condition interferes with a child's ability to learn.
3. Speech or language impairments: impairment to speech articulation, patterns, voice quality, etc. that interferes with the child's ability to learn or to relate with his/her peer group.
4. Visual impairments: a permanent or temporary visual condition that interferes with a child's ability to learn.
5. Serious emotional disturbance: a condition that is exhibited over an extended period of time that may include an inability to learn that is not explained by intellectual, sensory, or health factors. It might also include depression or prolonged unhappiness, acting-out behaviors, poor peer relationships, or fears associated with school situations or personnel.
6. Autism: a developmental disability that might include mental retardation, an inability to form interpersonal relationships, communication disabilities, stereotyped movements, and other unusual patterns of behavior.
7. Traumatic brain injury: an acquired injury to the brain that results in a full or partial loss of functioning in cognitive skills, psychosocial skills, or both, which interferes with a child's ability to learn or function in a school setting.
8. Orthopedic impairments: a motor disability that adversely affects a child's educational performance.
9. Other health impairments: when a medical condition that cannot be attributed to a listed condition interferes with a child's ability to learn.

10. Specific learning disabilities: a disorder in one or more of the basic psychological processes involved in understanding or in using language, spoken or written, which may manifest itself in an imperfect ability to listen, think, speak, read, write, spell, or do mathematical calculations.

11. Developmental delay: used for children from birth through age of eligibility for public school who experience delays in physical development, cognitive development, communication development, social or emotional development, or adaptive development.

It is fairly common to hear professionals place these 11 disability categories into three broad categories that include speech and language difficulty, academic difficulties, and other disorders. Many parents will have little trouble recognizing some of these disabilities such as mental retardation, hearing or visual impairment, traumatic brain injury, orthopedic impairments, and autism. In some cases the disability will have been identified prior to the adoption taking place. However, in other cases the disability will either be unrecognized or perhaps not developed at the time of the adoption.

The disabilities that are more commonly recognized and addressed within the educational system are those that may interfere with a child's ability to attain academic skills at the optimum level. These particular disabilities tend to be found in the areas of developmental delays, speech or language impairments, serious emotional disturbance, and specific learning disabilities. In addition, under the category of other health impairments, one would usually find a diagnosis of Attention Deficit Hyperactivity Disorder. These are the disorders that are most often seen in the local elementary, middle, and high schools.

Within our society it is common for parents and individuals to look at the word "disability" in a negative way. For the purpose of this chapter, don't think of a disability as a barrier that prevents the child from achieving the knowledge and skills necessary to function within the home, within a peer group, and within the society at large. Instead, think of a disability as a condition that interferes with the child's ability to achieve an educational, social, or behavioral goal.

If you suspect that your child has a learning disability, the place to begin is your local school. Talk with your child's teacher or the school principal. Make a written request that your child be evaluated for a learning disability. Most school districts will honor your request or give a denial within 10 days. You have the right to appeal their decision. Each school has a "Handbook of Parents' Rights" that will tell you the steps to take if you wish to appeal their decision. Follow those steps precisely within the time frame allotted. (You can also look to the Resources Guide at the end of the book for more help on dealing with disabilities.)

SPEECH AND LANGUAGE IMPAIRMENTS

Of the disabilities that may affect a child's educational achievement in more subtle ways, speech and language impairments are the ones most likely to appear early in a child's development. Speech and language impairments may occur as a result of impaired ability to produce spoken language, a process commonly known as articulation, which is known as an *expressive language disability*. Or the impairment may be the result of a *receptive language disability*, which is an impairment of the child's ability to understand spoken language.

Many parents have experienced amusement when their small child mispronounces common words. We smile when we hear the color yellow pronounced "yay-yo." Once a child is enrolled in school, however, his ability to properly articulate basic words is important if he wants to avoid becoming identified as a baby or being laughed at by other children. The proper use of language is often seen in our society as a sign of intelligence. It is important that when our child experiences a deficit in this area, we take steps to remedy that deficit.

Disorders of receptive language may contribute to a child's difficulty in the classroom, as well. Poor receptive language skills have been linked with reading difficulty and writing problems. When a child has difficulty understanding the spoken word, she may also experience impaired social relationships because she has difficulty properly interpreting what she is told. This frequent "misunderstanding" of what she is told serves to frustrate her as well as her peers and those in authority. Thus, the child may be isolated from her peers or may be frequently in conflict with authority figures.

Now, before you jump up to get the yellow pages and look for a speech pathologist, remember that there are developmental stages our children go through. The development of language occurs in stages that may be influenced by early childhood trauma or deprivation. Your child may have a language disability—or she may just need more time to catch up.

To identify the possibility of a speech and/or language impairment, parents can begin by doing some objective observation of their child as well as other children of the same gender and the same approximate age. One would look for problems with pronunciation, difficulty rhyming words, slow growth in vocabulary, and difficulty following instructions. You may also notice that your child has difficulty finding the desired word. You may see your child struggle with reading aloud or solving word problems. As your child goes into middle school or high school you may see a strong reluctance to begin and complete reading and writing assignments.

SPECIFIC LEARNING DISABILITIES

The classification of *specific learning disability* is used when a child has a disability that appears to be specific to a given area of academic functioning. Specific learning disabilities can be in the areas of basic reading and reading comprehension, math calculation and math reasoning, oral expression, and listening comprehension.

Difficulties with vision and/or hearing often factor into the presence of a specific learning disability. For example, chronic otitis media, also known as middle ear infection, can interfere with a child's ability to clearly understand words that are read aloud and may then interfere with the child's ability to associate a given word with the appropriate sound. A child may be unable to clearly see what is written on the board or may not clearly hear a teacher's instructions. If the child is self-conscious, he may be reluctant to point out that he has failed to hear or see. It is important for parents to remember that the fear of rejection or disapproval is never far below the surface for many adopted children.

Problems in the area of vision can come from the inability to see information clearly, or they may come from the inability to process visual information accurately. If visual acuity is the problem, typically vision correction is a relatively quick and inexpensive solution. However, visual processing deficits may not be quite so easy to diagnose or remedy. Poorly developed visual processing skills may result in the child having difficulty interpreting visual information. This is not due to a lack of intelligence but, rather, from the brain's underdeveloped ability to associate visual input with previously learned material.

An excellent—and commonly heard of—example of the visual processing problem is dyslexia. While the eye may see the information accurately, once it hits the part of the brain responsible for processing visual information, the information becomes mixed and chaotic. Letters don't appear in the sequence they were in, they may change shape, or the black print on white paper may simply blend together (black print on white paper blending together is referred to as Irlen Syndrome).

Problems in the area of auditory processing may create a presentation of symptoms or behaviors that mimic Attention Deficit Hyperactivity Disorder, in particular, the predominantly inattentive type. Children who have a deficit of auditory processing are likely to behave as if they cannot understand spoken directions, may have difficulty taking notes in the classroom, and may have difficulty expressing their thoughts in a manner that is easy for the listener to follow without creating frustration and confusion for both parties.

Children who have Central Auditory Processing Disorder (CAPD) will have difficulty filtering out or ignoring extraneous sounds and struggle to determine which of the sounds they should be focusing upon. Since most children are not known for patience and perseverance, their likely response to this war of sounds is to retreat and do nothing.

OTHER HEALTH IMPAIRMENTS—ADHD

Within the category of "Other Health Impairments" would be health-related conditions that do not fall into the other specific categories, although they do interfere with a child's ability to learn. Among the diagnoses that would be considered other health impairments, Attention Deficit Hyperactivity Disorder (ADHD) is probably the most commonly used. Attention Deficit Hyperactivity Disorder is a diagnosis that has three subcategories: (1) predominantly inattentive type; (2) predominantly hyperactive-impulsive type; and (3) combined type.

ADHD is a disorder of impaired self-regulation. The behaviors presented when a child has ADHD range from a lowered ability to pay attention to an impaired ability to stay on task to the extremely hyperactive child. While the hyperactive child is engaging in behaviors that draw the attention of others, as well as interfering with his ability to learn, the inattentive child is no less impaired.

Children who have a diagnosis of Attention Deficit Hyperactivity Disorder are often diagnosed with an additional learning disability. According to Russell Barkley, author of *Attention-Deficit Hyperactivity Disorder*, "It is not surprising to find that as many as 56 percent of children with ADHD may require academic tutoring, approximately 30 percent may repeat a grade in school, and that 30 to 40 percent may be placed in one or more special education programs."[5] If parents suspect that their child has some form of ADHD, it is important to seek an evaluation at the first sign of symptom presentation by the adoptee.

ADHD, especially the hyperactive-impulsive type, tends to have a negative influence on the child's ability to develop sustained attachments with members of her peer group. In fact, very often it is the parent of a child's playmate who finds ways to leave a child with ADHD out of the social setting. As such, the child with ADHD feels rejected on a regular basis. This can easily become a sustained belief that she is disliked or unloved. While we may try to convince the child otherwise, there is often sufficient evidence to the contrary.

Children with ADHD often benefit from calm structure. While they may battle the structure in the beginning, with time they benefit from structure and organization—whether they appreciate it or not. Children with ADHD may behave in a way that creates chaos. It is up to the parents or caregivers to help the child see the benefit of a calm and stable environment. An appreciation of "calm and stable" is something the child with ADHD has to learn; it won't come naturally. (You can see the Resources Guide for more help on this important topic.)

Serious Emotional Disturbance

The diagnosis of Serious Emotional Disturbance (SED) was developed as a category for educators to classify a child who engaged in behaviors that were dangerous to others, dangerous to self, or disruptive to the academic achievement of other students. It is important to remember that SED is not a psychiatric diagnosis in itself. While it is true that many children who do have psychiatric diagnoses present disruptive behaviors and disturbed emotions, a counselor is more likely to look for an underlying cause of these disturbances. In the school setting, however, simply identifying the behavior as disturbed is enough to push a child toward placement in special education.

This placement requires a meeting that includes the child's teacher, a school administrator or designee, a special education teacher, and the child's parent or guardian. It is at this meeting that parents have the right and the responsibility to advocate for the best needs of their particular child.

STRATEGIES FOR HELPING YOUR CHILD WITH LEARNING DISABILITIES

It is important for any parent who plans to advocate for their special needs child to become familiar with the system of the local education district. Each school district prints a pamphlet known as a parent's rights handbook. Not only does it offer expectations for students and parents, it also guides parents through the process of remedying conflicts that arise between the child and the school system.

To assist a child who has a learning disability, the first step a parent can take is a relatively simple one. Research has shown that children who struggle may improve their academic performance simply by having their parent near them while they do homework. Even when a parent may not be able to assist with the homework directly, the parent can be a calming influence when the child begins to experience frustration. This calming influence can counteract the child's desire to give up when the material in front of her challenges her.

Another way that a parent can assist a child with a learning disability is to understand the learning style of a particular child. For example, if your child is an auditory learner, then finding ways to present information verbally increases the likelihood that she will remember the information. The child may perform better if she listens to a lecture repeatedly rather than trying to take notes while the lecture is being given. A visual learner may perform better if he creates a map of a lecture rather than trying to write word for word what the teacher is saying.

For a special needs child to learn material necessary to survive in school and in life, she needs repeated exposure to the educational material. This does place a demand upon parents. This means that as the parent, you have to look for opportunities to reinforce what is being taught at school.

How do you do this? Be creative. When traveling, point out signs and ask your child to read a word; ask her to play rhyming games with words; ask him to identify numbers of buildings as you pass them. Set aside time to give your child the opportunity to tell the story of what he learned in school during the day, play spelling games together, and so on.

And remember to be *patient*. Depending on the disability, your child is unlikely to match other students in the classroom stride for stride. Although differences may be small when making daily comparisons, the gap does widen as time goes by. It is like giving a child one dollar every day while giving a second child 90 cents every day. The difference between 90 cents and one dollar is small when compared each day but widens dramatically over the course of months or years.

It's essential that we keep an eternal perspective in mind when it comes to our children's educational and emotional development. If your child is 21 years of age by the time he or she learns enough to be independent, that's great. It really doesn't matter if your child learns at 21 what some other child has learned at 16. What matters is that once the knowledge is learned, it is maintained and serves as a solid platform upon which your child can stand.

ACCESSING SUPPORT

Most of the parents I know who have special needs children have learned that to access services and support you have to be a cross between a pit bull and the Energizer Bunny. You have to have the energy to keep going and going and going despite the fact you can be denied repeatedly; and once you do access a service, you have to bite into it and never let go.

Begin by talking with an adoption specialist or social worker. These people are likely to have some good advice about available services and financial support. Types of services to look for would be tutoring, counseling, social skills training, or medical assistance.

You might browse the Internet and see if you can find local support groups. There are associations that have been developed for the purpose of addressing a single disorder. Connecting with other parents who have shared similar experiences can provide support, knowledge, and encouragement.

It is also important to recognize that some of the professionals you may encounter have their own ideas regarding (and treating) learning disabilities, especially surrounding ADHD and emotional disturbance. Very often, these physicians have sound reasons for the positions they take. However, if you feel uncomfortable or unconvinced about their methods, then it is incumbent upon you to seek a physician who will support your beliefs and meet the needs of your child. Remember that it is probably easier to change doctors than it is to change your child's condition. Please do not make the change impulsively; rather, make the change prayerfully.

WORKING WITH LEARNING SPECIALISTS

When working with a learning specialist, it is important that you understand both his approach and the foundation for his approach. It is not enough to assume that he knows what he's doing; assuming will cost you a lot of money and it may not generate the improvement you seek. Be sure to find a specialist who has numerous approaches to solving the same problem.

Think of this as you would one of the old episodes of *I Love Lucy*. When Lucy met Ricky's relatives and found that they didn't speak English, she didn't begin to speak in Spanish. Instead, she spoke in English louder and slower. Her adjustment didn't allow Ricky's relatives to understand her. In the same way, a teacher telling your child the same information repeatedly will not help your child assimilate that information. A different approach is what is required. Be sure that the specialist can give you a different approach. If she cannot, then it is time to shop for a new specialist. Always remember that the best specialist is the one who can help your child. That is the true test. The proof is in the improvement experienced by your child.

HOLDING ON TO THE TRUTH

Often, medical and disability concerns come as a great shock and surprise to parents. Questions arise: "Is it my fault?" "What did I do to deserve this?" "Can't God correct this problem?" There are many more questions that arise when we are hurt or frustrated by circumstances outside our control. So where is God in the life of a family with a child who is "less than perfect" for one reason or another?

Jeremiah 1:5 tells us that "Before I formed you in the womb I knew you, before you were born I set you apart." From this we see that the creation of a human being is extremely personal and intimate for God. Your child was already in God's planning stages long before she was ever conceived. Her concerns may be a mystery to you, but not to God.

It is easy to praise the Lord when your child is strong, healthy, smart, or attractive. It is much more challenging to give thanks for things that are viewed as less than perfect. If Scripture says we are "fearfully and wonderfully made; your works are wonderful," then God made no mistakes. The greatest challenge for all of us is not in loving a child, but to see a child (or adult) through God's eyes. Sadly, our society is quick to judge others by name-calling and giving hurtful labels to individuals.

Take comfort in knowing that God has a plan and a purpose for your child just the way he is. "'For I know the plans that I have for you,' declares the LORD, 'plans to prosper you and not to harm you, plans to give you hope and a future'" (Jeremiah 29:11).

In closing, remember that there is no labeling of imperfection in God's mind for your child. Children are a precious gift from the Lord (Psalm 127:3). Our responsibility as parents is to love, nurture, and care for their needs. Most importantly we must "train a child in the way he should go, and when he is old he will not turn from it" (Proverbs 22:6). You'll want to lead your child to a saving knowledge and personal relationship with the Lord, no matter what characteristics he or she is born with!

All parents experience trying times, days of frustration with raising children. We want our children to be healthy, happy, and successful in life. But when those stormy days come—and they will come for all parents—remember, your heavenly Father is right there with you. Call upon His name, and you'll find His comfort and help. "I lift up my eyes to the hills—where does my help come from? My help comes from the LORD, the Maker of heaven and earth" (Psalm 121:1–2). He made heaven and earth, and *your child!*

■ ■ ■

Michael Safko is a counselor in private practice with a doctorate in clinical psychology from Pepperdine University. Dr. Safko has worked with children, adolescents, and adults affected by poorly developed or abusive relationships in childhood.

Seventeen Years Later
by Raymond and Ann Holland

People make some of the same principal mistakes when they are contemplating adoption that they do when considering marriage. Everyone expects the new arrangement to fulfill all longings and dreams. The reality is that in both cases—marriage and adoption—the parties involved can expect to work very hard for a long time with no guarantees that life will turn out just the way they hoped. In most cases, the end result doesn't look anything like they expected, but it may be a greater blessing than they imagined.

My husband, Raymond, and I have learned that to make a marriage successful, we need to work at understanding and fulfilling the needs of the other, rather than trying to get our own needs met all the time. The same approach is necessary in adoption. Parents whose goal is to fulfill their own needs will never have a healthy relationship with an adopted child. And those who try to make that child conform to their vision instead of God's blueprint will only cause destruction.

When we adopted our daughter, Lisa, I had visions of a beautiful little girl I could dress up, who would be sweet and loving and would make me cards that said, "I love you, Mommy," or "You are the best mom in the world!" I did, in fact, get a beautiful little girl whom I did dress up for a year or so, until she decided she didn't want to wear pink dresses anymore. Since then I have put up with years of baggy clothes full of holes and tears. Many of those were ripped or cut by that same daughter, who sometimes deals with stress in destructive ways.

Why is she this way? Adopting our daughter was a beautiful and joyful experience for her father and me, a modern-day fairy tale. But only for us. Not for her. For our daughter it was a very painful experience. First, in the womb, she was exposed to her mother's ambivalent feelings. A mother responds to an unwanted pregnancy completely differently than she does to an unborn baby she regards with delight.

Second, despite the mother's ambivalence, the child bonds to the sounds, smells, and movement of her birthmother, and the ensuing separation is a painful shock. It is the death of the person she loves most.

Finally, our little girl experienced months of neglect in an orphanage in a former communist country. She received virtually no attention, no loving touch, no eye contact, and no soothing words. From birth she was left alone, even receiving her nourishment from propped-up bottles. Due to these tragedies at the beginning of her life, our beautiful girl still struggles with a big black hole inside that, at its worst, has caused her to seriously consider suicide and, at its best, has caused her to be extremely compassionate toward other hurting people.

One day Lisa abruptly said, "Mama, please don't be hurt by this" (she was only in elementary school) "but I wish I hadn't been adopted." Fortunately, God was at work that day, and I was able to respond that I wished she hadn't been either; I wished she had been able to be born and raised in her own birth family, the way God intended it to be.

Were her dad and I ready for years and years of trying to teach Lisa to leave the environment around her relatively intact? To convince her that it's okay to let us be the ones to initiate a kiss or hug sometimes, that eating is not the most important thing in the world and that hiding food remnants or wet underwear under her bed makes her parents rather cranky?

Was she ready for years and years of parents frustrated by her crossing of boundaries that seemed so obvious to us but not to her? Was she ready for the injustice of being denied privileges available to other kids her age?

Were any of us ready for the years and years of parent/teacher, parent/principal, parent/everyone-at-school meetings?

On the other hand, did any of us understand how we would learn to be more patient, loving people as a result of this very precious and unique relationship? Did we understand that we would learn to judge people by their innermost being and not just by their "covers"? Did we know that we would learn to recognize real trials and begin to accept occasional inconveniences?

Seventeen years, two months, and many, many experiences later, I can say that although I would not have sought out the above experiences, I would choose again to adopt. I would choose to adopt the young lady I am privileged to call my daughter.

When an Adoption Disrupts or Dissolves

by Renée Sanford

. . . God has said, "Never will I leave you; never will I forsake you."
So we say with confidence, "The Lord is my helper;
I will not be afraid. What can man do to me?"
—HEBREWS 13:5b–6

The camera pans the child's bedroom, colorfully decorated and well stocked with toys and books and stuffed animals. Another rags to riches, orphanage to American home story concludes. The viewer turns off the TV with a happy feeling knowing that a child who has spent the first few years of his or her life in a situation of trauma or neglect will now experience all the good things that a family can give.

But the camera turns off and the credits play before the whole story is told. The story has just begun. It takes real work to bring a child to a place where she can truly embrace this new family and find healing. And it's not always a happy ending.

Why talk about when adoption doesn't work out just as planned? If you are an adoptive or prospective adoptive parent, this chapter is just as crucial as any of the others in helping you succeed, because preparation is the best prevention.

Sadly, some parents are simply not prepared for the real picture of the child they are adopting. Other parents are in way over their heads when it comes to caring for a disabled or traumatized child. And in worst-case scenario situations, the adopted child may actually physically harm or sexually abuse another family member.

Whether you've been through an adoption disruption or dissolution in the past and are now adopting again, or you're presently going through a difficult circumstance with your adopted child, we want to offer a few tips on what you can do to protect all members of your family (including your adopted child) and things you should consider throughout the process.

UNDERSTANDING THE TERMS

Disruption is a term used to describe an adoptive placement that ends after the child is placed in an adoptive home and before the adoption is legally finalized. It results in the child returning to foster care, or being placed in another adoptive home. Disruption also can be the result of a legal decision not to terminate the parental rights of one or both birthparents. All prospective adoptive parents should be well informed of the difficult reality that before an adoption is final, there is always a possibility the placement will disrupt, sometimes for reasons beyond their control. Most state foster care systems call these placements "at-risk" or "legal-risk" in order to prepare all prospective adoptive parents that until the adoption is finalized, anything is possible. Christian families must face this fear head-on with full reliance that God is in control.

More than a decade ago my husband and I served as foster parents for two girls, sisters ages nine and six. After a few months, we were asked if we would be interested in adopting both girls. We felt God's peace to say yes. After all, we loved the girls! Besides, we were told that their birthparents' rights were going to be terminated. Shortly before the holidays, however, the courts decided against that course of action and a few weeks later the girls were moved out of our home and in with their mother. Within a year or two it was clear that was the right decision, but at the time all we could do was trust God, pray, and remain committed to loving the girls whether or not we ever saw them again. (Thankfully, we have!)

The term *dissolution* is used to describe an adoption that ends after finalization. In a dissolved adoption, children return to or are placed in foster care or with another adoptive family. Living arrangements are also altered when parents remain the legal parents but the child resides outside of the home. This may happen because the home is not adequate either to meet the intense needs of the child or to protect family members from harm.

It is important to note that even in this situation, adoptive parents can communicate unconditional love, commitment, and support to a child who needs to reside out of the home. Think of the heartbreaking situation where any of your children, through birth or adoption, ended up in prison. You would still be their parents even though they couldn't reside with you any longer.

PREVENTING ADOPTION DISSOLUTION

Jesus talked very clearly to His disciples about how they approach commitments: "Suppose one of you wants to build a tower. Will he not first sit down and estimate the cost to see if he has enough money to complete it?" (Luke 14:28). Jesus asks His followers to pay the cost of following Him—but He calls for counting the cost first.

This principle is particularly vital when making the decision to adopt. It means putting in the time and energy to really pray with an open heart before doing anything else. And to think hard. One of the foundations to peace as an adoptive parent is knowing with certainty that this was God's will for your family—not a plan you pushed through. That way, when the hard time comes, you will find security in the certainty of God's will, rather than collapsing under your current failure or pain.

The application process should be a practical tool for formulating realistic expectations for what your family can handle. Such examination means more than acknowledging that things might be different than you expect. It also means being realistic about your limitations, looking at yourself and your life up to this point, recognizing what you can tolerate and what you cannot. God has given different callings to different people. If you aren't called to adopt five or six children, rejoice that God gives you the chance to adopt one or two. If you know you would not easily parent a child with life-threatening disabilities, let God guide you to one of the thousands of other children who need you.

Making a wise match also involves practical considerations of age and spacing. Be aware that there are challenges when altering the birth order in the home.

As well, parents who have not yet parented teens would do well to consider waiting until their children are older before taking on a teen adoptee. A family with younger children would not be the best match for an older child with a history of sexually acting-out behavior.

Ask for complete information from the agency with whom you are working. This may be more difficult with an international adoption agency, but you have the right and the responsibility to make your decision based on all the information they possibly can give you.

Our family had been waiting for more than a year to be chosen as a possible home for a preschool child. We were adopting through the state child welfare system, so we had a good deal of information on each child for whom we applied, and our caseworker pressed us to be brutally honest with ourselves.

Because we already had three grown children, we had prayerfully decided that the healthiest situation for our family would be to adopt a daughter who was within three years of our then six-year-old son. When presented with the opportunity to adopt a much younger little boy, we were eager, but we considered the long-term commitment and the heightened competition issues that we would face if we adopted a boy. Within a few hours of that phone call, both of us felt peace in saying "no."

Several months and more disappointments later, we were presented with two more opportunities to adopt. The first was a girl with severe acting-out behavior who was exactly the age of our son. The second was a girl who was two and a half years younger. She, too, had experienced trauma and neglect. Our hearts went out to both girls—we had waited so long that we wanted to say that we would take whichever child we could be approved for first. But we also knew that having two children the same age would be a stress on both children in the home. We had taken adoption preparation classes, so we knew what some of those acting-out behaviors could really look like. In the end, we knew we couldn't do the kind of parenting that both the first child and our son needed.

With dependence on the Lord, we pursued and were able to adopt the younger girl. Stresses and acting out behaviors abounded, but her age and personality were a fit with the family. Our family was stretched but not snapped. Just as importantly, because of excellent educational opportunities, we were armed with good information. This allowed us to anticipate and recognize the challenges that came along as we enfolded our new daughter into our family.

Even with the best efforts at making a good match, parents will find more than enough surprises and challenges as they raise their adopted children. You might adopt a child who has severe birth defects. Or you may have been presented with a child who is quite different than you were led to believe. If you are trusting in God's knowledge, you can rest in the fact that He is not surprised. You can invest in the child He's given you and make decisions for this child and for your family, based on God's lifelong purpose in her life and yours.

WHEN YOU FEEL LIKE GIVING UP

Every parent on earth has terrible parenting days. But this is more than just a bad day—or a tough year. Instead, you've come to a state of emergency in which you are operating with an "it's him or me" mentality. When you even start getting close to an adversarial relationship—with survival going to the winner—it's time to get help. Emergencies can be handled with personal and professional intervention and support.

For those who are feeling frustrated and helpless or anxious and upset, take the time to consider the issues addressed below:

Have you pursued multiple options to address the issues with your child? Begin by seeking extensive counseling—not just for the child, but for the family as a whole. As parents you should seek out mentoring and support from people who have a clear picture of what's been happening in your home. Consider joining a support group. Stay in close connection with people in spiritual leadership and/or your church community. Be sure you have extensive prayer support. Be honest and transparent about your struggles with those who can uphold your whole family in regular prayer. Be active in accessing the resources offered in your community. Work consistently with the school—both teachers and counselors—to address your child's needs.

Have there been periods of stabilization? If you step back, can you see a cycle of behavior or struggle over the course of time? Does that cycle seem to bring some growth and improvement, even incrementally? If there have not been any periods of stabilization, but only continued disintegration, you need to find out exactly what's not working and why. Professional counseling can help you determine the root cause.

Examine the state of everyone in your family system. Pay attention to what is happening with other members of the family. Of course, adding a child to a family changes the family dynamics—and there's sure to be jostling and clashing. But do your other children (whether biological or adopted) show signs of abnormal distress, particularly personality changes?

What about your marriage? If there is an upheaval in your relationship, take notice. Entire families—not just adoptions—dissolve when the foundational marriage crumbles. One therapist relates how, after ongoing trauma with adoptive children, a father said, "I'm done," and walked. The mother couldn't continue to do it on her own and put the children in her state's foster care system.

What about your state of mental and emotional health? Parenting a hurt child is wearing. Any parent needs to practice good self-care. But if, in spite of best efforts and support, a parent finds herself or himself having difficulty keeping mental and emotional stability, call for emergency help. Do this for your child's sake, as well as your own.

Address these issues head-on. With the help of a skilled counselor, lay out what corrective measures could be taken to make your home a healthy place. Keep in mind that this will probably involve as many changes for the adults as it does for the child.

Examine the safety threats. Is your adopted child a physical threat to any individuals in your family? If so, what safety measure should be taken? Families routinely make accommodations for the danger-seeking behaviors of two-year-olds. Locks on cupboards and plugs in light sockets keep little people safe. Many families make other kinds of accommodations to keep their families safe: locking up dangerous items (not just guns but also knives, matches, and medications), installing alarms on bedroom doors, and keeping a strict supervision policy.

Sometimes, however, even the best plans can't keep a child from endangering himself or others, and the family lives in constant fear.

One adult sibling watched as her parents dealt with the unpredictable behavior of her young brother, adopted from an Eastern European orphanage. Because of his cognitive challenges, he did not understand how knives and guns could hurt both him and others. She dealt with her own fear of what would happen if things escalated, and she knew her parents had their own very real fears, as well.

Examine the expectations placed on the child. Is this child someone who simply doesn't fit in and disrupts the family ideal? Or does this child truly endanger the mental, emotional, and physical well-being of other family members? In other words, do you understand (and can you accept) the special challenges your child faces because of his trauma? Or do you simply blame the child's behavior on her "badness"?

In these situations, it is crucial for the parents to honestly examine their hearts before God. You may be weeping as you give Him all your hopes and dreams for your child and accept the loss of what will not be. Then you can work toward accepting and embracing what will be and letting it be good enough. Good enough that the child reaches her own potential (not yours) and good enough that you as parents provide nurture and care—whether or not it ever comes easily.

This acceptance is not just an understanding of the child's limitations. It also means accepting that you can still successfully parent without some of the rewards and good feelings that you expected. It might mean that a smile and a thank you is the warmest expression your son will give you. It means giving up the entitlement you might feel as parents. In the best-case scenario, these issues first are addressed before the adoption, but certainly they need to be reprocessed as both you and your child grow.

It's a challenging balancing act—keeping expectations very realistic, yet continuing to pour into these children as if they could reach beyond their expected potential. Make it your goal to delight in the potential that they will reach.

OPTIONS FOR OUT-OF-HOME CARE FOR AN ADOPTED CHILD

Often children have serious issues that require skilled care. Even a family with the best intentions and the biggest hearts may not have the training and resources to care for a severely challenged child. This applies to not just physical disabilities but also to developmental disabilities and issues of emotional or mental health and abnormal behavior. This also applies in serious situations where safety has become a concern for the family (including your adopted child's safety from his or her own behavior). Maybe your child has started acting out in dangerous and unhealthy ways.

In the cases we've just mentioned, parents may have to seek out-of-home care while still retaining legal status as the child's parents. This does not fit the technical definition of disruption, but it is experienced as a disruption in the lives of the parents and child just the same.

If you find that you need to seek out-of-home services, research the services carefully. The Department of Human Services in your state is a good place to start, but connecting with other parents who have adopted or support services could lead you to private agencies that better fit the needs of your child. To determine this, constantly ask, "What will best meet the needs of my child? Which living situation will best foster an ongoing connection between my child and our family?" Distance may not be as crucial as the philosophy and policies of the residential facility. If possible, seek out a Christian establishment, but make sure the program will meet the specific needs of your child.

TRANSITIONING INTO A NEW PLACEMENT

When a drastic change in the living situation is absolutely necessary (such as out-of-home care), the move should be done with the greatest care. Parents need to go the extra mile to make sure that the child is well cared for. Instead of blaming your child, acknowledge your own limitations. Give him a blessing by affirming his worth before God. Pray for your child—even if all you can emotionally manage is, "The LORD bless you and keep you; the LORD make his face shine upon you" (Numbers 6:24–25).

Ideally, transitions should take place in a carefully planned manner. Therapy should be ongoing (preferably with the same therapist) or started right away to establish some continuity. A good therapist will help the child make sense of what has happened in the past and what will happen in the future. Even if it is through correspondence, you can continue to offer emotional support to your child in his new living situation. Again, instead of focusing on blame, emphasize that the challenges were bigger than either you or your child was able to handle alone.

Transitions should include a time when the new caregivers visit the child in your home. If possible, she should also have opportunity to become accustomed to her new environment before the move. What will the child take with her? Don't just send her clothes, but also those things that will help her feel like she still owns "pieces" of herself and her life in her new home. Her life storybook should go with her—with new pages that explain the reasons for the move.

Of course, the ongoing crisis that brings a family to this decision doesn't leave a lot of extra emotional energy for ensuring an optimum transition. Still, prayerful dependence on God and intentional actions (even when you don't feel like it) are a lasting gift you can give to this child. Remember, God's story for this child is still so much bigger than what you can see, and you are part of that story.

A FINAL THOUGHT

As Christians, adoption is more than just a way to add a child to a family. We view the adoption commitment as a spiritual picture of our adoption into God's family (Galatians 4:5–6). We value lifelong commitments based on God's covenantal love, so we desperately want, and can choose to have, adoptive relationships—and other family relationships—to continue indefinitely. With this desire in mind, we honor God's Word by "counting the cost" when we build a family. And we depend on the Holy Spirit for guidance and healing in another arena of a broken world.

■■■

Renée Sanford is a social worker, author, book editor, public speaker, and vice president of Sanford Communications, Inc. Renée and her husband, David, live "on the road to Damascus" a few miles from downtown Portland, Oregon, with their two youngest children.

Joseph's Hope
by Paul McArthur

We already had four biological children when we decided to adopt two boys from Russia. We named them Daniel (age 7) and Joseph (age 5), hoping that they would be like the men of old who left their country and became great men of God.

When they first came, Daniel was our real challenge. He had many tantrums and outbursts, which were a result of having lived in an orphanage and being physically abused. Joseph was more compliant, but the doctor warned us that there were difficult times ahead with him.

We knew Joseph had difficulty learning. When he entered kindergarten, his learning issues became even more apparent. As time went on, he became increasingly disruptive. He wasn't angry and hostile, but he would get the other children wound up. More difficult issues arose when he displayed obviously unacceptable behavior. Sometimes it was a safety issue, such as not coming home from school right away.

When he was eight years old, we were still trying to teach him the same things over and over. We would ask, "Why did you do it?"

"Because I wanted to," would be his reply. No matter how severe the consequences, he wasn't learning. We realized he wasn't capable of learning.

When the safety issues became more serious concerns—when he posed a threat to himself and to others—we realized that it wasn't working. We couldn't keep him or others safe in our home. We knew puberty would only bring more issues. We were fearful that he would be easily influenced by hurtful or criminal people. We felt that we could not care for him adequately. And my wife, Carolyn, experienced the strain on a daily, deeper level than I did.

It was hard for me to face the struggles, but eventually, Carolyn and I pursued a new living situation for Joseph. We had become friends with a woman who worked as our adoption advocate and who was an adoptive parent herself. She shared with us that they had to put their boy in a place called "Hope House" because he had such severe handicaps.

Carolyn took Joseph down to Nampa, Idaho, to visit Hope House. We knew within a few months that this would be a good place for him. The process, however, took about a year. We placed Joseph into the care of Hope House in June of 2001, when he was 11 years old. It was not until later that Joseph was finally diagnosed with Tourette's syndrome as well as ADHD and FASD. Yet he had many of the classic symptoms long before the diagnosis.

Even though we knew Joseph could not live in our home, we still remained his parents. We didn't even investigate dissolving the adoption. We had given the children the promise of unconditional acceptance. We were not trying to get Joseph out of our life, but he needed a place that was safer and better for him.

We promised Joseph that he would always be part of our family, and he does consider himself part of our family. Joseph now lives at a young adult community in Houston, Texas. He was not able to stay at Hope House because of his sexually inappropriate behavior. We still have an active part in supervising his needs. He is on about five medications and receives SSI/DD support. We talk to him weekly by telephone.

When we went to visit him in Idaho, we took him back to the hotel to swim in the pool or to the park to play. Each time, he'd cry when we had to take him back to Hope House. One day, he and I were walking in the park, and he was telling me that he felt the staff didn't understand him. "Do you feel that I understand you?" I asked him.

"Well, you're my dad, so you understand me," he replied. Whether or not he's in my home, he understands that I will always be his father.

Still, this was the most gut-wrenching experience of our lives. We suffered with coming to terms with the fact that our love and nurture was not going to be the happy ever after for Joseph. And few people could understand.

We felt as though we couldn't keep explaining over and over why we had placed Joseph in a home. It was just too draining. Yet we also didn't have the luxury of trying to appear as if everything were fine. No matter what other people thought, we had to do what was right for our family. It was helpful to talk with people who had been through the same experience we had.

We valued the people who listened and understood that we weren't "dumping" Joseph, but that we were highly committed to his well-being. Some people saw that he was happy with us and wondered why he had to live somewhere else. They didn't understand. People with severe FASD need simple structure and routine that a normal home just can't provide.

In preparing to adopt, be aware that your picture of what that child is like may be based on Anne of Green Gables—anxious to be in a family, thrilled to be there. Most kids aren't able to think like that until they are adults. Remember, the adopted child never filled out any application to be in your family. We thought our parenting skills were better than average, but everything we had was still not enough.

Our other adopted children have had struggles, too, but they were able to make adjustments and stay at home. What has always reassured us is to think of what life would have been like for Joseph if he hadn't been adopted. In spite of everything, we know God purposed for Joseph to be in our family.

Afterword

*Sing to God, sing praise to his name, extol Him who
rides on the clouds—his name is the Lord—and rejoice
before him. A father to the fatherless, a defender
of widows, is God in his holy dwelling.
God sets the lonely in families . . .*
—PSALM 68:4-6

As adoptive parents, it is an incredible blessing to know that God has chosen us to be the families into which He set our previously lonely orphan children. The spiritual, legal, and practical reality is that our children are orphans no more—they are, indeed, our very own.

In the Rosati home, we often pray and thank God for making us a family through both marriage and adoption. To us, it is nothing short of amazing that the God of the universe knit together our family through the blessing and miracle of adoption.

We also know, however, that challenges usually accompany blessings. Adoption is no exception. As adoptive parents, those challenges can be very unique and, at times, overwhelming. They can make us feel as if we're drowning in grief, fear, and pain. They can even make us question our calling from God. Let me encourage you: He who has called us is faithful! And we can stand on His promise that there is great hope for the future.

It is our sincere hope at Focus on the Family that this *Handbook on Thriving as an Adoptive Family* was a blessing to you and your family. We pray it helped you understand that you're not alone in your struggles and provided practical assistance for whatever stage of the adoption and parenting journey in which you find yourselves.

We also want you to know that you can call us at 1-800-AFAMILY for confidential counseling and support. We want to walk alongside you down this remarkable road and help carry your burdens. We want to help your family thrive!

Above all else, we hope this book provides you with the hope that God is able to equip you to handle whatever may come your way. Remember, He has called us to this high calling as adoptive parents and our struggles are no surprise to Him, even when they surprise and discourage us.

So as you pray for and hug your precious children today, thank God for making you a family through the blessing of adoption and cling tightly to the One who placed your children into your family.

And, finally, please pray for the orphan children here in the U.S. and around the world who are still waiting for God to send them their own forever adoptive families. For more information on Focus on the Family's orphan care initiative, visit our Web site at www.iCareAboutOrphans.org.

Blessings in Christ,
Kelly M. Rosati, J.D.

Kelly M. Rosati is the senior director of the Sanctity of Human Life division at Focus on the Family, where she oversees the Adoption & Orphan Care Initiative. An attorney by training, Mrs. Rosati was the executive director of Hawaii Family Forum for 10 years, where she advocated for Hawaii's children and families in the legislature and media. She has been married to her husband, John, for more than 17 years, and they were blessed to adopt all four of their children through the U.S. foster care system.

Notes

Chapter 1

1. Dan Rafter, "Creating the Comforts of Home for an Older Adopted Child," *Chicago Tribune*, December 26, 2003, C1.
2. Proverbs 12:18.
3. See http://www.winstonchurchill.org/i4a/pages/index.cfm?pageid=388 (last viewed March 31, 2008).

Chapter 2

1. Bruce Perry, M.D., *Bonding and Attachment in Maltreated Children* (www.childtrauma.org), 2001.
2. John Bowlby, *Attachment and Loss. Vol. 1: Attachment* (New York: Basic Books, 1969).
3. Allan Schore, "The Effects of a Secure Attachment Relationship on Right Brain Development, Affect Regulation, and Infant Mental Health," *Infant Journal of Mental Health*, 2001, 22: 7–66.
4. B. Bryan Post, *The Great Behavior Breakdown,* audio CD Recording (Oklahoma City, OK: Post Institute for Family Centered Therapy, 2004). www.postinstitute.com.
5. L. Alan Sroufe, *Emotional Development* (New York: Cambridge University Press, 1995).
6. Bruce Perry, M.D., *Bonding and Attachment in Maltreated Children* (www.childtrauma.org), 2001.
7. Adapted from a simpler diagram by Foster W. Cline, M.D., *Understanding and Treating the Severely Disturbed Child* (Evergreen, CO: Evergreen Consultants in Behavior, 1979), 28.
8. John Bowlby, *A Secure Base: Clinical Applications of Attachment Theory* (Padstow, Cornwall: TJ International Ltd, 1988), 9.

9. Ibid., 15.

10. Heather T. Forbes and B. Bryan Post, *Beyond Consequences, Logic, and Control* (Orlando, FL: Beyond Consequences Institute, LLC, 2006).

11. S. E. Kay Hall and G. Geher, "Behavioral and Personality Characteristics of Children with Reactive Attachment Disorder," *Journal of Psychology: Interdisciplinary and Applied*, 2003.

12. Perry, 2001.

13. For more information, see www.childtrauma.org.

CHAPTER 4

1. Laura Christianson, *The Adoption Decision: 15 Things You Want to Know Before Adopting* (Eugene, OR: Harvest House Publishers, 2007).

2. "Day Care: Choosing a Good Center," American Academy of Family Physicians, July 2006, http://familydoctor.org/online/famdocen/home/children/parents/infants/030.html#top.

3. W. C. Martin, *Small Town, Big Miracle* (Carol Stream, IL: Tyndale House Publishers, Inc., 2007), 93.

4. Laura Christianson, *The Adoption Network: Your Guide to Starting a Support System* (Enumclaw, WA: Winepress Publishing, 2007).

5. U.S. Census Bureau, Census 2000.

6. Rebecca Barnes and Lindy Lowry, "The American Church in Crisis," *Outreach* magazine, May/June 2006.

CHAPTER 5

1. Paul Reisser, M.D., *Focus on the Family Complete Guide to Baby & Child Care* (Carol Stream, IL: Tyndale House Publishers, Inc., 2007), 274.

CHAPTER 6

1. Bruce D. Perry, M.D., Ph.D., Senior Fellow at The Trauma Center in Houston, Texas, www.childtrauma.org.

2. Deborah Gray, *Nurturing Adoptions: Creating Resilience after Neglect and Trauma* (Indianapolis: Perspectives Press, 2007).

3. Nancy L. Thomas, *When Love Is Not Enough: A Guide to Parenting Children with RAD* (Glenwood Springs, CO: Families by Design, 2005), 8.

CHAPTER 7

1. Julian Davies, M.D. and Julia Bledsoe, M.D., Center for Adoption Medicine, University of Washington. Speakers' notes from live presentation. Available at www.adoptmed.org/storage/adoption%20medicine%20handout.pdf (last viewed January 10, 2008).

2. Rita Taddonio, Director of SPARK (Child Development program) at Spence-Chapin Agency in New York (www.spence-chapin.org) in a 2003 online "expert chat" (http://www.adopting.org/adoptions/adoption-expert-chat-series-transcript-is-it-toddlerhood-or-adoption.html; last viewed January 10, 2008).

3. See http://www.sinetwork.org.

4. Julian Davies, M.D., "Transitional Feeding Difficulties." The Center for Adoption Medicine, May 17, 2005. http://www.adoptmed.org/topics/transitional-feeding-difficulties.html (last viewed January 10, 2008).

5. Julian Davies, M.D., "Sleep and Adoption." The Center for Adoption Medicine, October 9, 2005. http://www.adoptmed.org/topics/sleep-and-adoption.html (last viewed January 10, 2008).

6. Paul Reisser, M.D., *Focus on the Family Complete Guide to Baby & Child Care* (Carol Stream, IL: Tyndale House Publishers, Inc., 2007), 297.

7. Child Welfare Information Gateway Factsheet for Families: Adoption and the Stages of Development Ages 2–6 (http://www.childwelfare.gov/pubs/f_stages/f_stagesb.cfm).

8. Matthew D. Bramlett, Ph.Da., Laura F. Radel, MPPb, and Stephen J. Blumberg, Ph.Da., "The Health and Well-Being of Adopted Children," *Pediatrics*. Vol. 119 Supplement, February 2007, S54–S60.

9. Department of Health and Human Services, Centers for Disease Control and Prevention, "Child Development" Toddlers: 1–2 years old, Toddlers 2–3 years old, Preschoolers 3–5 years old, http://www.cdc .gov/ncbddd/child/toddlers1.htm (last viewed January 10, 2008).

10. American Academy of Pediatrics, "Parenting Corner Q & A: Developmental Milestones," June 2007. Adapted from *Caring for Your Baby and Young Child: Birth to Age 5,* 2004. Available at http://www.aap.org/ healthtopics/stages.cfm#early (last viewed January 10, 2008).

11. Sharon Glennen, M.D., "Predicting Language Outcomes for Internationally Adopted Children," *Journal of Speech, Language, and Hearing Research.* Vol. 50, 529–548, April 2007, doi:10.1044/1092-4388 (2007/036). See Dr. Glennen's Web site for English Language Milestones and other research at http://pages.towson.edu/sglennen/ index.htm.

12. Boris Gindis, Ph.D., "Language Development in Internationally Adopted Children," *China Connection,* Vol. 10, Issue 2, 2004, 34–37.

13. American Academy of Child & Adolescent Psychiatry, "Facts for Families #48: Problems with Soiling and Bowel Control." Available at http://www.aacap.org/cs/root/facts_for_families/problems_with _soiling_and_bowel_control.

14. Reisser, 83.

15. Deborah A. Borchers, M.D., FAAP, Member, American Academy of Pediatrics Committee on Early Childhood, Adoption, and Dependent Care. "Adoption: Positive Strategies for Early Childhood Educators." Available at http://www.healthychildcare.org/pdf/Adoption.pdf (last viewed January 10, 2008).

CHAPTER 8

1. David M. Brodzinsky, Marsall D. Schechter, and Robin Marantz Henig, *Being Adopted: The Lifelong Search for Self* (New York: Doubleday, 1992), 62.

2. American Academy of Child and Adolescent Psychiatry (http://www.aa cap.org/cs/root/facts_for_families/when_to_seek_help_for_your_child).

CHAPTER 9

1. Angela Huebner, "Adolescent Growth and Development," available at http://www.ext.vt.edu/pubs/family/350-850/350-850.html (last viewed January 10, 2008).
2. Dictionary.com.

CHAPTER 10

1. Nancy Verrier, *The Primal Wound: Understanding the Adopted Child* (Baltimore: Gateway Press, 1993).
2. Ibid., 1.
3. See Betty Jean Lifton, *Journey of the Adopted Self: A Quest for Wholeness* (New York: Basic Books, 1994), for a comprehensive review of the challenges adoptees face in their own self-construction.

CHAPTER 16

1. See http://nces.ed.gov.
2. See http://www.census.gov/prod/2003pubs/censr-6.pdf, page 2, table 1. See also http://www.census.gov/Press-Release/www/releases/archives/facts_for_features_special_editions/002683.html (last viewed January 10, 2008).
3. Annie Stuart, "Identifying Learning Problems in Adopted Children," http://www.schwablearning.org/articles.aspx?r=689; (last viewed January 10, 2008).
4. See http://www.law.cornell.edu/uscode/html/uscode20/usc_sec_20 _00001401——000-.html (last viewed June 24, 2008).
5. Russell A. Barkley, *Attention-Deficit Hyperactivity Disorder, Third Edition: A Handbook for Diagnosis and Treatment* (New York: Guilford Press, 2006), 126.

Glossary

Adopt – to legally bring a child into one's family

Attachment – the process by which a child forms stable and significant emotional connections with people; begins in infancy; if attachment has not occurred by age four or five, the child may experience difficulty in connecting socially with others

Closed Adoption – neither birth nor adoptive families share identifying information with one another; there is no relationship or communication between the two parties

Disruption – in the context of adoption, this occurs when a child is removed from the current placement after living there for some time; can also refer to a failed placement, particularly before the adoption is finalized

Dissolution – to void or reverse an adoption after finalization

Domestic Adoption – both the child and adoptive family are U.S. citizens

Emotional Age – refers to the emotional development level of the child; many children who experience trauma do not develop emotionally at the same pace as a typically developing child. A child may be 10 years old but emotionally only age six; therefore, he must be treated as a six-year-old to help him reach the developmental milestones that may have been missed

Fetal Alcohol Effects (FAE)* – a lesser severity of FAS, often with no outward physical manifestations or mental retardation

Fetal Alcohol Spectrum Disorder (FASD)* – a catch-all category encompassing both FAS and FAE on a continuum

Fetal Alcohol Syndrome (FAS)* – the most severe form of in utero drug/alcohol effects, almost always characterized by altered facial features, stunted growth, and/or mental retardation

Individualized Educational Plan (IEP) – a written plan outlining a child's educational goals as well as any special support that may be required to achieve those goals; usually completed by parents and educators

International Adoption – the process of adopting a child from another country; not all countries allow adoption by U.S. families

Legal Risk – this refers to the type of foster-to-adopt placement where the parental rights of a child have not been terminated prior to placement; the potential adoptive family is made aware of the "legal risk" that the birthparents' rights may not be terminated. If parental rights are terminated, the adoptive family can choose to finalize the adoption

Open Adoption – birth and adoptive parents know one another and maintain some level of communication; level and amount of communication is decided between the two parties

Post-Adoption Depression (PAD)** – an increasingly common anxiety disorder among parents who are emotionally unprepared to cope with the challenges of parenting adopted children

Private Adoption – typically refers to a domestic infant adoption by working with a private agency or adoption lawyer

Reactive Attachment Disorder (RAD) – a condition affecting children who have not had sufficient attachment in early developmental phases; characterized by the inability to establish age-appropriate social connections and maintain relationships

Relinquishment – refers to a birthparent who voluntarily chooses an adoption plan for his or her child and waives his or her parental rights; the child can then be adopted

Residential Treatment – extended or long-term stay facilities with intensive, therapeutic treatment for individuals who do not or cannot function safely and/or satisfactorily in their own home environments; often a last resort

Semi-open Adoption – limited communication between birth and adoptive family members; usually consists of photos and brief updates and often conducted through a third party (such as the adoption agency)

Termination of Parental Rights (TPR) – process by which an individual's parental rights are removed; often occurs when mandated by the court; after TPR, the child can be adopted

Transracial Adoption – an adoption in which a family adopts a child of a different race

Typically Developing Child – refers to a child who has achieved the appropriate developmental milestones and is continuing to progress normally; can be a child who entered the family either biologically or through adoption

---

*As defined by Dr. Steven Gray
**As defined by Laura Christianson

Bonus Chapters and More Online

There's more!

Be sure to log on to www.iCareAboutOrphans.org to find more informative, practical, and up-to-date resources on adoption.

At www.iCareAboutOrphans.org you'll find three "bonus chapters" (modules of articles) on:

- "Characteristics of Successful Adoptive Families" by Debi Grebenik
- "Birth Family Relationships" by Mardie Caldwell and Renée Sanford
- "Your Child's Life Story" by Jayne Schooler

At www.iCareAboutOrphans.org you'll also find a number of additional stories of adoption addressing virtually all of the subjects covered in this book. Why more stories? Because "Experience is the best teacher . . . especially other people's experiences!"

While you're online, be sure to check out the many other adoption resources offered at www.FocusOnTheFamily.com.

Resources Guide

The following products, authors, and organizations are not endorsed by Focus on the Family. Discerning parents will find a wealth of useful information, but caution is advised. Not all resources are written from a distinctly Christian worldview, and some statements or claims may conflict with sound biblical teachings.

BOOKS

Atwood, Thomas C. and Jayne E. Schooler. *The Whole Life Adoption Book: Realistic Advice for Building a Healthy Adoptive Family* (Colorado Springs, CO: NavPress, 2008, revised updated version).

Burlingham-Brown, Barbara. *"Why Didn't She Keep Me?": Answers to the Question Every Adopted Child Asks* (South Bend, IN: Diamond Publications, 2005).

Christianson, Laura. *The Adoption Decision: 15 Things You Want to Know Before Adopting* (Eugene, OR: Harvest House Publishers, 2007).

Christianson, Laura. *The Adoption Network: Your Guide to Starting a Support System* (Enumclaw, WA: WinePress Publishing, 2007).

Eldridge, Sherrie. *Forever Fingerprints: An Amazing Discovery for Adopted Children* (Warren, NJ: EMK Press, 2007).

Eldridge, Sherrie. *Twenty Life Transforming Choices Adoptees Need to Make* (Colorado Springs, CO: Piñon Press, 2003).

Furnstahl, Shari Rusch. *From Stumbling Blocks to Stepping Stones: Help and Hope for Special Needs Kids* (Carol Stream, IL: Tyndale House Publishers/Focus on the Family, 2007).

Gillespie, Natalie Nichols. *Successful Adoption: A Guide for Christian Families.* (Franklin, TN: Integrity Publishers, 2006).

Gray, Deborah D. *Attaching in Adoption: Practical Tools for Today's Parents* (Indianapolis, IN: Perspectives Press, 2002).

Gray, Deborah D. *Nurturing Adoptions: Creating Resilience after Neglect and Trauma* (Indianapolis, IN: Perspectives Press, 2007).

Hopkins-Best, Mary. *Toddler Adoption: The Weaver's Craft* (Indianapolis, IN: Perspectives Press, 1998).

Kitze, Carrie A. *I Don't Have Your Eyes* (Warren, NJ: EMK Press, 2007).

MacLeod, Jean and Sheena Macrae, editors. *Adoption Parenting: Creating a Toolbox, Building Connections* (Warren, NJ: EMK Press, 2006).

McCreight, Brenda. *Parenting Your Adopted Older Child: How to Overcome the Unique Challenges and Raise a Happy and Healthy Child* (Oakland, CA: New Harbinger Publications, 2002).

O'Malley, Beth. *Lifebooks: Creating a Treasure for the Adopted Child* (Winthrop, MA: Adoption-Works Press, 2000).

Pavao, Joyce Maguire. *The Family of Adoption* (Boston: Beacon Press, 2004).

Purvis, Karyn B., David R. Cross, and Wendy Lyons Sunshine. *The Connected Child: Bring Hope and Healing to Your Adoptive Family* (Columbus, OH: McGraw-Hill, 2007).

Stoller, John L. *Parenting Other People's Children: Understanding and Repairing Reactive Attachment Disorder* (New York: Vantage Press, 2006).

Swanberg, Dennis and Diane Passno. *Why A.D.H.D. Doesn't Mean Disaster* (Carol Stream, IL: Tyndale House Publishers/Focus on the Family, 2003).

TeBos, Susan and Carissa Woodwyk. *Before You Were Mine: Discovering Your Adopted Child's Lifestory* (Grand Haven, MI: FaithWalk Publishing, 2007).

Van Gulden, Holly and Lisa M. Bartels-Rabb. *Real Parents, Real Children* (New York: Crossroad Classic, 1995).

ORGANIZATIONS

Adoption Today
246 S. Cleveland Ave.
Loveland, CO 80537
(970) 663-1185
(970) 663-1186 FAX
www.adoption.org/adopt/adoption-today-magazine.php
This adoptive-parent-owned magazine is a helpful guide for adoptive families, with an easily accessible format.

Adoptive Families
2472 Broadway, Suite 377
New York, NY 10025
(800) 372-3300
www.adoptivefamilies.com
This award-winning adoptive-parent-owned magazine is a loved resource
    for adoptive families.

ARIS (Adoption Referral and Information Service)
(425) 614-4444 or (888) 777-1538
www.adoptionreferralservice.com
ARIS is a Washington-based referral service, linking adoptive parents
    with therapists, education specialists, physicians, and resources. For
    information on setting up similar programs in your area, contact ARIS
    director Yolanda Comparan, MSW.

ATTACh (Association for Treatment and Training in the Attachment
    of Children)
P.O. Box 533
Lake Villa, IL 60046
(847) 356-7856
www.attach.org
ATTACh is a national resource on attachment issues. They publish a
    newsletter, have listings of therapists, and offer a helpful national
    conference annually.

ChildTrauma Academy
Feigin Center, Suite 715
Texas Children's Hospital
6621 Fannin
Houston, TX 77030
www.childtrauma.org
This educational series for parents and caregivers provides access to accurate
    and useful information from leading trauma professionals.

Center for Cognitive-Developmental Assessment and Remediation
www.bgcenter.com
Developmental psychologist Dr. Boris Gindis offers helpful articles for
educational planning on this Web site.

CHADD (Children and Adults with Attention Deficit Hyperactivity Disorder)
8181 Professional Place, Suite 201
Landover, MD 20785
(800) 233-4050 or (301) 306-7070
Fax: (301) 306-7090
www.chadd.org
CHADD is packed full of information about education, medication, home
routines, counseling, and local support groups.

Child Welfare Information Gateway
www.childwelfare.gov
This is a service of the Children's Bureau, Administration for Children and
Families, U.S. Department of Health and Human Services. The CWIG
accesses information and resources to protect children and strengthen
families. It also provides publications, referrals to services, and searches
of their informational databases.

Christian Alliance for Orphans (CAO)
www.ChristianAllianceforOrphans.org
This organization exists to provide orphan care and adoption-related ministries
and organizations with partnership opportunities, connecting resources,
and networking capabilities. National media campaigns also serve to raise
awareness.

Families Moving Forward
http://depts.washington.edu/fmffasd
This program is offered as a home visiting intervention model, which can
be mimicked in settings where FASD (fetal alcohol spectrum disorder)
diagnosis takes place.

Fostering Families Today
www.fosteringfamiliestoday.com
This magazine offers well-written articles with solid information. It is
    particularly helpful for older adopted children.

FRUA (Friends for Russian and Ukrainian Adoption Including Neighboring
    Countries)
P.O. Box 2944
Merrifield, VA 22116
www.frua.org
Adoptive families will find this resource helpful no matter where they've
    adopted from. Individuals and couples can sign up for their *Family Focus*
    newsletter, make use of their active online discussion group, order audio
    CDs, or register to attend their national conference.

Institute for Family Development
www.institutefamily.org
Their Homebuilders program is a national intervention model for effective
    and evidence-based treatment.

The Iceberg
P.O. Box 95597
Seattle, WA 98145
Iceberg_fas@yahoo.com
This newsletter combines stories, advocacy, and research findings to support
    families with Fetal Alcohol Syndrome and effects.

International Adoption Medical Program
Box 211 UMHC
420 Delaware St. SE
Minneapolis, MN 55455
www.med.umn.edu/peds/iac
This organization is at the leading edge of medical, psychological, and social
    issues facing adopted children and their families.

Kinship Center
www.kinshipcenter.org
Offers adoption-related materials covering important aspects of parenting and professional support.

National Council for Adoption (NCFA)
225 N. Washington Street
Alexandria, VA 22314-2561
(703) 299-6633
www.adoptioncouncil.org
This organization seeks to promote the positive option of adoption through laws, policymakers, adoption resources, and adoption facts.

NOFAS
National Organization on Fetal Alcohol Syndrome
1815 H St. NW, Suite 750
Washington DC 20006
(800) 66 NOFAS
(800) 666-6327
www.nofas.org

Pact, an Adoption Alliance
3450 Sacramento St., Suite 239
San Francisco, CA 94118
Voice: (425) 221-6957
Fax: (510) 482-2089
www.pactadopt.org
This placement and education service also specializes in supporting families raising adopted children of color in an interracial or transracial home environment.

Raising Black and Biracial Children
RBC
1336 Meadow View Ln., #1
Lancaster, CA 93534
RBCeditor@aol.com
This magazine offers a wealth of information on African-American, interracial, and transracial adoptive and foster families.

Sibshops
www.siblingsupport.org
Siblings love these local workshops designed to support their needs as siblings of special needs children. Visit their Web site for a national directory of workshops.

Society of Special Needs Adoptive Parents Newsletter
(604) 687-3364
snap@snap.bc.ca
This practical quarterly newsletter offers the latest information on special needs issues, including FASD.

David and Renée Sanford own Sanford Communications, Inc., which works closely with leading authors, ministries, and publishers to develop life-changing books and other resources. Their professional credentials, life experience, and passion for helping adoptive families well qualify them for this project. David and Renée were trained and served as foster parents to two sisters in 1996. They were then trained as adoptive parents in 2002 and adopted their daughter Annalise through the Oregon State Child Welfare system in 2004.

David and Renée have been married 26 years and are the parents of five children: Elizabeth (married to Billy Honeycutt), Shawna (married to Jordan Goertz), Jonathan (age 20), Benjamin (age 11), and Annalise (age 8). They have two grandchildren, John (age 3) and Havilah (age 1).

David, Renée, and their two youngest children live "on the road to Damascus" a few miles from downtown Portland, Oregon. You can visit them online at www.sanfordci.com.

FOCUS ON THE FAMILY®

Welcome to the Family

Whether you purchased this book, borrowed it, or received it as a gift, we're glad you're reading it. It's just one of the many helpful, encouraging, and biblically based resources produced by Focus on the Family® for people in all stages of life.

Focus began in 1977 with the vision of one man, Dr. James Dobson, a licensed psychologist and author of numerous best-selling books on marriage, parenting, and family. Alarmed by the societal, political, and economic pressures that were threatening the existence of the American family, Dr. Dobson founded Focus on the Family with one employee and a once-a-week radio broadcast aired on 36 stations.

Now an international organization reaching millions of people daily, Focus on the Family is dedicated to preserving values and strengthening and encouraging families through the life-changing message of Jesus Christ.

Focus on the Family MAGAZINES

These faith-building, character-developing publications address the interests, issues, concerns, and challenges faced by every member of your family from preschool through the senior years.

FOCUS ON THE FAMILY CITIZEN®
U.S. news issues

FOCUS ON THE FAMILY CLUBHOUSE JR.™
Ages 4 to 8

FOCUS ON THE FAMILY CLUBHOUSE®
Ages 8 to 12

BREAKAWAY®
Teen guys

BRIO®
Teen girls 12 to 15

BRIO & BEYOND®
Teen girls 16 to 19

PLUGGED IN®
Reviews movies, music, TV

For More INFORMATION

 ONLINE:

Log on to
FocusOnTheFamily.com
In Canada, log on to
FocusOnTheFamily.ca

 PHONE:

Call toll-free:
800-A-FAMILY
(232-6459)
In Canada, call toll-free: 800-661-9800

Rev. 6/08

More Great Resources
from Focus on the Family®

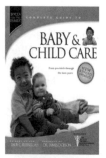

Complete Guide to Baby & Child Care
by Dr. Paul Reisser and the Physicians' Resource Council
There's one book parents reach for at night when their newborn has an unusual symptom . . . one book that thousands of doctors recommend as a practical medical reference for families. It's the *Complete Guide to Baby & Child Care*. Now updated with the latest research, these 900+ pages address the physical, mental, emotional, and spiritual needs of your child. With advice that spans from pre-birth to the teen years, the *Complete Guide to Baby & Child Care* even keeps up with your child's rapid growth.

Small Town, Big Miracle
by Bishop W. C. Martin with John Fornof
Possum Trot, an East Texas town so small it's not on most maps, hardly sets the stage for big miracles. But when a local pastor and his wife adopt two children, something amazing happens . . . their church follows in their footsteps! Who would have thought that God would inspire this small-town church community to take in 72 of the foster system's most troubled kids? You'll be moved and inspired by this heartwarming tale of modern-day miracles.

Saving Levi
by Lisa Misraje Bentley
A 6-week-old baby boy with burns over 70 percent of his body was left to die in a field in China. Odds of his surviving were stacked against him, yet through e-mail, prayer, and word-of-mouth, people came forward to help. In *Saving Levi*, you'll be amazed by the story of how one little boy's incredible fight for life brought people together from around the world to prove the power of God.

FOR MORE INFORMATION

Online:
Log on to FocusOnTheFamily.com
In Canada, log on to focusonthefamily.ca.

Phone:
Call toll free: 800-A-FAMILY
In Canada, call toll free: 800-661-9800.

FOCUS® ON THE FAMILY

BPZZXP1